Media and Religion | Medien und Religion

edited by | herausgegeben von

Dr. Anna-Katharina Höpflinger
Ludwig-Maximilians-Universität München

Prof. Dr. Stefanie Knauss
Villanova University, USA

Dr. Marie-Therese Mäder
Ludwig-Maximilians-Universität München

Prof. Dr. Daria Pezzoli-Olgiati
Ludwig-Maximilians-Universität München

Volume 3 | Band 3

Michael Leo Ulrich

Religion – Marketing's Unwitting Godparent

A Case Study of Coffee Branding and Consumer Loyalty

Nomos

MEDIEN UND RELIGION

The Deutsche Nationalbibliothek lists this publication in the Deutsche Nationalbibliografie; detailed bibliographic data are available on the Internet at http://dnb.d-nb.de

a.t.: München, Ludwig-Maximilians-Univ., Diss., 2018

ISBN 978-3-8487-5799-2 (Print)
978-3-8452-9881-8 (ePDF)

British Library Cataloguing-in-Publication Data
A catalogue record for this book is available from the British Library.

ISBN 978-3-8487-5799-2 (Print)
978-3-8452-9881-8 (ePDF)

Library of Congress Cataloging-in-Publication Data
Ulrich, Michael Leo
Religion – Marketing's Unwitting Godparent
A Case Study of Coffee Branding and Consumer Loyalty
Michael Leo Ulrich
281 p.
Includes bibliographic references.

ISBN 978-3-8487-5799-2 (Print)
978-3-8452-9881-8 (ePDF)

1st Edition 2019

Table of Contents

Acknowledgements

First and foremost, my thanks go to Prof. Dr. Daria Pezzoli-Olgiati, and Prof. Dr. Dr. Peter Seele, my first and second supervisors. When Daria Pezzoli-Olgiati approached me, some six years ago, asking whether I would be interested in writing a PhD thesis, I did not know what I was getting myself into. I did not realise that my work as a researcher would first make me lose the parameters of my established way of reasoning. Yet, with Daria Pezzoli-Olgiati and Peter Seele's help and guidance, those parameters, enriched by a myriad of facets, formed a new set of multiple paradigms, allowing me to see and cognise the world, past and present, in an entirely new way.

Many thanks also go to the members of the research group *Medien und Religion*, foremost to Dr. des. Baldassare Scolari, Dr. Marie-Therese Mäder, and Dr. Nathalie Fritz, who reviewed my drafts, suggested possible different approaches, provided me with the needed literature if missing, and never withheld their moral or academic support. Special thanks also go Paul Sidiropoulos. The intellectual exchange with him was a source of great inspiration and constructive criticism.

Many thanks then go to Marlen Tschudin, Elisabeth Tester, Christine Hunziker, and Michael Hecker for their continued support in conducting the socio-empirical survey in Switzerland, Germany, and China. Special thanks also go to Meng'an Ding, who translated the questionnaire to Mandarin, and conducted and documented the socio-empirical survey in Shanghai.

Finally, my thanks go to my partner and my mother. Both gave me the vital emotional support that, as any PhD student knows, is much needed to complete such a task successfully. A PhD thesis is never completed by one person alone, in isolation. Therefore, many thanks to all the persons named above, and to all of those who I did not mention here.

Preface

There are certain things you expect, and certain things you don't expect. For instance, you don't expect a car dealer, any car dealer, to be the epitome of honesty. Nor do you really expect to understand a French person speaking English. And, when on a flight to London, you should only expect tourists to drink tea; the English have long given up that habit. In my case, I did not expect Swiss professionals in their forties – lawyers and teachers, highly rational beings and deliciously indifferent to most things – to feel truly passionate about coffee brands.

What had happened? Well, I was given, as a present, an Amici coffee-machine. Amici is a coffee brand of Italian origin, founded in Switzerland by Francesco Illy, one of the sons of the founder of illycaffè, and his wife Annemarie (Amici, n.d.).[1] I already had a Nespresso coffee machine at home, so I took the Amici to the riding stable. I told my fellow riders that they would no longer have to drink that horrible coffee from the dispenser. I continued speaking, but little did I realise that my next remark would change my life – at least my life as a scholar: I mentioned that, when faced with the choice to either bring the Amici or the Nespresso machine, I had chosen the Amici because I believed it made better coffee than Nespresso. This innocent statement provoked an unexpected response from two women (both professionals). They simultaneously gasped: "Oh!?!" I responded with "Oh what?" which, admittedly, was not the most polite way to answer. Regardless, a heated proclamation of Nespresso's supremacy over all rival coffee brands ensued. And it sadly ended with hard feelings. I was amazed. I enjoy coffee very much, but after all, it's just coffee.

Several weeks later, I made a slightly critical remark about Nespresso in the presence of one of my mother's friends (who passed on shortly thereafter and could no longer participate in my Nespresso interviews) who immediately rushed to Nespresso's defence. It was in that moment that I, for the first time, began to think of Nespresso drinkers not just as coffee consumers, but as *adherents*. After she had finished proselytising, there was no doubt that Nespresso had ended this woman's lifelong search for the best coffee. The answer was found, the journey ended. She sounded not unlike my evangelical aunt, who had also found what she was looking for. In a

1 For a website in English, see Illycupscolletion (n.d.).

somewhat bizarre, totally unexpected, but astonishingly homological way, my mother's friend and my aunt seemed to share the same experience. This basically counterintuitive explanation of a coffee drinker's behaviour with a concept, so to speak a mini-theory, that would be attributed more to the field of the study of religion, and one which reminded me of the common adage - that progress in science is often triggered by, at first sight, counterintuitive results.

That got me started. What is it about Nespresso that turns consumers into adherents, at least the ones that crossed my path? I began to read about brands in general and to study the financial statements documenting their sustained contribution to their owners' business success. The question then began to arise in me, whether a theoretical concept pertaining to the field of the study of religion, and not, as one would expect, to the field of marketing, would perhaps be better suited to explain Nespresso's outstanding success, both, in the commercial sense and more specifically, in the sense of its clients' unswerving loyalty.

Abstract

Situated at the intersection of the study of religion and marketing, this study focuses on one of the most successful marketing campaigns in recent history. Approaching marketing campaigns within a theoretical framework pertaining to the study of religion, this investigation aims to discover whether the meaning-making mechanisms of that exemplary, extremely powerful and successful marketing campaign can be compared to, or are even analogous to, the way religious symbolism functions. Based on visual semiotics, this investigation explores precisely how Nespresso's campaign of the successful charging of an ostensibly profane commodity with symbolic attributes is effectuated. Because conventional marketing theories fail to provide an in-depth explanation of Nespresso's dazzling success, this study seeks fresh answers. Taking a perhaps unorthodox approach, it proposes an explanation of a to-date largely unexplained phenomenon.

The methodological framework for this study, outlining the procedure followed by the analysis, is developed along the lines of James M. Buchanan's theory of economic clubs, which introduces the insider-outsider pattern as a prerequisite for the construction of scarcity and exclusivity. The relevant parts of Buchanan's findings are then combined with the tenets of Stuart Hall's cultural theory, as well as the contributions from visual culture theory, as advocated by Brent Plate, Daria Pezzoli-Olgiati, and Gillian Rose. Furthermore, the circuit of culture described by Hall is used to structure the analysis and its results. Based on this synthesised methodological framework, Nespresso's medial representation is then analysed according to Clifford Geertz's approach to religion.

To substantiate the findings of the visual analysis, a socio-empirical quantitative consumer survey is carried out using interviews based on questionnaires to compile the required data. On the grounds of that body of data, selected statistical hypotheses are tested and rejected, demonstrating the validity of the proposed theoretical explanation of the observed phenomenon – that is, the more than exceptionally high operating profit margins. The quantitative survey is followed by a qualitative survey with focus groups. The aim of the qualitative survey is to further substantiate the findings of the quantitative survey. Finally, based on the characteristics of the data compilation, it is shown to what degree the findings can be generalised.

As a closing remark, it is worth noting that by examining the high performativity of symbolism, so widely practised in religion, this study sheds light on the potential appropriation by the business community. Identifying, on the theoretical level, structural and functional analogies between religion and marketing, this interdisciplinary study outlines the often-overlooked economical dimension within the study of religion.

1 Introduction

1.1 An unexplained business phenomenon

Nespresso's global market share of 27% in 2011, successfully built and maintained, with an operating profit margin[2] beyond 30% (Revill, 2012), and Apple's global market share of 25% in 2012 (Elveren, 2013), combined with operating profit margins well in excess of 30% (Stock Analysis on Net, 2014) are, in comparison to their industries' average performances, truly exceptional. For instance, in May 2015, the average operating profit margin in the US food and beverage industry was 5.2% (Investopedia, 2015).

> In the case of Apple, this picture of outstanding commercial success is further amplified when its worldwide profit share is taken into consideration.
>
> Apple has a relatively tiny slice of the smartphone market, measured by phones shipped to consumers. According to the latest data from IDC [International Data Corporation], iPhones were 17.6% of smartphones shipped last quarter. Android-based phones were 78.1% of the phones shipped. But if you measure the smartphone market by profits, Apple has practically a monopoly. Analyst Tavis McCourt at Raymond James estimates Apple has 87.4% [sic!] of smartphone profits. The next closest is Samsung, with 32.2% of smartphone profits. Yes, those numbers add up to over 100%. That's because everyone else is losing mon-

---

2 The "operating profit margin", or simply the "operating margin" is a key accounting figure used to capture the commercial success of a firm. It gives analysts an idea, as a percentage figure of total sales, of how much profit a firm makes. The operating profit margin measures a firm's profit before interest payments and taxes are deducted. Therefore, it also illustrates a firm's capacity to service its debt and pay taxes that are due. Evaluation means comparison; therefore, the absolute figure in itself is to some degree less significant than a comparison to the corresponding figure of a competitor or another industry. To that end, it can be useful to compare the quarterly or yearly change in the operating profit margin to determine whether a firm is becoming more or less profitable. Naturally, in a commercial context, the higher the margin, the better.

> ey, and so McCourt gives the rest of the world's phone makers negative profit share. (Yarow, 2014)

Nespresso has been similarly successful with the introduction of new coffee flavours, packaged into easy-to-handle capsules. As Bloomberg reported in February 2013:

> Nestlé SA (NESN) has found something even better than single-serve coffee costing twice as much as ground java: a version that costs eight times [sic!] as much. While consumers worldwide rein in spending, the Swiss company in October [2012] introduced Hawaii Kona Special Reserve, a limited-edition coffee for its Nespresso machines. At $2 a shot, it cost four times the price of regular Nespresso. It sold out within weeks, and the company says more such offerings are in the works. (Doherty, 2013)

Considering, that a regular Nespresso capsule already costs roughly twice as much as a non-brand coffee capsule, such a phenomenon is truly exceptional and calls for an explanation that goes beyond the standard analysis of marketing,[3] budget and brand identification, or consumer loyalty.

A branded good is not like any other good – for producers, it is special, often a source of great revenue and profit. This maxim has been known within the study of marketing for quite some time. Forbes regularly publishes a list of the world's most valuable brand names (Forbes, 2014). In November 2013, Apple ranked first, with an operating profit margin of 29% in 2013 (Stock Analysis on Net, 2014). Nespresso's results were equally impressive. According to an analyst at the Zurich Kantonalbank, in 2012, Nespresso's operating profit margin was in excess of 30%, with a global market share of 27% (Revill, 2012). In 2012, Nestlé SA, the company owning Nespresso, generated an overall profit margin of 15.2%. The biggest contribution came from powdered and liquid beverages (i.e., including Nespresso) with an operating profit margin of 22.5% (Nestlé Media Press Releases, 2013). That figure is an average for the whole of all powdered and liquid beverages, including Nespresso, Nescafé, Nestea and Nesquik (Nestlé Asset Library, 2011) suggesting that Nespresso, with an operating profit margin in excess of 30%, is one of the largest, if not the

3 The term "marketing" is used according to the definition of the American Marketing Association (AMA): "Marketing is the activity, set of institutions, and processes for creating, communicating, delivering, and exchanging offerings that have value for customers, clients, partners, and society at large" (AMA online dictionary, n.d. a).

largest contributor within that group.[4] The magnitude of those figures is, from a commercial standpoint, indeed awesome and, so far, theoretically unaccounted for. The explanatory power of the theoretical body prevailing in marketing is insufficient to explain in greater depth *why* anybody would pay roughly €0.40 (the equivalent of US$ 0.55[5]) for a cup of coffee brewed at home, given that a regular cup of filter coffee can cost as little as €0.04 (Czycholl, 2013). Similarly, in the case of Apple's iPhone, the question arises as to why anybody would spend several days and nights in a queue just to be among the first to own a new mobile telephone (Prigg, Parsons, & Margolis, 2012).

Seen from the perspective of a firm, these questions can be rephrased with reference to the firm's marketing campaign: What lies at the root of a marketing campaign so successful that it enables a firm to build and defend, over a sustained period of time, a global market share of 20% and more, while simultaneously generating an operating profit margin which is, as in the case of Nespresso, a multiple of the industry's average (CSI Market, 2014; Eurostat, 2017)? As outlined below, these considerations lead to the question this study proposes to answer. Yet, this study's focus does not include Apple's noteworthy success. The scrutiny of more than one marketing campaign would lie beyond its scope. This study's focus lies exclusively on Nespresso's successful celebrity marketing campaign for its highly profitable capsule coffee business, in which it collaborated, in the campaign for European markets, with Hollywood actor George Clooney (Nestlé FAQs, 2014). The focus lies on the time span from 2006 to 2014. From a marketing point of view, this study adopts a thus far, unexplored, new perspective: Nespresso's marketing campaign will be examined within a theoretical context pertaining to the study of religion, with the aim of discovering whether its success can possibly be attributed to a structural and functional analogy between religion on the one hand and the marketing campaign on the other – a structural and functional analogy that can be described in the mechanisms put to work by the marketing campaign, which are also inherent in, and characteristic of, religious symbolism, with commensurate impacts and analogous effects.

An analysis of Nespresso's campaign, according to the hermeneutics of the study of religion, raises the question to which degree a presence of a

---

4 If the group average is 22.5%, then a figure in excess of 30% (for Nespresso), which is at least 7.5% above the average, indicates that Nespresso's individual contribution to the group is way better than the group's average.

5 Prices and the exchange rate refer to June 2013.

religious, sacred quality within something as profane as a mere commodity, has already been addressed by scholars of the humanities. As will be expanded upon below, Karl Marx, Walter Benjamin and Norbert Bolz have all shown that there is another dimension adhering to a commodity beyond its purely profane or secular surface, or use-value – a dimension, that can possibly be captured, made visible, and be explained with the help of this study's theoretical framework. In a manner of speaking, this study addresses the *reverse* of the question of how religion morphs into a brand – a question, as will be discussed below, that Mara Einstein, Jörg Stolz, Jean-Claude Usunier and others have so brilliantly addressed. The question addressed by this study, instead, is the question of precisely how a profane, secular commodity is successfully turned into a brand of quasi-religious content in the sense that the product is turned into a brand, with respect to rivalling products, establishing an order of seemingly ontological nature with itself at the top – an order, which is accompanied by a commensurate consumer-ethos issuing in the continued consumption of the advertised commodity. In this context, finally, it must be mentioned explicitly, in order to prevent any misunderstanding, that it is not the aim of this study to show, or allege, that drinking Nespresso *is* a religion. The study's aim, as will be demonstrated below, is solely to show, on a theoretical level, that a structural and a functional analogy exists between Nespresso's marketing campaign on one hand, and religion on the other.

1.2 Structure and design of the study

As stated above, this study aims to explain Nespresso's outstanding commercial success with an approach based on a potential structural and functional analogy between religion and marketing. The analysis of the corpus, three Nespresso commercials, released in 2006, 2012 and 2013 as well as the collection of primary[6] data through a socio-empirical survey, is carried

6 Whether data collected through questionnaires are indeed, in the strictest sense of the word, of a "primary" nature shall not be addressed in the context of this study. Some of the questions in the questionnaire are based on the interviewee's memory, his or her recalling of moods, for instance – moods he or she had in connection to the consumption of Nespresso. In that sense, that data could also be regarded as being of a "secondary" nature as, in the strictest sense, primary data would refer to the information that was generated literally in the moment of consumption. Yet, in the context of this study, data collected through questionnaires and in focus groups, are referred to as primary data.

out using categories of analysis based on Clifford Geertz's definition of religion. The methodology, followed by the analysis, is theoretically substantiated by the contributions made by Stuart Hall, which have also been widely-used in the field of the study of religion, in particular in the contributions made by Daria Pezzoli-Olgiati, Brent Plate and Gillian Rose, as well as by James Buchanan's economic theory of clubs. In that sense, the analysis of the production of meaning through the process of encoding and decoding will be structured according to the circuit of culture, first introduced by du Gay, Hall, Janes, Mackay, and Negus (1997).

As already stated, the analysis focuses on the performativity of the audio-visual corpus in the representation of a narrative, scrutinising the co-involvement of the commercials' viewer, resulting in meaning-making as well as in identity-formation and, finally, in the implicit instigation of the viewer to act like the principal characters in the commercials' narrative. These elements form a pattern in both religion and marketing. The analysis of this pattern, or structure, is then followed by the analysis of the primary consumer data that was collected in a quantitative and qualitative mixed-method survey. This second analysis uses the statistical method of hypothesis - testing to support the findings of the audio-visual analysis. In this sense, the socio-empirical data helps to substantiate the results of the audio-visual analysis based on theory. As the audio-visual analysis, the analysis of the socio-empirical data also uses the categories from Clifford Geertz's definition of religion as they constitute an effective heuristic tool of analysis allowing to capture, on the theoretical level, both the structural and functional characteristics of a system of symbols, irrespective of whether or not such a system is of an explicitly religious nature. A discussion of the findings, the cogency and validity of the conclusions and implications, and their limitations, leads to the final conceptual output/offering, and to the contribution this study hopes to make - to expand the theoretical reach of the study of religion.

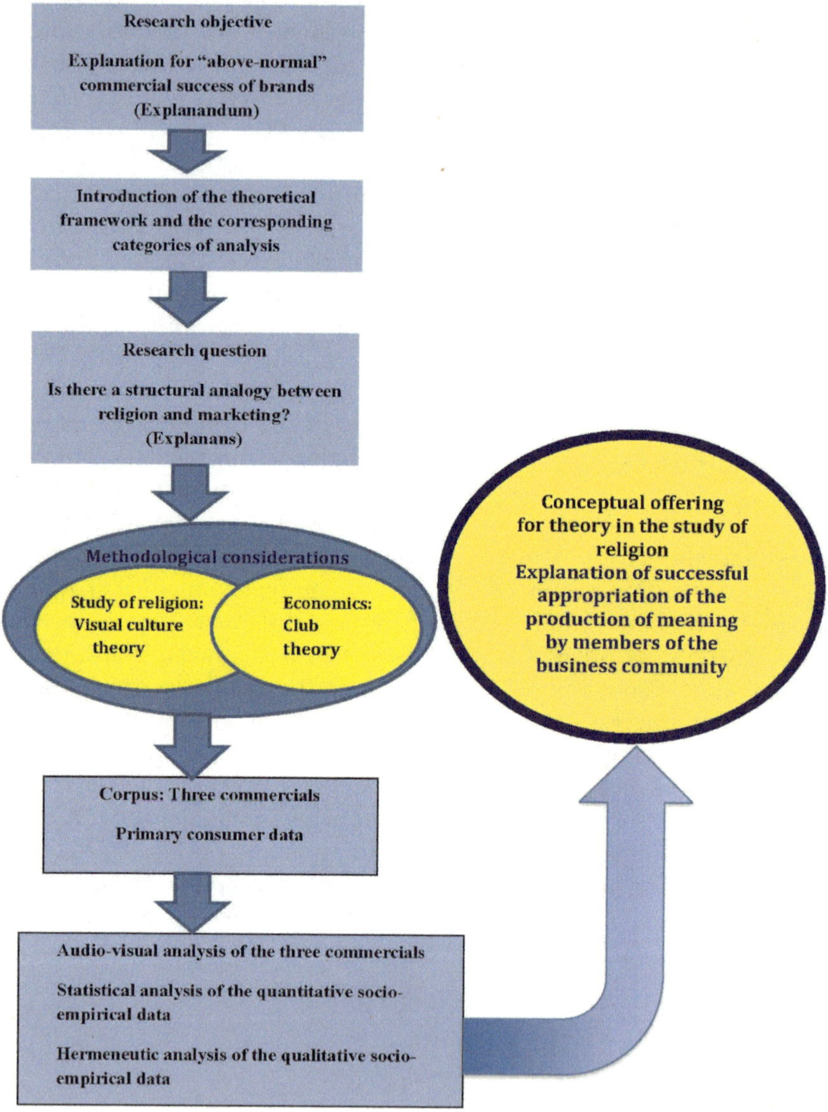

Figure 1: Research design (generated by the author with Word, 2013)

1.3 Aims of this study

The aim of this study is to determine precisely *how* outstandingly successful marketing campaigns generate their power, and whether such power is garnered through mechanisms that, when viewed through the lens of the study of religion, possibly owe their effectiveness to a structural and functional analogy between religion and marketing. This study is thus located at the intersection of traditionally separate academic disciplines, exploring a so far little-understood, and therefore also largely unexplained commercial phenomenon. In its search for understanding, and its attempt to find an explanation, this study then uses terms, concepts, methods and theories that have become well established within the study of religion.

To date, a possible structural and functional analogy between religion and marketing that could explain the phenomenon under scrutiny has not yet been addressed by research. Aiming to rectify this omission is where this study comes in and is precisely the contribution it hopes to make. At this point, it is worth mentioning again that this investigation limits itself to the scrutiny of the Nespresso marketing campaign centring on Hollywood actor George Clooney. Moreover, it must be stressed again that this study does not intend to prove or even allege that the consumption of Nespresso, or, by the same token, Nespresso's successful capsule *is*, or *has become* a religion. It aims to theoretically demonstrate that a potentially existing structural and functional analogy between religion and marketing can be employed to explain the phenomenon under scrutiny. This study is therefore also clearly demarcated from the remit of the psychology of religion, as it does not, at any point, allege or infer that the regular or occasional consumption of Nespresso is a religious act or equivalent to such an act.

To date, in-depth research examining why certain marketing campaigns function so well, or, along the same line of reasoning, research examining according to which possible structural and functional logic a marketing campaign turns a plain, everyday commodity with seemingly limited use-value into a firm's cash cow, is still missing. With respect to marketing's failure to produce a theoretical body with satisfactory explanatory power, Stephen Brown speaks of the *myopia of marketing* (Brown, 1993, p. 25). Such myopia is naturally pernicious to an in-depth scrutiny of marketing-related phenomena. Consequently, the question whether some marketing campaigns, geared perhaps in the most indiscernible way, to invest the marketed commodity with an elevated exchange-value, is based on structures and mechanisms traditionally observed in the context of religion, has not been addressed. Nor has the question been raised whether, in a marketing context, a categorical transformation of the commodity's perceived value can deliberately be constructed, and if so, what it takes to accomplish such a feat. Perhaps answers to those questions could be found if it were argued that a seemingly profane commodity is potentially much more than just that: that there could be, perhaps, other, far-reaching dimensions invoked, dimensions that can transform a commodity into a meaning-producing symbol – and render consumers willing to pay almost any price. In a search for fresh answers, this study expands the scope of its analysis beyond the realm of the purely marketing-based study of how a commodity's use-value can be increased by refined product placement, or by presenting it as the choice of the rich and famous. This study aims to find out whether what is at work, is not a continuous increase in a commodity's use-value, as perceived by consumers to the effect that it fetches a very high unit-price, but a categorical transformation of a commodity's character, dramatically opening a gap between its apparent use- and exchange-value. By going beyond the scholarly discipline of marketing into the remit of the study of religion, this study examines if, and how such a categorical commodity transformation, moving it from the commercially profane to the symbolically charged, is brought about. And because, on that trajectory axis, semiotics plays a crucial and decisive role, the contribution of semiotics thereto is also discussed in detail.

It needs to be mentioned that even though this study, placed at the intersection of the study of religion and economics, is, amongst other things, about marketing, consumers and consumer behaviour, the approach taken is not consonant with the well-established concepts of economic anthropology, as captured by the term "homo economicus", in which humans, for analytical purposes, are axiomatically assumed to act rationally. Instead, a currently observed academic discussion, with possibly far-reaching implications, provides an important premise of this study: Landmark studies have begun to question the validity of the economic anthropology of the homo economicus. While that designation was minted in the early 20th century, the concept itself was forged earlier, primarily in the 18th century. Adam Smith's contribution here, was perhaps crucial.[7] Today, however, this anthropological theorem is beginning to waver. Even though most economists would agree that the concept captured by the term homo economicus has primarily served, and continues to serve, as an analytical tool

7 For further reading on this topic, please see Manstetten (2000/2004), Binswanger (2011), and Hirschman (1977/2013).

that helps, on a theoretical level, to understand certain economic phenomena without pretending that humans are purely and exclusively rational beings, peer researchers such as Jochen Hörisch (2011) and Christoph Binswanger (2011) have pointed out, that the homo economicus no longer seems to provide a sufficiently adequate model to explain the phenomena observed in reality. Moreover, whilst Binswanger's findings also shed light on Adam Smith's affiliation to stoic philosophy by illustrating that stoic philosophers and their anthropology were an inspiration for Smith, Martha Nussbaum (1994/2009) has demonstrated how stoic philosophy advocated for the total excision of passion and desire.[8]

These genealogical considerations cast doubt on that still, largely prevailing economic anthropology as a hegemonic concept, and in this sense, the findings of the above-cited scholars lead to a key premise of the present study: the current understanding in economic anthropology fails to fully explain certain patterns of consumer behaviour because its primary theory has a fundamental flaw, namely the exclusion of the passionate and desire-driven, and by implication, the imaginary side of human nature. It is, of course, not the aim of this study to establish a new theory of economic anthropology or even to continue in a critique thereof. Simply, the concept of the homo economicus has been excluded from this study on account of its relative weaknesses. Moreover, non-consideration of conventional economic anthropology leaves room for an in-depth exploration of the determinants of consumer behaviour in addition to the traditionally conceived, and well-known rational motivators.

Adopting as it does, an interdisciplinary approach, this study also hopes to advance the current discussion, as to whether a theory pertaining to the field of economics can make a vital contribution to the explanation of a religion-related phenomenon. In the context, for example, of the scholarly discussion on whether the theory of rational choice can be used to explain the core issues of religion that concern sociologists, Steve Bruce (2014) has argued that this only seems to apply if there has been a notable decline in levels of religious belief and practice in a given society, as can be observed in the modern, industrial liberal democracies of the West. In his critique of Laurence Iannaccone's contribution, Bruce (1999) concluded that economistic theories can only be sensibly applied to the field of religion after some degree of secularisation has set in: "The grand irony is that it is only when attitudes to religion change in ways most of us are happy to call

8 As will be explained subsequently, advertising also works with consumers' desire.

'secularization'[9] that it becomes possible to apply the principles of economics to religious behaviour. [...] Only in largely secular societies [...] is it possible for ordinary people to treat religion in a utility-maximising manner and hence for analysts to explain their behaviour in terms of economistic rational choice ideas" (1999, p. 203).

Regarding the issue of secularisation, it needs to be emphasised that this study neither addresses nor wants to contribute to the scholarly discussion as to which degree or whether secularisation has or has not taken place in liberal Western societies. The term "secularisation" is used with the implication of a "decline in obedience to divine authority and the decline in the use of social power to enforce religious conformity" (Bruce, 2014, p. 198) as well as a "decline in levels of religious belief and practice" (p. 199).[10] Further implications are "the differentiation of the secular sphere from religious institutions and norms [and] the marginalisation of religion to the private sphere [...]" (Bruce, 2014, paraphrasing Casanova, 1994).

A breakdown of religious norms, as well as the possibly connected increased individual freedom to choose in all matters important to individuals, are two of many characteristics of a process which Stolz and Usunier refer to as a "modernisation process" (Stolz & Usunier, 2014, p. 5), a perhaps less controversial term than "secularisation". Suffice to say, many scholars appear to prefer the term "modernisation process" to "secularisation" (Norris & Inglehart, 2004; Dawson 2011; Gauthier, Martikainen, & Woodhead, 2013). In this study then, as already mentioned, the term "secularisation" is understood as a decline in the moral authority of religious institutions, leaning towards the notion of a "modernisation process", without the implication of a generic decline in religiousness.

As previously stated, this study does not address the issue of the rationality of human behaviour as, for example, stipulated by the theory of rational choice. It does, however, consistent with Bruce's line of argument, use, for methodological purposes, James M. Buchanan's economic theory of clubs. Moreover, as is addressed below, this study is, again consistent with Bruce's argument, carried out against the backdrop of a postmodern, largely secularised society.

With respect to placing this study in a postmodern frame, a brief excursion is warranted here to clarify this study's use of the notion of "postmodernism". It is important to notice that this study does not aim to contribute

9 All the quotations are given in exactly their original form with no emphasis, quotation marks or brackets added or omitted.

10 For a discussion of the secularisation theory, please see Pollack (2011).

to the discussion regarding "modernism" and "postmodernism", their notional content and, with respect to time, their correct historic positioning. Its reference to postmodernism only serves an analytical purpose to provide a hermeneutical framework for a meaningful analysis. With respect to epochs and the notions used to describe them, Peter Seele writes:

> Epochs are – it seems necessary to spell this out clearly – interim notions. The discussion regarding "modernism", "postmodernism", and "postpostmodernism" confirms this thesis of interims. Epochs are proposed construals regarding the past, proving their worth and perpetuating themselves by conveying, in their presence, a reference to the past.[11] (Seele, 2008, p. 74)

In view of this, this study uses a construal of the term postmodernism in accordance with Fredric Jameson's interpretation, who sees in postmodernism a cultural dominant, a so-called "force field" affecting all types of cultural productions (Jameson, 1991). The main feature of postmodernism, according to Jameson, is depthlessness: "The first and most evident [significant difference between the high-modernist and the postmodern moment] is the emergence of a new kind of flatness or depthlessness, a new kind of superficiality in the most literal sense […]" (Jameson, 1991, p. 9). With respect to the prominent, perhaps all-pervasive role of markets in our day-to-day lives, Jameson puts forth an argument which is valid for both, markets as well as the products traded and sold therein:

> […][T]he excitement of the once tire-some old fifties representation of the free market derives from its illicit metaphorical association with a very different kind of representation; namely, the media itself in its largest contemporary and global sense. The operation is […][a] postmodern one […], in which two systems of codes are identified in such a way as to allow the libidinal energies of the one to suffuse the other […].Horkheimer and Adorno observed long ago […] the peculiarity of the structure of a commercial "culture industry" […]. The media offers free programs in whose content and assortment the consumer has no choice whatsoever but whose selection is then rebaptised "free choice." In the […] tendential identification of the commodity with its image (or brand name or logo), another, more intimate, symbiosis between the market and the media is effectuated, in which boundaries are

11 Translation by the author, 2016.

> washed over (in ways profoundly characteristic of the postmodern) and an indifferentiation of levels gradually takes the place of an older separation between thing and concept (or indeed, economics and culture, base and superstructure). For one thing, the products sold in the market become the very content of the media image, so that, as it were, the same referent seems to maintain in both domains. (Jameson, 1991, pp. 274-275)[12]

What Jameson describes here is the emergence, as a consequence of the annulment of the separation of thing and concept, of a contingent super-elevation of the commodity. And this, in turn, opens a wide range of new marketing and advertising[13] possibilities. With respect to the notion of postmodernism as it is used in this study, this annulment of the separation of thing and concept and its implications for marketing are its main features.

Addressing this very issue, Venkatesh, Sherry, and Firat (1993) maintain that postmodernism "treats our conceptualisations of the individual subjectivity (e.g., the consumer). It is also concerned with social formation (e.g., markets)" (Venkatesh, Sherry, & Firat, 1993, p. 216). As a conclusion, they state that "marketing research need no longer be confined to the presentation of tables, equations and figures [...]. Its presentational forms could range from poetry to scientific discourse, from narratives, descriptions, story-telling to visual and symbolic representations" (Venkatesh, Sherry, & Firat, 1993, p. 218). With respect to this study, the enquiry into one of those narratives, is precisely the contribution this study hopes to make: An in-depth analysis of the system of symbols present in Nespresso's representation, aiming to shed light on the structural, and functional characteristics of Nespresso's postmodern marketing-success story.

---

12 For a further in-depth discussion of marketing in the context of postmodernism, see Venkatesh, Sherry and Firat (1993), Brown (1993), Firat and Venkatesh (1993), Firat, Dholakia and Venkatesh (1995), Cova (1996), Firat and Shultz (1997.).

13 In this study, the term "advertising" is used according to the definition of the American Marketing association (AMA): "The placement of announcements and persuasive messages in time or space purchased in any of the mass media by business firms, nonprofit organisations, government agencies, and individuals who seek to inform and/or persuade members of a particular target market or audience about their products, services, organisations, or ideas" (AMA online dictionary, n.d. b).

In the next chapter, the proximity of religion on one hand, and marketing on the other is considered, examining whether a possibly existing analogy, or overlap actually warrants this study's general line of argument.

2 Religion's Overlap with Advertising and Marketing

Narratives and storytelling are an integral part, not only of marketing strategies, yet of most, if not all, religious traditions as well. Irrespective of whether the stories are told, and whether their messages are conveyed by words, images, and/or sounds, or by any combination of those, the messages carried by the stories tend to imply a worldview and a corresponding ethos, irrespective of the context of the narrative – religious or related to marketing. This contiguity – or overlap even – of religion with advertising and marketing will be scrutinised more closely in the following chapter.

2.1 Advertising and marketing

Corporations are, under law, legal persons. They are, so to speak, our fellow citizens. However, contrary to most people, they only have one objective: to earn, on a legal basis, sustained maximum profits[14] for the corporation's owners. It is important to keep that in mind for a good understanding of the role played by both, advertising and marketing, in the context of a firm's objectives: A possible myriad of objectives only serves that one particular prime objective: profit. By stating this, no criticism is implied. A successful scrutiny of marketing, and advertising for that matter[15], in the context of this study simply presupposes a clear, concise, and matter-of-fact understanding of a firm's objective. Firms tend to function along utilitarian lines, dividing the world they operate in into two spheres: pleasure and pain. Everything with a positive impact on a firm's profit is part of the former sphere, and everything with a negative impact is part of the latter. And, in this respect, marketing and advertising, are parts of a firm's toolbox in its endeavour to generate maximum profit for shareholders. From a

14 The experienced accountant might want to add, that some companies might aim to minimise profits for tax reasons, and that companies aim, instead, to earn as much cash as possible. This study does not make this technical difference. Indeed, large profits might be hidden for tax purposes, however, in the context of this study, this is of no concern.

15 The relationship between advertising and marketing is explained below.

methodological standpoint, the relationship between marketing and advertising can be explained by pointing to its fractal nature: Whilst marketing as such can be viewed as one of the principal methods in a firm's arsenal to generate maximum profits, advertising, in turn, is one of the principle methods of marketing. And finally, to also include the commercial in this methodological typology, a commercial is one of the methods used by advertising.

It is hard to sell to people what they already have, or do not really need – for example, another coffee brand. Therefore, a corporation finding itself in that situation, selling a consumer product into a saturated market, must make an effort to the effect, that a potentially redundant product is perceived, by consumers, as something other than what the product appears to be at first sight; the product must be seen as something consumers do not yet possess – and as something they desire and are thus willing to spend their money on. Under the presupposition that humans are beings of need, they are all in need of something. With respect to Nespresso's efforts to launch a new coffee brand then, Nespresso faced the challenge of turning coffee into something else, to heave it to another level, away from the overcrowded market place where sellers compete with nearly identical products for the attention and the money of satiated consumers. So, the question then becomes, what a coffee capsule, admittedly a clever piece of innovation, could be morphed into – something, the targeted would-be consumers do not yet have. To live up to that challenge of "transubstantiation", marketing will need to pull out all the stops as the solution will, in a materialistically satiated society, most likely lie in the realm of the immaterial and the imaginary, in the world beyond the reified – and that world, most probably, is not readily there, it must be constructed.

Nespresso products can be purchased in one of the 450 or so Nespresso boutiques worldwide (Nestle-Nespresso, 2016a), or online. An online purchase requires the client to become a Nespresso Club Member first. One of the consequences of registration is that Club Members can be easily contacted by Nespresso. When, in 2004, Nespresso asked their Club Members who they would like their Nespresso ambassador to be, they suggested Hollywood actor George Clooney (Nestle-Nespresso, 2016b). Subsequently, beginning in 2006, the Nespresso marketing campaign placed George Clooney in a series of commercials, wherein he moves through a world of aestheticised coffee consumption. Advertising in the sense of the American Marketing Association, as aforementioned, is the placing of a message. In the case of the Nespresso commercials, the message is not openly directed towards the recipient. The viewer is not addressed directly. The commercials, instead, provide the viewer with a glimpse of a beautiful world of coffee consumption. Perfectly designed Nespresso boutiques, exquisite tasting areas, and beautiful female Nespresso clients meld with Clooney's charming humour and wit, representing a world of coffee consumption which, in its apparent perfection, can only exist in the imaginary, or so it would seem – and yet, those Nespresso boutiques do exist in reality, with their beautifully designed tasting areas where clients can indeed enjoy a cup of Nespresso of their choice. Thus, the audio-visual representation of Nespresso's coffee world, a representation of an imagined narrative, becomes real through consumers themselves, if the commercial's viewers and would-be consumers actually respond to the commercial in the way presumably intended by the commercials' producer, that is, Nestlé Nespresso SA. As Nespresso's commercial success suggests, they actually do. Nespresso's coffee capsules must be something targeted consumers are motivated to spend their money on – possibly something greater than just another coffee brand amidst a multitude of substitutes.

Following the first Nespresso commercial featuring George Clooney in 2006, that special world – Nespresso's world – was subsequently, in a series of follow-up commercials, represented again and again. Thereby, a specific conception of a coffee world, and of a specific way to enjoy coffee was conveyed to the viewer of those commercials. Moreover, in as much as the would-be consumer feels a motivation in him/her to participate in that world, an ethos emerges. Such ethos, implying a should – a blueprint for action so to speak – is all the easier to follow as those exquisitely designed Nespresso boutiques alongside the equally appealing tasting areas do, as aforementioned, indeed exist in the real world. Consumers can easily go and visit those Nespresso boutiques, and, so to speak, reiterate and re-enact, in parts at least, the experience of the characters featured in the commercials. The fictional and imaginary content of the commercial thus becomes, in parts at least, real. Thus, through a specific use of the method of advertising, a marketing campaign can indeed create both, a concept of a particular worldview – even though the world in question is, in this particular case, limited to Nespresso's coffee world only – and an ethos, a blueprint for action. In that sense, marketing possibly has an overlap with religion.

Of course, that statement needs to be accurately substantiated. Suffice for now to allude to Geertz's definition of religion, which, in short, sees religion as a system of symbols offering a worldview and an ethos. As the discussion of Geertz's definition of religion in subchapter 2.2.2 shows, its use in this study is both warranted and legitimatised as it permits, as a heuristic analytical tool, a precise explanation of the phenomenon under scrutiny. Whether, in that context, advertising can be seen as a system of symbols is discussed later in this study. First, however, as the said overlap, comprising a worldview and an ethos, suggests a multifaceted interaction of the consumer with the commodity, the following two subchapters present a discussion of the commodity and the consumer, examining the feasibility of the claim underlying this study, that a commodity can, in principle, be morphed into something of considerable symbolic charge, and that consumers are, in principle, willing to go along with that, and finally, that they themselves make a decisive contribution to such a charging and super-elevation of the commodity.

2.1.1 A closer look at the commodity

With respect to a possible analogy between religion and marketing, it is appropriate to check whether there are, in the academic literature, any contributions investigating whether a plain commodity might possibly possess other dimensions that go beyond its apparent use-value. And indeed, over many years, a considerable body of knowledge addressing a possible connection between the material and practical dimension of a commodity (i.e., its use-value) – or a consumer good in the context of this research – and a more transcendent dimension adherent to it has been developed. Karl Marx speaks of the dual character of commodities:

> At first glance, a *commodity* seems to be something obvious and trivial. But its analysis brings out that it is quite intricate, abounding in metaphysical hair-splitting and theological niceties. So far as it is a *use-value*, there is nothing mysterious about the commodity [...] But, as soon as [it] steps forth *as a commodity*, it changes into something that has extrasensory features attached to its sensuous existence. [...] [Yet,][t]he mystical character of the commodity does not arise [...] from its use-value.[16] (Marx, 1867/1872/2009, p. 83)

As such, Marx sees no direct and simple relationship between the practical use-value and what he calls the mystical character of the commodity, or, in other words, its societal value. For example, a commodity, or a service that may have a comparatively high use-value, may well have a comparatively low societal value, such as cleaning services in a hospital. According to

16 Translation by Hans G. Ehrbar 2002 (Marx, 1867/1890/2002.).

Marx, the discrepancy between use-value and societal value of commodities is a phantasmagoria mirroring a corresponding, and, with respect to that discrepancy, constitutive societal structure (Marx, 1867/1872/2009, pp. 84-85). In his focus on the production of commodities, Marx identifies the producer's social position as the main root of the commensurate, transcended societal position of the product. Thus, the product's societal value, and consequently its exchange-value, mirror the producer's position in society back to him or her, whilst it appears as though these qualities were immanent in the product itself (Marx, 1867/1872/2009, p. 85). Only in the realm of religion does Marx identify a similar phenomenon, where the products of human minds, like gods and goddesses, seem to be independent entities invested with their own lives and interests, interacting with one another as well as with humans:

> In order, therefore, to find an analogy we must take flight into the misty realm of religion. There the products of the human brain seem to be independent beings endowed with a life of their own, which enter into relations with each other and with the human race. So, it is in the realm of commodities with the products of people's hands. This I call the fetishism, which sticks to the products of labour as soon as they are produced as commodities, and which is therefore inseparable from the production of commodities. [...] [T]his fetish-like character of the world of commodities has its origin in the peculiar social character of the labour which produces them.[17] (Marx, 1867/1872/2009, p. 85)

Thus, Marx argues that the commodity acquires the characteristics of a fetish, an otherwise lifeless object that has been imbued with an elevated and enhanced meaning, and that objective societal circumstances become societal circumstances of objects:

> [...] [T]he social standing of the producers, asserting and perpetuating [the] social conditions and characteristics of their jobs, their professions, assumes the form of a social relation between the products of their labour themselves.[18] (Marx, 1867/1872/2009, p. 84)

Due to this replication of the producers' social position in the relative value of a commodity with respect to other commodities, that is, in the relative value attributed to the products of the producers' labour, Marx ascribes to the commodity itself a mysterious quality:

17 Translation by Hans G. Ehrbar 2002 (Marx, 1867/1890/2002.).
18 Translation by the author, 2015.

> [...] What is mysterious about the commodity form is therefore simply that the social characteristics of men's own labour are reflected back to them as objective characteristics inherent in the products of their labour, as quasi-physical properties of these things, and that therefore also the social relation of the producers to the aggregate labour is reflected as a social relation of objects, a relation [existing] apart from and outside the producers.[19] (Marx, 1867/1872/2009, p. 84)

That phantasmagorical quid pro quo is expanded and elaborated on by Walter Benjamin in his Passagenwerk (Benjamin, 1991a, & b). However, whereas Marx sees in the objective societal circumstances the causal base of the resulting superstructure of the commodity-fetish, or, in other words, the societal circumstances of objects, Benjamin, in Konvolut K 2.5 (Benjamin 1990a, pp. 495-496), characterises the relationship between base and superstructure as one of "expressive connectivity". He writes:

> At first it seems as if Marx wanted only to establish a causal relation between superstructure and base (infrastructure). But the observation that the ideology of the superstructure reflects these relations in a false and distorted manner goes beyond this. The question is, namely: if the base (i.e., the infrastructure in the literal sense), to a certain extent, determines the conceptual and practical material of the superstructure – this determination is, however, not one of simple reflection – how is it then to be characterised [...]? As its expression – the superstructure is the expression of the base.[20] (Benjamin 1990a, p. 495)

Thus, Benjamin believes the "fetish-quality inherent to the commodity" (Tiedemann, 1991, p. 28)[21] is not the mirror, but rather the expression of the base. Furthermore, Benjamin attributes the dimension of imagination to this expressive connectivity. When introducing that dimension of imagination, which, in this study, is referred to as the imaginary[22], he writes: "The fetish-quality inherent in the commodity adheres to the commodity-producing society itself, yet not in the way it actually is, but in the way it imagines and understands itself to be whenever it abstracts from the fact that it indeed does produce commodities. The image of itself that society

19 Translation by Hans G. Ehrbar 2002 (Marx, 1867/1890/2002).
20 Translation by the author, 2015.
21 Translation by the author, 2015.
22 For a further discussion of the imaginary, see Pezzoli-Olgiati (2015).

thereby produces and which it tends to call its culture, is what is described by the notion of phantasmagoria" (Benjamin 1991b, p. 822).[23],[24] In this context, "abstraction" stands for a decoupling from the confining characteristics of the societal base. The imaginary then, freed from confinement of the base structure, becomes a limitless, open space that can be filled with close to any content. In this sense, as Bolz illustrates (Bolz, 2002, pp. 64-65), for Benjamin, capitalism qualifies as a religion, a cult religion entirely centered on the worship of commodities. The commodity as such, is the fetish of that cult religion, in which the cult precedes the doctrine – a cult, similar to pagan religions, without both, dogmatics and theology. Thus, the enthronement of the commodity – with its exchange value as the object of worship, or glorification – is the religio-sociological explanation of the so-called phantasmagoria, a key concept in Benjamin's work.[25] Thus, commodities obviously can serve as vessels, as carriers of the imaginary. They can be used or exploited as projection screens *for*, as well as, manifestations *of* the imaginary. As does Marx, Benjamin speaks of commodity fetishism (Bolz, 2002, p. 65). Yet, whilst also confirming the fetish potential of commodities recognised by Marx, Benjamin expands the concept by liberating it from the confining aspects of the commodity-producing base-structure. The introduction of the imaginary dimension, limited only by the imaginativeness of a society's members, sets, regarding this study, the stage for the construction of a theoretical framework with respect to the elevation of commodities, or, in other words, successful branding. If marketing, and branding succeed in propelling the imaginary in the desired direc-

---

23 Translation by the author, 2015.

24 For further reading on the related topic of brandscaping, that is, the representation of a brand in a particular space (landscape), see also Sherry (1998).

25 Benjamin's analysis does not, however, limit the dimension of the sacred to the commodity-fetish alone. For Benjamin, capitalism itself is a religion: a pure cult religion without theology and without dogmata. Similar to ancient pagan cults, the religiosity of capitalism has a direct and practical focus: the permanent, and uninterrupted commodity cult with commodity-fetishes, charged with the imaginary, as its objects of worship. Again, it is important to differentiate here between the use-value of a commodity and its exchange-value: the object of worship is the *exchange-value* of the commodity, not its practical use-value (Bolz, 2002, pp. 64-65). And the expressive quality pertains to only the exchange-value of the commodity – therein lies the expression of the societal base, an expression enriched by the imaginary.

tion, a commodity can, in principle, acquire close to almost any symbolic charge.[26]

Taking Benjamin's argument one step further, and placing it into the context of a postmodern, globally interconnected society where consumers often have, on average, a comparatively high purchasing power, it can be observed that even profane consumer goods are, at times, morphed into something far more exciting than their use-value would imply, namely into brands of abounding appeal.

However, such appeal does not come about all by itself, it is the result of a complex process, devised by marketing, implemented and guided by advertising. As was previously discussed in chapter 1.3, the annulment of the separation of thing and concept, a presupposition of successful postmodern marketing, has far-reaching implications for the possible potency of the aforementioned dimension of the imaginary: This dimension of the imaginary is addressed by visual culture theory as well as by the neo-formalist film theory, which are both discussed in subsequent chapters. This dimension is therefore, a pivotal point of this study, paving the inroad for marketing by establishing the link between marketing and advertising on one hand, and the consumer on the other. It provides, so to speak, the docking point wherein marketing profoundly connects to the consumer. The commodity becomes the vessel, the carrier of an expression enlivened by the imaginary that surrounds the commodity like a nutritive solution, feeding and charging the commodity with its concepts that were, in turn, instigated by the narrative told through the language of advertising – a narrative which is, ultimately, re-enacted by the consumer. As far as the consumer is motivated to become a part of the concepts transported by the commercials and reified in the commodity, the consumer's desire for the concept becomes a desire for the commodity itself. Marketing, in this sense, if it is successful in stirring the would-be consumer's desire to be, in some way, part of the commercial's narrative, steers it towards the advertised product. In other words, the consumer's imagination, supported by advertising, guides their decision to choose a certain product, which is tantamount to choosing the concept that has been amalgamated with the product. Thereby, that concept issues in an ethos, a blueprint for the consumer's actions. Therefore, expressed in a terminology pursuant to Geertz's

26 For a more recent study examining the requirements that have to be fulfilled for a commodity to assume, in the consumer's perception, a status of sacredness, see Belk et al. (1989).

definition of religion, the consumer's imagination is the locus of a model *of* the world, a concept or a worldview, and a model *for* the world, a specific ethos. Subsequently, in subchapter 2.2.2, Geertz's definition is discussed in detail. First, however, a closer look at the consumer is warranted.

2.1.2 A closer look at the consumer

In addition to examining the role of commodities, with respect to their above-mentioned super-elevation into objects of worship, it is also essential to shed light on the worshipper, or in commercial terms, on the consumer of such fetish-commodities charged with imaginary qualities. Later, based on the findings of the audio-visual and the socio-empirical analysis, this study examines whether such charging of a commodity is done solely by its material producer, that is, the supplier, or whether such charging is co-produced, and reproduced by the consumer also. Therefore, what is needed first, is a discussion of the type of consumer presupposed in this study, as well as that consumer's societal context.

As already mentioned, this study does not work with the anthropology of the homo economicus. Consumers are primarily approached as beings with generally many unsatisfied needs and wants. It is rare that a human has all of his, or her needs catered for. Furthermore, if the basic needs are met, then more refined needs such as self-esteem and respect by others move to the foreground. At any rate, humans, it can be assumed, are rarely completely free of feeling that something, whatever that may be, is missing. Therefore, consumption, as a favoured method to meet needs and wants, assumes a pivotal role.[27]

In a society with a high degree of differentiation[28], religion has to surrender some of its tasks and functions to other, secular systems (Stolz, 2010, 2013). In this sense, referring to Walter Benjamin's concept of the above mentioned "capitalist religion", Bolz maintains that the postmodern consumer's behaviour includes patterns exhibiting elements of a cult-worshipping consumer items rather than God or gods. For instance, in reference to Volkswagen's "Autostadt" in Wolfsburg, Germany, he points to such patterns: "The automobile is an object of worship that requires a sanc-

27 For a further discussion of this topic, see Maslow (1943/2013).

28 A society with a high degree of differentiation is, for instance, a society in which religious institutions are not (or no longer) concerned with health care or public education.

tuary" (Bolz, 2002, p. 91). In contrast to the cult of worshipping consumer goods, in many postmodern societies, traditional institutionalised religion, instead, is on the decline. Indeed, it is largely practised, if at all, in a moderated form where believers hesitate to accept and abide by the core dogmas of their own religious denomination (Bolz, 2002, pp. 27-28), as is exemplified, for instance, by Roman Catholic spouses getting divorced. In that general societal setting, consumption has assumed functions that go beyond the mere use of consumption items according to their use-value. Of course, what is alluded to here, are the implications of the aforementioned super-elevation of the commodity.

Generally speaking then, the consumer-type addressed in this study is an individual living in a postmodern, consumption-oriented, largely secularised society with a high degree of social differentiation. Regarding the identity of such a postmodern consumer, Firat and Shultz maintain that "the postmodern identity is highly fluid and contested. Indeed, [...] postmodern consumers are said to be playful with identity, comfortable with multiphrenic selves" (Firat & Shultz, 2001, p. 191). Multiphrenia[29], the skill, the capability of living and thinking in different realities alongside one another, is accompanied by a condition which Firat and Shultz call "hyperreality". They write:

> Hyperreality, the condition of the constitution of social reality through powerful signification and representations of hype or simulation (Firat & Venkatesh, 1993), is also the process of construction of the (social) identity of the consumer. This process of identity construction plays the most significant role in how a consumer perceives oneself, how s/he identifies her/his purpose and reason for being, and constitutes meaning. (Firat & Shultz, 2001, p. 193)[30]

With respect to different identities, Firat and Shultz then tested the hypothesis that postmodern consumers, adopting different selves, are thereby trying to actively manage the impressions they give in different situations, feigning different selves (Firat & Shultz, 2001). However, that hypothesis had to be rejected. They write: "[W]hen postmodern consumers adopt different selves, they immerse into each experience to become and live the identity in its own right. For them, it is not managing an impression, but

29 For a detailed description of multiphrenia, see Gergen (1991).
30 For a further discussion of the concept of hyperreality, see Eco (1986) and Jameson (1991).

actually *becoming* the self, which they represent in each experience. Each self, that is, is a true experience [...]" (Firat & Shultz, 2001, p. 199).[31]

The contingencies of a consumer's reification desire in a product, and of an idea's reification in a product, were presented above. Another question concerns the role marketing, in a satiated consumer-oriented society, plays in those processes. To be able to address that question, another look at the consumer is warranted. The postmodern consumer implied in this study typically belongs to the winners of the globalisation process, that set in after the fall of communism in the late 1980s and early 1990s. In many countries, the resulting abundance of material goods and services led to a situation in which the scarcity of goods and services, a paradigm of economic theory, has itself become scarce. When the American psychologist Jerome Seymour Bruner wrote: "Above the subsistence level, you do not need anything until you have it" (Bruner, 1979, pp. 145-146), he meant that consumers, once they are used to and familiarised with a certain product or service, will be unwilling to let go of it. Seen from a purely practical point of view, the key to commercial success is to make people desire a product they do not need, and thus have no innate demand for. Nevertheless, once a consumer is introduced to such a product, Bruner claims that he or she will be unlikely to stop consuming it. It is therefore the task of a marketing campaign to kindle a consumer's desire and to simultaneously interpret the kindled desire on behalf of the consumer in such a way that he or she knows exactly what product to crave. Moreover, with respect to the creation of demand for the apparently unnecessary, the imagination's contribution is decisive: It is in the would-be consumer's imagination where a commercial's meaning is conceived, where the concepts conveyed by the advertising's narrative unfold, ultimately leading, if consumption is triggered, to factual realities boosting the supplier's profit margin.

As stated above, the question of precisely *how* the Nespresso campaign kindles the consumer's desire leads to the analysis of the audio-visual enactment of the marketing campaign, to the Nespresso commercials, and their intricate workings and functional mechanisms. In this context, a contribution made by Elizabeth Cowie (1990) is essential. She writes:

> [...][W]hile on the one hand fantasy can be characterised as a series of wishes presented through imaginary happenings, on the other hand it

31 For a further discussion of the postmodern consumer, see McCracken (1986), Firat (1991), Brown (1993), Woodruff (1997), Firat and Shultz (2001), Holt (2002), Hamouda and Gharbi (2013).

> is also a structure: fantasy as the mise-en-scène of desire, the putting into a scene, a staging, of desire. (Cowie, 1990, p. 149)

Cowie connects the notion of fantasy to the concept of the imaginary, adding to it a specific structure, viz. the structure that comes with the staging of desire. For the purpose of the analysis of the audio-visual corpus, that is, the commercials, this link between the imaginary, fantasy and desire is helpful as it allows for an explanation of why the actions portrayed by the commercials' protagonists, that is, the consuming of Nespresso, are so easily imitated, why the portrayed ethos is so readily learnt by viewers.

With respect to a film's audience, Cowie maintains that the individual subjects are not only the viewers of a fantasy shown to them, but they might also see themselves participating in the fantasy. Gillian Rose summarises Cowie's contribution as follows: "Cowie's (1990) key point about fantasy is that the subject need not only be the audience of a fantasy. The subject may also imagine that they participate in the fantasy as well [...]" (Rose 2012, pp. 178-179). Furthermore, viewers watching the fantasy, that is, the film, may imagine their participation in the shown fantasy "in ways that correspond to the dynamics of their own fantasies" (Rose 2012, p. 179).

So, not only does the audience of a fantasy imagine that they are participating in it, but their participation takes shape according to the dynamics of their *own* fantasies. This constitutes a crucial point: the viewer's participation in the fantasy of a commercial according to the choreography of his or her own fantasy permits the commercial and the personal fantasy to meld into one story. And, as Cowie points out, fantasy is the staging of desire. The commercial, prompting the viewer's own fantasy, becomes the medium that stages the viewer's desire. Moreover, by showing the viewer the protagonists' fantasy desire, the commercial also interprets the viewer's desire for him, or for her. As the two fantasies, the commercial and the personal, merge into one story, the awakening of desire becomes embedded in the commercial's storyline, and personal desire coalesces with the content constructed by the commercial. Pursuant to Bruner's contribution, one could say that even if a viewer, prior to learning about Nespresso, had not felt that something like capsuled-coffee was missing in his or her life, is highly likely to feel a desire for Nespresso once he or she has participated in the commercial's fantasy. Put more easily, the viewer's desire does not rear its head until the viewer knows about the product promoted through the commercial's fantasy.

Desire is connected to emotion. And an emotion can give rise to desire. If the commercial stirs agreeable emotions in the viewer, he or she might feel the desire to try the advertised product. Nussbaum sees a strong connection between emotions and action. She writes, "emotions are closely connected with *action*; few facts about them are more obvious" (Nussbaum, 2001/2008, p. 135). The question now arises concerning the actions that are likely to follow the awakened desire. To answer that question, a closer look at the values put forth by the commercial's narrative is needed. Nussbaum, in this regard, identifies a connection between the acknowledgement of value, and the motivation to act, saying: "Sometimes, […] value-acknowledging, in combination with the situational perceptions […], will straightforwardly give rise to motivations to act" (Nussbaum, 2001/2008, p. 135). The commercial gives the viewer's desire its direction by seemingly attributing, through its narrative, a value to a certain object and/or action.[32] In this sense, as stated above, it is the marketing campaign, specifically the commercial that interprets the viewer's – the would-be consumer's – desire (Bolz, 2002, p. 97). Thereby, the commercial becomes the determinant with respect to both: the viewer's object of desire and the subsequent actions.

If the viewer participates in the commercial's fantasy according to the dynamics of his or her *own* fantasies, he or she is likely to perceive the awakened desire as truly his or hers, and the object of desire as what he or she really wants. In that case, the fantasy presented by the commercial is no longer just a generic fantasy, but becomes an individualised, personal fantasy. Thus, the craving, the desire for the advertised product is likely to be perceived as genuinely real. The viewer's own fantasy then – despite being a fantasy – takes on, in the individual's mind, a factual quality. In anticipation of the subsequent discussion regarding the use of Geertz's definition of religion in this study, it can be said that an "aura of factuality" results from this coalescence of fantasies. Expressed in the terms of Geertz's definition of religion, such an "aura of factuality" makes "the […] motivations [to act] seem uniquely realistic" (Geertz, 1966/2010, p. 4). And, until such desire is satisfied, the consumer is likely to perceive an unfulfilled need and, as a result, is likely to feel the motivation to purchase the product or object of desire.

The participation in the commercial's fantasy according to the dynamics of the viewer's own fantasies has yet another, far-reaching implication. Ac-

---

32 The specific role the viewer plays in the attribution of value to a certain object or action, that is, the viewer's role in the process of meaning-making, will be discussed in greater detail in chapter 5.2.1, in connection with the introduction to this study's approach to commercials.

cording to the American philosopher Harry Frankfurt, the consumer's desire for a product with an emotional and symbolical charge – that is, for a successfully branded product – is accompanied by a second-order desire: A desire to participate in the idea represented by the branded product, or fetish, and to be henceforth transformed as an individual and, in a transcendent sense, completed by it. Consumption becomes the "medium of a culture of the self" (Bolz, 2002, p. 102), allowing for the staging of the self and for the creation, or invention of an identity (Bolz, 2002), rendering the consumer whole: For the consumer, the fetish-commodity, due to the aforementioned postmodern annulment of the separation of thing and concept, becomes a means to a personal transformation and completion of the self. In this sense, marketing has most likely outgrown the realms of innocence, simply informing potential consumers of the practical value of a product.

Next, before discussing Geertz's definition of religion, an overview of religion in the perspective of cultural studies is offered, providing a frame of reference in order to examine the hypothesised analogy between religion and marketing in a traceable and comprehensible way.

2.2 *Religion in the perspective of cultural studies*

2.2.1 General overview

In the words of Toby Miller, cultural studies as a field of study is "animated by subjectivity and power – how human subjects are formed and how they experience cultural and social space" (Miller, 2006, p. 1). Similarly, Graham Murdock sees cultural studies engaged in the questions of "how discourse and imagery are organised in complex and shifting patterns of meaning and how these meanings are reproduced, negotiated, and struggled over in the flow and flux of everyday life" (Murdock, 1995, p. 95). It is not the scope of this study to plough through the plethora of existing definitions of cultural studies. What the two examples illustrate, however, is the apparent consensus amongst scholars that cultural studies is concerned with the production of meaning. With respect to the notion of "culture" itself, Hall, one of cultural studies' main representatives, maintains that "[p]rimarily, culture is concerned with the production and the exchange of meanings [...] between the members of a society or group. [...] [It] depends on its participants interpreting meaningfully what is happening around them, and "making sense" of the world in broadly similar ways" (Hall,

1997/2003a, p. 2). Moreover, "culture is about feelings, attachments and emotions as well as concepts and ideas." (Hall, 2003a/1997, p. 2) Similarly, according to Jeff Lewis, "culture is that shared (imagined-meaning) space where the media and audiences interact" (Lewis, 2008, p. 4). Here, the word "shared" implies, or presupposes rather, communication and therefore *language*. In this context, obviously, language is of prime importance. Hall also attributes to language a pivotal role because it is the "privileged medium in which we make sense of things, in which meaning is produced and exchanged" (Hall, 2003a/1997, p. 1). Or, in other words, a focus on "the particular mechanisms by which meaning is produced and circulated – the forms of culture as opposed to content [...] has directed attention to the communication process itself and the medium in which meaning is constructed – i.e., *language*" (du Gay, Hall, Janes, Mackay, & Negus, 1997, p. 12-13). Thus, in cultural studies, "the production of meaning through language – what is sometimes called signification - occupies a central role in the analysis of culture" (du Gay et al., 1997, p. 13). In this context, it is important to note that the term "language" is understood to include "sounds, written words, electronically produced images, musical notes, even objects [...]" (Hall 2003a/1997, p. 1). Cultural studies, in this sense, is inherently interested in signs, in semantics.

A language that must be mentioned in the context of this study is advertising. Generally speaking, "advertisements are one of the most important cultural factors moulding and reflecting our life today" (Williamson, 1978/2002, p. 11). And, more specifically, du Gay et al. (1997) maintain: "Advertising is the cultural language which speaks on behalf of the product. Advertising makes commodities speak" (p. 25). In this sense, the language of advertising communicates meaning, and is itself a signifying practice. And furthermore, in as much as advertising is successful in turning would-be consumers into actual consumers, the practices related to the use, or the possession of the advertised commodity are potentially also signifying practices, as they are, for consumers, meaningful practices: "What matters for *culture* is that these practices [...] are meaningful. They are organised, guided and framed by meaning. They are meaningful for the participants involved. We call them signifying practices" (du Gay et al., 1997, pp. 17-18).

Similarly, with a view to the production of meaning in a religious context, it does not, in the perspective of cultural studies, matter whether the signs used, taken individually, do or do not have a religious meaning. What matters is the way in which the signs are used. Depending on what is meant by the term "religion", signs that have, for a given culture, no obvious religious connotation can still be used on the semantic level and thereby produce meaning of a religious quality. The context of signs generates religious meaning. Or, in other words, what matters is the practice, the communication process itself. In Hall's words: "[Meaning] is constructed through signifying – i.e., meaning-producing – practices" (Hall 1997/2003b, p. 28). In this sense, religion is to be understood, like advertising, as a signifying practice.

As mentioned above, with a view to religion in the perspective of cultural studies, it *cannot* be argued that on the semantic level, only signs that are within a given culture and clearly recognisable as "religious", are qualified to connote religious phenomena. Instead, with a view to the fluidity of meaning of close to any sign, this study argues along another line. Whilst signs that are clearly recognisable as religious are indeed used on the semantic level, as, for example, the Illy commercial discussed below clearly demonstrates, that need not necessarily be so. Signs with no obvious religious connotation may as well generate meaning of a religious quality. What matters is not the individual sign per se, but the respective cultural practice. Regarding the attribution of meaning to objects, actions, and people "the emphasis on cultural practices is important. It is [the] participants in a culture who give meaning to people, objects and events. Things 'in themselves' rarely if ever have any one, single, fixed and unchanging meaning" (Hall 2003a/1997, p. 3).

It can be summarised that in the perspective of cultural studies, both advertising, one of marketing's principal methods, and religion, are signifying practices. Given that the terms "advertising" and "marketing" have already been addressed above, and with a view to the overlap between religion and marketing, the notion of religion this study works with, needs to be addressed next.

2.2.2 Clifford Geertz's contribution

With respect to the use of a definition of religion in scientific work, that is, in the social sciences and the humanities, Linda Woodhead argues that "the social scientific study should [...] become more self-conscious and self-critical in its approach to 'religion' [...] [I]t is necessary to have some critical awareness of what concept(s) of religion are in play, and to be able to justify their applicability in particular contexts of use" (Woodhead, 2011, p. 122). Scholars should therefore be able to argue in a plausible manner why in their work one definition of religion is preferred over another.

This study attempts to carve out a structural and functional analogy between religion and marketing. In this sense, both religion and marketing, mirror a pattern representing a worldview[33] and an ethos – factuality, how things "are" and a blueprint for action. Geertz's definition ideally captures that structure of worldview and ethos. In this sense, it is a very useful and well-suited heuristic tool of analysis. It reads as follows: "A religion is 1) a system of symbols which acts to 2) establish powerful, pervasive and long-lasting moods and motivations in men by 3) formulating conceptions of a general order of existence and 4) clothing these conceptions with such an aura of factuality that 5) the moods and motivations seem uniquely realistic" (Geertz 1966/2010, p. 4).

Geertz's definition illuminates the various aspects of religion: Religion as a "system of symbols" captures the forging of ideas, of the imaginary, into subsumable forms, that is, symbols, and their subsequent configuration into a system of symbols that serves as an extrinsic source of information. The source is extrinsic to the religious subject, or, in the context of this research, to the consumer. As a source of information, the system of symbols provides a blueprint or a model of, as well as a model for, the configuration of social and psychological processes that steers and governs public and private behaviour. In this sense, the system is both a model *of* and a model *for* the world. As the system of symbols is manipulated "so as to bring [it], more or less closely, into parallel with the pre-established non-symbolic system [or non-symbolic, profane reality]" (Geertz, 1966/2010, p. 7), it becomes a model *of* the world. On the other hand, in the manipulation of non-symbolic reality according to its parameters, the system of symbols serves as a model *for* the world. As will be shown in this study, the Nespresso marketing campaign also is both: a model of the world, allowing a glimpse into the coffee world of those who belong to Nespresso's Shangri-La, the insiders, or members of the club, but it also is a model for the world, or the coffee world, implying "how it should be", and displaying the right course of action that is only ignored by those who elect not to be part of that world or those who are not invited to join that world, to be a part of that world.

33 In the context of marketing the term "worldview" is not used in the sense of its eschatological meaning. "Worldview" with respect to marketing refers to the classification, the "canonisation" in relation to the advertised brand.

The second element in Geertz's definition, the "powerful, pervasive and long-lasting moods and motivations" (Geertz 1966/2010, p. 4) established by the system of symbols indicates two different emotional aspects, which differ in terms of the circumstances and conditions wherein they make sense: moods and motivations. Geertz says:

> [...] [P]erhaps the most important difference, so far as we are concerned, between moods and motivations is that motivations are 'made meaningful' with reference to the ends toward which they are conceived to conduce, whereas moods are 'made meaningful' with reference to the conditions from which they are conceived to spring. We interpret motives in terms of their consummations, but we interpret moods in terms of their sources. (Geertz, 1966/2010, p. 12)

This degree of discriminatory power and the differentiation between moods and motivations facilitate a precise analysis of two observed effects of the marketing campaign under investigation: the observed creation of identity on the part of Nespresso consumers refers to the notion of moods, and the consumers' observed determination to perform, or avoid, certain actions refers to motivations.

The third element of Geertz's definition, the formulation of "conceptions of a general order of existence", provides adherents and believers, or consumers for that matter, with the tools needed to deal with chaos. As Geertz, quoting Langer (1960), phrases it:

> Therefore, our most important assets are always the symbols of our general *orientation* in nature, on the earth, in society, and in what we are doing: the symbols of our *Weltanschauung* and *Lebensanschauung*. Consequently, in a primitive society, a daily ritual is incorporated in common activities, in eating, washing, fire-making, etc., as well as in pure ceremonial; because the need of reasserting the tribal morale and recognising its cosmic conditions is constantly felt. The Church brought men daily (in some orders even hourly) to their knees, to enact if not to contemplate their assent to the ultimate concepts. (Geertz, 1966/2010, p. 14, quoting Langer 1960, p. 287)

In this sense, the pivotal functional role of the ritual as a practice of religion must be emphasised. As will be explained later, it is in, and through, the ritual that the two models (the model of the world and the model for the world) merge – giving rise to the creation of faith, to the emergence of religious conviction, and shaping the believer's (or the consumer's) spiritual consciousness. "[...][M]en attain their faith as they portray it" (Geertz, 1966/2010, p. 29).

Finally, "clothing these conceptions of a general order of existence with an aura of factuality" (Geertz 1966/2010, p. 4) is a part of Geertz's definition that reflects a fundamental principle of any religion: In order to know, one must first believe. From a religious perspective, the adherent corrects and completes everyday reality according to a more comprehensive system. The religious perspective provides a worldview that is not of a hypothetical nature. Furthermore, from *within* that perspective, an interest in factual evidence, successfully explained by the religious model – the system of symbols – leads to and culminates in the creation of verisimilitude. And, finally, that aura of factual reality, reflected back on to and absorbed by the system of symbols, becomes a core element of the above-mentioned ritual. It endows the ritual with the performative power to reaffirm the religious perspective, thereby perpetuating the creation of faith. Obviously, such verisimilitude, once absorbed and reflected by a system of symbols, ensures that the moods and motivations established by the system of symbols, and reinforced by rituals, consequently appear as uniquely realistic.

The clearly, very high level of abstraction of Geertz's definition allows for its application in a variety of scenarios, even those that at first glance seem to have nothing in common with one another and that do not display an affinity to religion. Indeed, the high degree of abstraction permits the identification of religion in the Geertzian sense in scenarios and contexts, marketing and advertising, for example, where it is neither expected nor surmised.

In this study, advertising, marketing's principal method and one of its indispensable pillars, is approached as a language using signs and symbols. Geertz's definition can then actually be likened to a checklist, including all the required elements of a system of symbols – any system of symbols – must have in order to qualify as a religion. It is precisely the broad scope of the definition that makes it ideally suited to this study, as it permits the comparison of two seemingly unrelated fields like religion and marketing. Indeed, this study would potentially flounder without the open scope and the contextual qualities of Geertz's definition. In a Geertzian sense, and supported by Woodhead (2011), it is at any rate not possible to determine, once and for all, the meaning of religion. This fundamental impossibility applies to both the ethical as well as the factual perspective (with respect to a worldview). In addition, as this study neither tries to come up with a new substantial definition of religion nor intends to claim that consuming Nespresso is a religion, it does not require a definition of what religion *is*. Because it exclusively aims to elaborate, on a theoretical level, whether a structural and a functional analogy between religion and marketing can be identified, the study requires an analytical tool that enables a comparison of two separate systems of symbols. Geertz's definition has been selected precisely because it is open enough to accommodate such a comparison.

In addition thereto, if one is willing to see a definition of religion, for a moment, as a concept, it is worthwhile to consider a contribution made by Richard Amesbury. He writes: "The point [...] is neither that these concepts [...] are *not* true, nor that we have no means of evaluating their "correspondence to reality" and so must remain agnostic with respect to their truth, but that they provide the contexts *within which* the distinction between truth and falsity can meaningfully be applied" (Amesbury 2002, p. 162). In this sense, with a view to the aforementioned contextual qualities of Geertz's definition, it must be emphasised that it is precisely these qualities that provide the points of reference required to meaningfully establish whether, or not, a structural and functional analogy between religion and marketing exists.

2.2.3 Chances and limits of this approach

In order to approach, on the theoretical level, possible structural and functional analogies between marketing on one hand, and religion on the other, it is, for analytical purposes, necessary to work with a definition of religion capable of capturing such analogies, in order to adequately register and chart them. As was outlined above, Geertz's definition, an analytical heuristic tool is, due to its *contextual nature*, ideally suited to that purpose, and therefore, to this study.

Moreover, as in marketing, the marketed product speaks through advertising, its language, it is indispensable to work with a definition of religion that is applicable to semiotics, to signs and systems of symbols. Again, Geertz's definition, due to its universal nature, can indeed be applied in contexts such as marketing, which seem at first sight, especially if only superficially analysed, too disconnected from religion to even warrant a study of possible analogies. The use of Geertz's definitions allows for a fine-tuned analysis possible to carve out, on a theoretical level, the nuances and characteristics of religion present in marketing which would, if another definition of religion were used, easily be overseen and would therefore remain hidden. To bring into the open what would otherwise remain hidden: That is the chance and the potential of this approach.

Next, as this approach presupposes a knowledge of the nature of signs and symbols, in the following, a brief introduction to semiotics is given. The prominent role of semiotics in marketing was first addressed by Roland Barthes in the 1960s (Barthes, 1964/1967). In that context, Barthes also sheds light on the crucial role of industry in deciding which signs enter the semiological[34] language:

> But in most [...] semiological systems, the language is elaborated not by the 'speaking mass' but by a deciding group. In this sense, it can be held that in most semiological languages, the sign is really and truly 'arbitrary' [...] since it is founded in artificial fashion by a unilateral decision; these in fact are fabricated languages, 'logo-techniques'. The user follows these languages, draws messages (or 'speech') from them but has no part in their elaboration. The deciding group which is at the origin of the system (and of its changes) can be more or less narrow; it can be a highly qualified technocracy (fashion, motor industry) [...]. (Barthes, 1964/1967, p. 31)

As such, the choice of signs and the related construction of meaning attributed to them naturally, have strong implications with respect to who has the prerogative of interpretation. That issue, which is related to the power to determine and fix the meaning of terms and notions, thereby manipulating language with respect to the concepts it is able to catch, express and communicate, will be addressed later in the context of Hall's semiotic paradigm.

Regarding the term "sign", this study uses a typology based on the works of Ferdinand de Saussure and Charles Sanders Peirce, differentiating between three types of signs (Rose 2012, p.113, & p. 119). Each sign consists of a signifier and the signified. The signified can be described as the meaning of the sign and is equivalent to a concept. The signifier, by contrast, is an object, an image, an action, a sound, an alphabetic character or a string of characters that stands for and is assigned to the signified. For instance, the concept of an object designed to drink coffee is the signified, and the corresponding signifier in the English language is the, ultimately arbitrary, sequence of the three Latin characters C-U-P. Furthermore, it has no bearing whether the signifier is actually a written word, an action, or object,

34 The notion "semiology" refers to the study of signs according to the tenets put forth by de Saussure, that is, the study of signs in a classically textual context only. In the context of this study, term "semiotics" is used instead, implying the study of signs in a wider context, including commercials.

perhaps portrayed in an audio-visual narrative or whether it has purely imaginary qualities, being part of a fantasy.

Peirce suggests that signs can be grouped into three categories (Peirce, 1931/1974, p. 143). If the signifier has a strong similarity to the signified, then the sign is said to be iconic. For instance, the road sign below is an iconic sign because the signifier, that is, the image shown on the physical sign bears a strong resemblance to the assigned signified, the concept: "slippery when wet".

Figure 2: Iconic sign (Walmart, 2018)

In the case of indexical signs, there is no resemblance between the signified and the signified. Instead, in the case of "[i]n indexical signs, there is an inherent relationship between the signified and the signifier" (Rose, 2012, p. 119). For instance, the signifier either points towards the signified, or is an effect thereof. Smoke is an indexical sign standing for fire. Or, to give another example, once a coffee capsule has assumed, through a decoding of a commercial's narrative along the lines of "drinking Nespresso is preferable to chatting with George Clooney", a conceptual meaning of "the best coffee ever", then, that coffee capsule has become an indexical sign. The Nespresso coffee capsule, in this case the signifier, points towards the promised signified. The coffee capsule then is both, a promise and a guarantee regarding the best coffee ever.

Finally, in the case of symbolic signs, there exists "a conventionalised but clearly arbitrary relation[ship] between signifier and signified" (Rose 2012, p. 119). A good example is traffic lights. A red light indicates for instance that traffic must stop. Clearly, there exists neither a relationship of similitude nor of an indexical nature between the signifier and the signified.

Some signifieds can be part of an indexical and/or a symbolic sign. For instance, in the case of the above-mentioned signified "the best coffee ever", that signified also became, through the process of the successful marketing campaign, attributed to a specific signifier in the shape of the sequence of the alphabetic characters N-E-S-P-R-E-S-S-O. In that case, the signifier and signified form a symbolic sign, as there is neither an obvious resemblance between the two elements nor is there a compelling reason why the said signifier must be attributed to the ultimately arbitrary sequence of the characters N-E-S-P-R-E-S-S-O.

Not only can a specific signified be part of an indexical as well as a symbolic sign, a specific signified might also be attributed to more than just one signifier. Nespresso, for example, gives each specific coffee blend or flavour, respectively, a different name. And the various colours of the coffee capsules each correspond to one specific blend. Therefore, a specific blend, or flavour, and the corresponding colour go with a name – the capsules are named. For example, the name of the Nespresso capsule in the colour of gold, with a slight tinge towards beige, is *Volluto*. Clearly then, if the arbitrary sequence of the characters V-O-L-L-U-T-O comes to be associated, through marketing's successful conventionalising, with "the best coffee ever", that capsule's name, and the capsule's colour become both signifiers of a symbolic sign.

Next, there are two notions that need to be introduced: "referent" and "code". With respect to codes, Hall maintains: "Codes fix the relationships between concepts and signs. They stabilise meaning […]" (Hall, 1997/2003a, p. 21). As will be discussed in detail in chapter 4.1.1, codes are often culture-specific, and they are subject to change. Diachronically, they might change slowly, instead when manipulated, by marketing for example, they can change rapidly with the effect that new codes emerge. A referent then is the "actual object in the world that the sign is related to" (Rose, 2012, p. 113). In the case of the symbolic sign mentioned above where the arbitrary string of the three characters C-U-P (the signifier) means an object of a height of about three inches that can contain liquids and is usually equipped with a handle (the signified), the referent is the actual real-life cup in someone's cupboard. In this context it is important to note that an imaginary signifier also has a potential real-world referent. If it is possible to first imagine a fantasy, and then, in a second step, to actually act upon it, then such an action, once carried out, will be the imaginary signified's referent. In this sense, as this study will show, the viewer of a commercial, if he or she purchases the advertised product, completes the production of meaning by becoming him- or herself a part of the fantasy's reified, real-life referent.

A point worth noting here is the cultural dimension of the imaginary. Pezzoli-Olgiati writes: "Since the concept of imaginary is deepened to analyse communicative practices in the public sphere where religious references are transported and generated, it seems more precise to use the term '*cultural* imaginary'," (Pezzoli-Olgiati, 2015, p. 27). By the same token, advertising, as a cultural language, can also be viewed as a communicative practice, taking place in the public sphere. Due to that public character of advertising, the audience includes a large number of actual and would-be consumers. Furthermore, the meaning constructed by one particular individual viewer in response to seeing the commercials might well be similar, or even close to identical to the meaning constructed by other viewers, if they share the same cultural map. An imaginary signified then, for instance the meaning "the best coffee ever" indexically linked to the letters N-E-S-P-R-E-S-S-O, might well become part of a cultural imagination shared by many. In this sense, marketing can create a cultural map shared by many consumers.

As was discussed above, the attribution of signifier to signified, in many cases, is arbitrary and largely follows general convention (Rose, 2012, p. 119). Yet, established conventions and codes can be manipulated and altered. Codes are implicated in the sign because they fix the relationship between the signified and the signifier. Now, in the case of a change of the conventionalised, connotative meaning of a sign, the sign's signifier becomes attributed to another concept, and a new code is created. In this instance, the signifier, for example the picture of a cup, acquires a totally new meaning or connotation. If, for instance, a cup connotes a cosy moment on a cold winter's evening, a shift in connotation may engender an entirely different meaning. If, for example, an audio-visual narrative is successful in initiating a process that ultimately issues in the investment of a profane product with a meaning and a standing, and ultimately with an exchange value that is, at first sight, hard to comprehend, then, such a feat is rooted in the occurrence of a shift of the signified from the original signifier to a new-one. Connotative meanings can travel. The regrouping and rearranging of signifiers and signified, creating new codes is, seen in this context, the task of the cultural language of advertising. If completed successfully, what emerges is, limited of course to the context of the advertised commodity, a new code, and connected thereto, a new worldview and a corresponding ethos, accompanied by moods and motivations that "seem uniquely realistic" (Geertz, 1966/2010, p. 4).

Finally, it is important to give due diligence to the difference between the denotative and the connotative level of a sign, or its signified, respectively. Denotative meaning is usually straightforward and widely accepted. Iconic signs often have a strong denotative dimension. If the signified is, once again, a "cone-shaped bone china container, narrowed at the bottom, with a handle and a height of three inches" then a picture of a cup is an iconic sign with a strong denotative quality. However, like indexical and symbolic signs, iconic signs can also have a strong connotative quality. If, for example, the signifier, that is, the action portrayed in an audio-visual narrative, often involves a cup, and if the action's signified is "the best coffee ever", then the signified, that is, the meaning, can indeed be associated with the cup as well. In other words, on a connotative level, the cup itself acquires, through metonymy, a new and different meaning, itself becoming a symbolic sign.

Naturally, this approach to the phenomenon under scrutiny also comes with limits. Advertising, as outlined above, is a language communicating with audio-visual signs and symbols, respectively, whose meaning is fixed by codes. Inasmuch as culture is about shared meanings (Hall 2003a/1997, 1997/2003b), a meaningful interpretation of codes requires familiarity with their cultural backdrop. In this respect, David Morgan writes: "Vision is a socially […] constructed operation, depending on […] how […][the human body] engages the interpretive devices developed by a culture in order to see intelligibly. […] Seeing […] operates on the foundation of covenants with images that establish the conditions of meaningful visual experience" (Morgan, 2005, p. 34). In addition thereto, visual communication naturally implies a viewer, in the case of an advertisement, the would-be consumer. As Hall shows (1993), the codes carried and communicated by the advertisement have to be deciphered, read, or, in Hall's words, decoded by the viewer.[35] Ultimately, it is the viewer who produces the meaning of the advertisement through interpretation. So to speak, the viewer translates the codes of the advertisement and attributes a specific meaning to them. This is a hermeneutical undertaking, involving interpretation and translation. For a viewer of the advertisement to decipher the codes in roughly the ways intended by its producer, the viewer must have previous knowledge of the meaning of the signs used in the advertisement. The viewer must know what the codes stand for. For instance, a viewer who does not know who George Clooney is, is highly unlikely the get the puns in the advertisements discussed below. It is not enough to just recognise George

35 Hall's paper "Encoding, Decoding" is discussed in chapter 4.1.1.

Clooney as a handsome man. It is important to know that George Clooney, at the time when he first appeared as Nespresso's product ambassador for Europe, was considered by the media to be one of the most handsome, if not *the* most handsome male Hollywood actor.[36] In 2006 for instance, the editors of the US American *People Magazine* elected him, for the second time after 1997, the "sexiest man alive" (ABC news, (n.d.); RP Online, 2017)[37]. Only if the viewer of the advertisements has this information does he or she fully get the pun carried by the advertisement's narrative. The "sexiest man alive" implies a difference to all men alive. If knowledge of that difference is cumulated with the knowledge that George Clooney is a celebrity, a world-famous Hollywood actor (i.e., another two differences, or outstanding features, because naturally, most men alive are neither world-famous nor Hollywood actors), then it becomes clear that George Clooney, in the advertisement, appears as a signifier standing for the world of glamour as well as the sexiest and, by implication, most desirable man alive. So obviously, George Clooney comes into the advertisement with a lot of information charged upon him. Williamson calls that a "referent system"[38] (Williamson, 19782002, p. 26). "[…][I]t is only by referring back to this system as a system of *differences* that the sign can function: it is hollow of meaning in itself, its signified is only a distinction rather than a 'content;" (Williamson, 1978/2002, p. 26). Quoting Saussure, Williamson adds:

> [I]n all cases, then, we discover not *ideas* given in advance but *values* emanating from the system. When we say that these values correspond to concepts, it is understood that these concepts are purely differential, not positively defined by their content but negatively defined by their relation[ship] with other terms of the system. Their most precise characteristic is that they are what others are not. (Williamson, 1978/2002, p. 26 quoting Saussure, 1972/1986, p. 115, § 162)[39]

---

36 For instance, in 2004 on Femalefirst, a UK-based social-media platform concerned with celebrity news and gossip, users voted George Clooney the world's most beautiful man: Clooney, 43, beat off stiff competition from 'Ocean's Twelve' co-star Brad Pitt, who finished second in the survey, with England football captain David Beckham coming third" (Femalefirst, n.d.).

37 There are just two other men (alive or dead) who also were twice elected "sexiest man alive" by the *People* magazine: Brad Pitt in 1995 and 2000, and Johnny Depp in 2003 and 2009 (RP Online, 2017).

38 For an introduction to semiotics, see sub-chapter 2.2.3.

39 This quote corresponds, word for word, to the passage quoted by Williamson. Williamson, unfortunately, does not indicate the number of the page where that quote can be found, she only indicates that her source was published in the year

Clearly, the translation of the advertisement's language into the meaning most likely intended by the advertisement's producer, or in other words, successful hermeneutical work, presupposes a certain type of viewer: a viewer who has all the relevant information regarding the signifier's (George Clooney's, in this case) relative position in the referent system. If George Clooney were only perceived as a handsome man, for instance a handsome waiter, then the commercial's pun would not work. Equally, it presupposes a viewer who translates a high degree of sexiness into a high degree of desirability. If that link is not made by the viewer of the advertisement, then the pun goes unnoticed.

Taking into account these considerations, it becomes apparent that the approach chosen by this study, that is, seeing advertisement as a language working with codes and symbols that have to be deciphered, can only produce new insights and plausible findings in a very specific context: Foremost, what is presupposed is a viewer with all the above discussed information regarding the signifier's referent system.[40] A knowledge thereof is presupposed in order to understand the advertisement's pun. It could be argued that if such a specific context, which can also be likened to a specific *cultural* context, implying a fairly narrowly specified type of viewer is abandoned, then the conclusions made by this study cannot possibly be upheld.

Questioning an alleged objectivity of the study of religion as well as giving due consideration to the subjectivity of the research with all its limitations and challenges is a crucial process (Pezzoli-Olgiati, 2012). Regarding the subjectivity of research, Pezzoli-Olgiati highlights the importance of a profound hermeneutical reflection in order to recognise, carve out and, if needed, correct or at least discuss the epistemological consequences thereof. Her analysis of the nature of visual research sheds light on the inescapable subjectivity of the individual researcher's gaze: "There is no explaining nor understanding of visual sources without the affective, emotional, as well as intellectual involvement of the spectator. Visual research is imbued with the subjective perception and the socio-cultural milieu of

---

2000. Saussure's book *Courses in General Linguistics*, translated from French in 1986, is presently sold in the nineteenth printing. The passage, quoted by Williamson, unfortunately does not correspond, word for word, to the corresponding passage of the 1986 translation. This is most likely so because Williamson's source uses a different translation.

40 For a discussion of the consumer presupposed by this study, please see chapter 2.1.2.

the researcher"[41] (Pezzoli-Olgiati, 2012, p. 348). The researcher, in the analysis of the viewer, needs to be conscious of any analytical bias of which he or she is the cause.

> Visual media and cultures of visual practice are two significant and interrelated parts of visual culture studies in the context of religion. The scientific gaze is, as another constitutive element, a part thereof. Thereby, the researcher assumes a position of observation of self-reflexivity with regard to hermeneutical considerations.[42] (Pezzoli-Olgiati, 2012, p. 348)

In this regard,

> [...] the relationship between the researcher and the visual sources he or she is investigating [is relevant]. Although these considerations may be regarded as secondary, nonetheless, within a general methodological reflection, they should not be underestimated or ignored. In fact, the admission of one's own involvement as a viewer of the images on which one is undertaking research, opens the door to the crucial issue of the role of the particularity of subjectivity in academic enquiry. (Pezzoli-Olgiati & Rowland, 2011, p. 11)

The hermeneutical work carried out in this study requires that my perspective is made transparent. As will be discussed in subchapter 7.3, the view adopted by me includes, owed to the interdisciplinary nature of this study, the microeconomic perspective. Microeconomics is both a mathematical method to understand a firm's and a consumer's behaviour as well as an ideology maintaining that a firm's objective is the maximisation of profit, and, with a view to Buchanan's economic theory of clubs, that a consumer's objective is to maximise his or her benefit. In this sense, the deciphering of the advertisement's language is analysed according to the implied, ultimate objective of a firm, that is, the maximisation of its profit, and by the same token, as a means to that end, the consumer is approached as a person who needs to feel that he or she maximises consumer benefit by consuming the advertised commodity.

Considering these concerns, a hermeneutical approach to the coding and decoding of an audio-visual corpus, as in the case of this study, raises the fundamental epistemological question regarding how much insight is at all possible. The researcher is bound to see the object of a study through

41 Translation by the author, 2015.
42 Original in German; translation by the author, 2015.

his or her particular lens, according to his or her views, tenets, and paradigms. Whether the insights gained reveal more about the object studied or the researcher is an interesting question with a multitude of answers. What is certain, however, is that this issue requires the researcher's undivided attention to and willingness for self-reflexivity lest the research, its findings, and its conclusions lose their explanatory power and significance.

Given all of the above described issues, one has to be mindful of the fact that the findings and conclusions of this study will most likely not allow for a full generalisation. They are most likely to be conditional insights that are valid only if all the conditions required for the argumentative architecture of this study are met. In conditions other than described and presupposed by this study, the conclusions might be significantly different. Therefore, whilst the use of Geertz's definition of religion provides a valid analytical hermeneutical tool, capable of detecting and locating structural and functional analogies between religion and marketing, this comes at a price: If the context of the data, of the analysed phenomena is changed, that is, if the conditions are altered, the study's conclusions are likely to lose their validity. Consequently, the extent to which they can therefore be generalised is bounded.

2.3 Religious symbols in coffee advertising

2.3.1 Religions symbols in advertising

Religious symbols have been used in advertising for quite some time. For example, back in 1991, the autumn campaign of the Italian fashion label Benetton included a photograph showing a Catholic priest kissing a nun, dressed in a traditional white habit, on her mouth. The picture, created by Oliviero Toscani, whose collaboration with Benetton ended in the year 2000, is an over the shoulder (the priest's shoulder) close-up shot of the nun's face (Selwyn-Holmes, 2009). The nun's eyes are closed. Due to the perspective chosen, it remains unclear whether or not the priest's eyes are also closed. However, given the calm stillness of the moment of deeply felt romanticism captured by the photograph, it can be inferred that they are possibly closed as well. This photograph lead to a world-wide controversy as it broke a religious taboo. "In Italy, bowing to pressure from the Vatican, the use of the image was finally prohibited" (Selwyn-Holmes, 2009). Responding to that controversy, Benetton stated that the ad was merely "the affirmation of pure human sentiment" (Stonewallgazette, 2010). Obviously, Benetton succeeded in getting the public's attention by portraying culturally, and religiously, sensitive issues.

Similarly, in 2011 Benetton's marketing campaign included a picture of Pope Benedict XVI kissing a senior Egyptian imam (MailOnline, 2011). The advertisement was also placed in Rome near the Vatican City. As might be expected, the Vatican rejected Benetton's campaign as "completely unacceptable" (Königkrämer, 2011). Benetton, withdrawing that picture from its campaign, stated that the campaign's objective was exclusively its battle against a culture of hatred (Königkrämer, 2011). In the sense that religious dignitaries can be seen, semiotically, as symbolic signs carrying meaning, it can be said that apparently, Benetton had again managed to gain widespread publicity with a controversial marketing campaign using religious symbols.

Perhaps equally controversial, the Austrian energy drink producer Red Bull, in 2007, just prior to Christmas Eve launched an animated commercial (cartoon) showing the Holy Family being visited not by the three Wise Men, but by *four*, the fourth bringing Red Bull. In the cartoon, Mother Mary, turning to her husband Joseph, comments on the offering of Red Bull, remarking that she already has an ox. Similar to Benetton's campaign, this derogatory portrayal of the nativity scene was the source of much public attention (Der Gloeckel, 2008). The Catholic church in Austria, however, decided not to comment on that commercial.

Many more examples of the use of religious symbols in advertising could be listed.[43] What needs to be mentioned here, however, is that all of the examples portrayed above used religious symbols in a direct and upfront way. The intention is to shift, by braking cultural taboos, the advertised brand to the centre of public attention. Yet this study takes a different approach: It tries to look into the more hidden, structural and functional properties of the Nespresso marketing campaign.

2.3.2 Focus on coffee advertising

Religious symbols have also been used in the promotion of coffee brands, however, contrary to the aforementioned examples, in a non-controversial manner. In 1950 for instance, Lavazza, an Italian coffee brand, issued a set of six trade cards named "Santi", serial number eight, depicting the holy

43 For a further discussion of the use of religious symbols in advertising, see Höpflinger (2014) and Nardella (2015.).

deeds of six Roman Catholic saints.[44] In 1995, finally, Lavazza started a campaign still running today labelled *Paradiso*. It is centred around the religious figure of St. Peter as well as a Roman Catholic image of heaven *as* paradise[45]. Featuring Tullio Solenghi, an Italian comedian and stage actor, the commercials tell non-controversial stories of a mortal, recently arrived in heaven, meeting St. Peter who, in one commercial, offers to go down to earth, into a supermarket, to buy two packets of Lavazza *crema e gusto* (Lavazza, 1995a; Lavazza, 1995b). In other, subsequent commercials there appear famous historical figures like Leonardo da Vinci (Lavazza, 1995c; Lavazza, 1995d) or, going by his external appearance, Giuseppe Verdi (Lavazza, 2012a; Lavazza, 2012b). The stories told in the commercials are all non-controversial. They all share one common pun, which is that in heaven, or paradise, they actually do drink coffee and, moreover, when they drink coffee, they exclusively choose Lavazza.

In one particular Nespresso commercial, which was released in 2009, George Clooney, leaving a Nespresso boutique, dies as he is hit by a piano falling from the sky. In his subsequent conversation with St. Peter, it becomes clear that the inhabitants of heaven have a craving for Nespresso. Sitting with St. Peter on a white sofa, with two young blonde women, obviously angels, on either side, all four clad in white, St. Peter reveals to George Clooney that in that place, there are no film producers. Clooney comments: "It's heaven" (Nestlé-Nespresso, 2009). According to Nespresso's then director for International Marketing & Strategy Guillaume le Cunff: "The commercial makes an impression due to its bold action combined with lots of humour"[46] (Horizont, 2009). Clearly, as the above-mentioned Lavazza commercials, that commercial was also not controversial. From the author's perspective, the story as well as the self-referential passages in the conversation make it witty and funny.

Mokarabia, another Italian coffee brand, released a commercial in 2013 showing thirteen men grouped around a table, all drinking espresso from Mokarabia cups. A soft guitar tune is playing in the background, no words

---

44 A set of the trade card series no. 8 is in the ownership of the author.

45 The Italian notion "paradiso" can be translated as "heaven". The stories in the commercials are not located in paradise in the sense of "garden of Eden". Instead, they are located in a place that, in the Roman Catholic tradition, can immediately be identified as heaven. In that tradition, St. Peter is also seen as the gatekeeper of heaven based on Matthew (16:19), where Jesus says to Simon Peter: "I will give you the keys to the kingdom of heaven." Other Christian denominations reject that view.

46 Translation by the author, 2016.

are spoken, until, at the very last moment, a female voice comes from nowhere praising Mokarabia coffee: "Caffè Mokarabia – L'arte italiana del buon gusto"[47] (Mokarabia, 2013). Naturally, arguing with Erwin Panofsky, a viewer with some knowledge of Christian religion will immediately recognise the iconographical analogy with *The Last Supper* of Christ as, for instance, portrayed by Leonardo da Vinci[48]. And, continuing with Panofsky, moving on to an iconological interpretation, a viewer familiar with the main tenets of Christianity will most likely connect to the symbolic message. The wine drunk at *The Last Supper* stands for the renewal of God's covenant with his people, and therefore, for Christ's continued presence. In Mokarabia's commercial, Mokarabia takes the wine's place and thus, it can be argued, appropriates the symbolic meaning of a bond, no doubt between viewers, or would-be consumers, and the brand. Officially, Mokarabia speaks a more moderate language. Marco Zanetti, its owner, testifies: "In this campaign, we wanted to associate 'caffè' espresso with the arts, another exquisite product of our country"[49] (Beverfood, n.d.).

Quite clearly, religious symbols, and narratives, have made their way into coffee advertisements. And, for instance with a view to Mokarabia's last supper, seen iconographically in Panofsky's sense, there are clear analogies between the motif in the commercial and the religious motif of *The Last Supper*. Yet, those analogies will not be scrutinised further as this study does not address the presence of explicitly religious symbols in advertising or in marketing campaigns. Instead, it aims to carve out the more hidden, structural and functional analogies between religion and marketing.

---

47 Caffè Mokarabia – The Italian art of good taste. Translation by the author, 2016.

48 For a brief introduction to Panofsky's contribution to iconology see Rose (2012), pp. 202-205; for a further discussion see Davis (2011) pp. 196-209 and pp. 234-274; for a detailed introduction see Panofsky (1955/1982).

49 Translation by the author, 2016.

3 The Research Question

3.1 State of research

Not surprisingly, academic research regarding Nespresso has focussed, so far, on the traditionally debated issues like the evolvement of a faltering campaign into a new, more promising format (Markides, 1999) or the replacement of an unsuccessful business model with a more promising alternative (Matzler, Bailom, von den Eichen, & Kohler, 2013), to give just two examples. Yet, regarding an understanding of why the campaign built around George Clooney was so successful and of the factors that success is owed to, current research has, to date, not drawn upon a possible functional and structural analogy between religion and marketing as an explanation for Nespresso's continued and exceptionally high operating profit margins. A study, for instance, examines the effects of the consumption experience of Nespresso clients on the creation of a competitive advantage for the firm (Roederer, 2012). Three different aspects of a client's consumption experience, in connection with the purchase and consumption of Nespresso, are identified, helping to establish Nespresso's special brand identity. They are: The client's (1) experience of the product itself when he or she makes a Nespresso at home, (2) the experience in connection to the actual purchase of the product, either online or in one of the more than 450 Nespresso boutiques, in both cases avoiding the sometimes annoying shopping conditions in overcrowded supermarkets, and (3) the experience of Nespresso's media communication which itself rests on three pillars: The web-based Nespresso Club, the Nespresso boutiques and the Nespresso campaign "What else?" with George Clooney. Whilst this study offers, in a descriptive way, a good insight into the individual elements of Nespresso's marketing campaign, it does not offer a theoretical explication of the phenomenon under scrutiny.

With respect to the aforementioned absence of a discussion regarding a possible presence of a functional and structural analogy between religion and marketing, it is self-evident that research has not, as of yet, addressed the *particular* use of semiotics that seems to be constitutive to the establishment of said analogy. However, as will be further discussed below, in a generic manner, the role of semiotics in marketing has been the object of academic research. In this respect, a paper published in 2004 merits mentioning (Mick, Boroughs, Hetzel, & Brannen, 2004). That paper presented a comprehensive compilation of current peer research in the field of semiotics and marketing, contributing to the knowledge of marketing and consumer behaviour. In their conclusion, the authors stated that: [...] [S]emiotic consumer research has advanced beyond focusing on specific products, to augment knowledge about more universal topics such as gift-giving, fetish, memory, and identity" (Mick et al., 2004, p. 52). Furthermore, addressing a desideratum of their study, they wrote: "Increased research attention to other central consumer research topics, such as brand preferences and choice as well as word-of-mouth behaviour, would be a valuable step toward further validation of the merits of semiotics for marketing and consumer research (Mick et al., 2004, p. 52).[50]

And this is exactly what this study aims to accomplish: the development of a theoretical model capable of explaining consumer behaviour and consumer choice with respect to Nespresso, thus ultimately providing an understanding of Nespresso's dazzling commercial success. Structured as a monograph, this investigation addresses Nespresso's marketing campaign as a representative campaign to sell a product that is neither indispensable nor unique. Indeed, one could probably live happily without it and, if not, there are countless substitutes. Nevertheless, as this study shows, Nespresso adherents do not share this view of the product's expendability.

With respect to a consumer's identity-formation through consumption, it has been argued by many scholars (Firat & Shultz, 2001; Bolz, 2002; Hamouda & Gharbi, 2013), that consumption can indeed be a constitutive act of identity construction on part of the consumer. Yet, such identity construction, of course, presupposes a commodity, a consumer item, which can indeed bring about the said consumption-based experience. The charging of the commodity, its metamorphosis into a fetish commodity, or, in other words, the hyping of its exchange-value is thus a necessary precondition for this to work. And, as the results of the socio-empirical survey of this study will show, the worldly, spatial context related to the purchase of a consumer good also plays a constitutive role therein. With respect thereto, that is, the setting in which consumption then takes place, with shops functioning as the stage of a ritual-like enactment of the ideological surplus attributed to the commodity or to its exchange-value, respectively, Bolz uses the term "sanctuary" (Bolz, 2002, p. 91). With respect to the creation of the exchange value of the commodity, he provides an initial, general explanation. A commodity about to become a fetish-commodity, or in

50 For a discussion of semiotics in advertising see Williamson (2002).

other words, a product that is about to become a brand, first stands for an idea and will eventually, if the branding process is successful, have fully absorbed that idea, thereby becoming the idea's equivalent, so to speak its concrete manifestation. For example, "automobile" will thus stand for freedom (Bolz, 2002), and by the same token, Nespresso will represent the epitome of coffee culture. This metamorphosis or reification of an idea imbues consumption with functions other than the mere fulfilment of a profane, practical need. Consumption, then, enables the consumer to appropriate the idea the product stands for. The practice of purchasing thereby becomes a means to shape and refine personal identity – a function that has traditionally been, and still is, performed by religion. It is thus, as previously mentioned, this functional analogy that gives rise to the idea of a possible, conceptually upstream, structural analogy between religion and marketing. However, whilst Bolz describes the melding of an idea with a consumer item, he provides no precise examination of how this process takes place. Nor does he go as far as to look, on the theoretical level, into a possible structural analogy between religion and marketing. Similarly, neither do Firat and Shultz nor Hamouda and Gharbi address the said analogy as the possible pivotal point that could provide the understanding needed, on a theoretical level, to explain the phenomenon under scrutiny – a gap, this study aims to fill.

The next first step is to shed light on the degree to which current research has contributed to increased knowledge and insight into the role of marketing within the wide field of religion. In anticipation of the explanation and observations below, it can be said that, within the study of religion, research connecting the fields of religion and marketing has to date been carried out solely from the perspective of the marketing of religions or the marketing of religious beliefs, respectively. Mara Einstein, for instance, has argued that religion actually takes the form of a commodity (Einstein, 2008): "Religious organisations have taken on names, logos or personalities, and slogans that allow them to be heard in a cluttered, increasingly competitive marketplace. Purpose churches (those associated with *The Purpose Driven Life* phenomenon), Alpha Churches [online Christian Church], Joel Osteen [American televangelist], Kabbalah – these, and others, are what I am calling faith brands" (Einstein, 2008, p. xi). Examining "the similarities between religion and marketing/branding and its implications for identity creation" (Einstein, 2008, p. xii), Einstein argues from the perspective of religions being transformed into brands. Her profound analysis expounds how successful branding of the religious is accomplished, effectively converting the sacred into a secular, branded commodity. The reverse line of thought inquiring into whether the success of branded products could be explained by a structural analogy between religion and marketing, transforming a profane product into a brand with a quasi-religious charge, however, is not addressed by Einstein. Similarly, Stolz has maintained that, "it is clear, that some religious organisations have been effective at marketing and branding and that this has helped them to grow considerably [...]" (Stolz, 2014, p. 21). Along the same lines as Einstein, Stolz has approached the issue of complementary dynamics between religion and marketing from the vantage point of religion, without examining whether the reverse direction could constitute a valid theorem.

When it comes to the role of religion within marketing research, it can be said that the study of religion, could indeed make a valid contribution from an as yet, untried perspective. With respect to normative power, a quality also attributed to religion, research has been carried out in the field of fashion marketing and luxury brands, evidencing that "a consumer's [...] self-concept underlies bandwagon luxury consumption" (Ko & Megehee, 2012, p. 1395), whereby the degree to which a consumer has status-seeking predispositions, is susceptible to normative influence, and has a need for uniqueness plays a constitutive role (Ko & Megehee, 2012, p. 1395). Yet, that study does not address the question whether normativity claims in the context of marketing are, to some degree at least, analogous to normativity claims in the context of religion, nor does it address the question of precisely how such a normative influence is constructed and carried out and why it works.

On the issue of marketing and emotions, a considerable number of studies of relevance to academic research have been conducted, (Aaker, Stayman, & Vezina 1988; Mukhopadhyay & Johar, 2007; Oliver, 1992; Richins, 1997). Whilst they address the production of meaning – even to the effect of the creation of a fetish commodity – they do not make any reference to precisely why such production of meaning seems to function so well, nor do they proffer a theoretical contemplation of a possible structural and functional analogy between marketing and the mechanisms of religious meaning-making that could explain the emotionalisation of a product.

With respect to the issue of motivation and emotions, today's standardised body of knowledge in marketing, as presented in a myriad of textbooks, makes multiple references thereto: "Our emotional reactions [...] influence the likelihood that we will engage in an activity [...]" (Solomon, 2013, p. 145). Or: "Some consumer behaviourists distinguish between so-called rational motives and emotional motives. [...] Emotional motives imply the selection of goals according to personal or subjective criteria (e.g., pride, fear, affection, or status)" (Schiffman, Lazar Kanuk, & Wisenblit, 2010, p. 92). Along the same line of reasoning, "a recent study found that emotions arising from buying or not buying, when facing an unintended purchase, impact the impressions of advertising viewed subsequently" (Schiffman et al., 2010, p. 92). Yet despite the focus on the emotions raised by marketing campaigns, all of the aforementioned contributions and studies fail to produce a theoretical body that offers an explanation of sufficient depth as to the structure and the functions needed to successfully stir those emotions. They furthermore neglect to define what it takes to translate those emotions into consumer motivation to act – and yet it is the action of consumers that, as the final step, generates the immense success of certain marketing campaigns.

A model for consumer devotion was presented by Pimentel and Reynolds (2004). Their study is based on secondary data levied in the context of earlier studies. Therein, alongside behavioural patterns related to consumption, they include behavioural patterns related to fandom. They write: "The term 'devotion' implies religious fervour, and indeed, a college football team (or other object of devotion) holds elements of the 'sacred' for the devoted fan. Informants often referred to their fandom as religion, and used religious terms such as 'conversion' and 'saint' when discussing it"; (Pimentel & Reynolds, 2004, p. 2). Based on a list of twelve properties of sacredness, including kratophany and ritual, they develop a model that includes the sacralisation of a product as a pre-requirement for a consumer's normative commitment. Arguing in part with Belk, Wallendorf and Sherry (1989) who, in turn, base their argument on the contributions made by Émile Durkheim and Mircea Eliade, Pimentel and Reynolds' (2004) sociological and phenomenological approach implicitly treats the phenomena, under scrutiny, as equivalent to religion. With respect to the interviewees, for instance, they write: "Informants frequently described their loyalty as "like religion". One man told us, "My oldest son has the spirit" […]" (Pimentel & Reynolds, 2004, p. 15). These repeated references are perhaps best summed up by the contribution of one informant that is reported to have said in connection to fandom: "It's like religion to me" (Pimentel & Reynolds, 2004, p. 41). That study then, avoiding putting forth a definition of religion itself, relies on what could be called an implicit definition of religion in use by the informants themselves. Therefore, their model's explanation of a consumer's commitment is based on the consumer's own classification of the nature his or her commitment as "religious". What that study, however, circumvents, is the establishment of a wider theoretical framework that could provide an explanation of the interviewees' testimonies beyond their self-declarations.

A study, examining the effect of transcendent customer experience (TCE) on the formation of brand loyalty and community-building found that "TCEs can help strengthen all aspects of brand community" (Schouten, McAlexander, & Koenig, 2007, p. 364). TCEs are defined to be either "flow" or "peak" experiences. "A peak experience is an ephemeral, yet powerful, personally meaningful, and potentially transformational experience" (Schouten et al., 2007, p. 357). A peak experience is described to be "less like a deliberate process and more like an epiphany" (Schouten et al., 2007, p. 358). The study supports the view that TCEs "appear to have a halo effect" (Schouten et al., 2007, p. 364). Based thereupon, the authors draw an analogy to religion, giving the example of religious conversion: A new member of a religious community who joined the community subsequent to an epiphany might exhibit a strong loyalty because the new religion possibly offers a framework helping to understand the epiphany, and because the new religion might offer texts and rituals that support future transcendent experiences. The authors of the study then conclude that TCEs in a commercial context help foster brand loyalty. Yet, that insightful study does not develop a wider theoretical body that would explain the observed analogy between religion and marketer- or marketing-related TCEs.

Another study investigating the brand cult in connection to Macintosh (Apple) found that brand-related myths play a constitutive role with respect to the extreme devotion some Macintosh consumers have towards that brand (Belk & Tumbat, 2005/2006). They conclude that, based on myths analogous to religion, "[t]he Mac and its fans constitute the equivalent of a religion" (Belk & Tumbat, 2005/2006, p. 207). The claim that extreme brand loyalty and devotion, in the case of the Macintosh community, *is* the equivalent of religion, however, is not supported by the development of a theoretical body. Also, the authors do not give a definition of religion. This lack of notional clarity and the absence of a theoretical framework are two desiderata of that study.

A similar lack of theoretical depth characterises David Lyon's account of the nature of religion, and consumption, or consumerism, in postmodernity. With respect to consumption, Lion identifies, inasmuch as access to certain consumer goods symbolises the consumer's societal position, consumption as part of a "system of symbolic rivalry, in which people construct their selves through acquiring commodities that make them distinct from others [...]" (Lyon, 2000, p. 79). However, Lyon does not elaborate this thought. Describing the quasi-religious connotations of postmodern consumerism, he fails to give a comprehensive theoretical framework supporting his argument. His book largely remains an interesting account, a casuistry so to speak, of religion's new forms of manifestation and the role of consumerism in postmodernity.

Ragas and Bueno, in their instruction book regarding the creation of a cult brand, make some allegations to religion (Ragas & Bueno, 2002). For example, they say that a cult brand needs, like a religion, a significant meeting place. Or, with respect to cult brands, an adherent's belief makes up his or her reality. However, whilst giving a complete checklist for the creation of a brand, they do not, on the theoretical level, explore the connection between cult brands and religion any further.

A study by Muniz and O'Guinn, whilst addressing the importance of the sociocultural and connected ritual-related aspects in the creation of "brand communities" (Muniz & O'Guinn, 2001), neither broached nor contemplated a structural analogy between religion and marketing as a possible, and valid explanation for the observed phenomenon. Similarly, a study by Muniz and Schau, whilst examining the spiritual aspects as well as aspects of religiosity in the Apple Newton brand community (Muniz & Schau, 2005), did not address questions as to wherein such religiosity could be rooted. Exemplary of a myriad of studies in marketing's remit, neither of those two studies went as far as explaining, or even trying to explain, the phenomena under scrutiny by means of a potential structural analogy between religion and marketing.

As Mick and Oswald (2006) have shown, since the 1980s, numerous scholars have addressed the role of semiotics in marketing and its contribution to the field. For example, a study on semiotics and marketing (Mick, 1998) shed light on the vital contribution of semiotics to the production of meaning in a communication process. Later then, Megehee and Woodside (2010) examined how advertising constructs and decodes a visual narrative, thus establishing meaning. Deploying a visual method later, also outlined by Gillian Rose (2012), their study argued that most communication is nonverbal and that consumers primarily think in stories via pictures. However, despite its examination of the creation of archetypes, or stock characters[51] by visual means, the study did not address the construction and production of meaning throughout an entire marketing campaign over an extended period of time. Nor does it encourage the generalisation of its findings, as it limited its focus to one individual consumer only. In summary, it

51 Examples of stock characters are the antihero, the Latin lover, and the absent-minded professor.

can be said that over the past twenty years, a myriad of studies applying Saussure's and Peirce's principles to marketing in virtually all conceivable configurations have been published. However, these analyses have a common limitation: none of them has considered the possibility that marketing – by using semiotics in a very specific way – could successfully create a framework of meaning analogous to the structure of religion.

Whilst many academic studies have addressed particular elements that lie at the heart of a successful marketing campaign, to date, none has proposed a paradigmatic model that could bring about an in-depth understanding and a satisfactory explanation of such success. In the search for fresh answers, this investigation considers the possibility of a structural and functional analogy, on the theoretical level, between religion and marketing. Rooted in the study of religion, it puts forward a previously untried intellectual approach to marketing, thereby aiming to make a constitutive contribution to the often-overlooked economic dimension within the study of religion.

Finally, the reader might permit a look beyond the boundaries of academic writing. One book in particular, published in 2004, should be mentioned. Written by Douglas Atkin, a professional working in the advertisement industry, the argument presented in the book opens with a strong proposition: "Brands are the new religion" (Aktin, 2004, p. xi). Seen from an academic perspective, it would perhaps be easy to ignore that book. For instance, its content and main predication are not neatly embedded in the body of documented academic research. Nor is it, for example, clear which definition of religion Atkin works with. Nonetheless, the book offers a well-documented casuistry of the power of brands with respect to the production of meaning. What is missing, again, is the presentation of a theoretical body that could explain such power.[52] And this is the contribution this study hopes to make. Finally, it must be said again, this study does not claim that "brands *are* the new religion", nor does it in the least equate marketing with religion. It tries to show, on the *theoretical* level, that analogies exist between religion and marketing: both, of a functional and structural nature. The next chapter then, drawing on Geertz's definition of religion, looks more closely into those analogies.

52 Two other books, also both written outside the tradition of academic writing, should not go unnoticed: *The Brand Gap* (Neumeyer, 2005) and *The Brand Flip* (Neumeyer, 2015). They both contain comprehensive heuristics with respect to the creation of a brand. What they do not offer, however, is an equally comprehensive theoretical framework.

3.2 Analogies between religion and marketing

As mentioned in chapter 2.3.2, on the iconographical level, there are clear analogies between the thirteen men depicted in the aforementioned Mokarabia commercial and, for instance, Leonardo da Vinci's fresco of *The Last Supper*. Similarly, the way St. Peter is portrayed in the Nespresso commercial, namely in the role of the gatekeeper of heaven, shows, in a vernacular manner, at least some iconological analogies to the representation of St. Peter in the Roman Catholic tradition, for instance to the fresco in the Sistine Chapel by Pietro Perugino, showing how Jesus gives St. Peter the keys to heaven. Equally in Lavazza's campaign, where St. Peter is a somewhat funny, likeable heavenly housekeeper, an iconological analogy, in the sense that St. Peter is in charge of a heavenly place, exists.

However, first it must be said that in the case of the Mokarabia commercial, the analogy, on the iconographical level, between the commercial and Leonardo's masterpiece should not be confounded with an analogy between *religion and marketing*. Commercials are not the equivalent of marketing. Commercials are a form of advertisement. And advertisements are one of marketing's principal methods. One could argue, with respect to Leonardo`s masterpiece, that the visual representation of religious scenes is equally a method with respect to the representation of a worldview and the corresponding meaning and its subsequent reproduction by the observer. In that sense, one could argue for an analogy with respect to the methods used in the production of meaning in religious contexts and marketing.

On the iconological level, in the case of all of the three mentioned examples, Nespresso, Lavazza and Mokarabia, quite obvious iconological, symbolic analogies exist. For instance, as mentioned in subchapter 2.3.2, Mokarabia is trying to create a feeling of connection between its brand and the viewer. Yet, that is not where the focus of this study lies. Instead, this study is interested in examining whether or not analogies, structural and functional, exist between religion and marketing, even if they are, on the iconographical level, clearly absent. The question is whether a marketing campaign can create structures and functions that are analogous to religion, even if the campaign, its advertisements and commercials do, on the iconographical level, almost exclusively, neither use nor allude to religious symbolism. For that reason, in this study, three Nespresso commercials were chosen for the analysis that do not contain, on the iconographical level, any reference to religious symbolism. As the analysed commercials do not include any symbols of an overtly religious nature, the analogies, of course, can neither be found on the pre-iconographical nor on the iconographical level. The analogies, should they successfully be identified, should be anticipated on the iconological level. In the absence of a pre-iconographical and iconographical content that would easily render them visible and serve as an explanation, this study aims to uncover them with the help of Geertz's definition of religion. His definition makes the analysis required for this research possible as it implies categories of analysis like "worldview" and "ethos", enabling the researcher to identify, on the theoretical level, analogies to religion in an unexpected context.

3.2.1 Structural analogies

The structural analogies this study hopes to uncover refer to the dichotomic nature of religion. In the Geertzian sense, religion systematically offers both: a model of the world, a worldview, and a model for the world, an ethos.[53] In addition to offering a specific model of the world, of what, in an ontological sense, the world *is*, it implies a "should", aiming to guide an adherent's "dos and don'ts". Seen in the Geertzian perspective, what is noteworthy in religion's dual nature is that the two sides of its structure are simultaneously present. The following excursus into Australian aboriginal totemism exemplifies this. Australian aboriginal totemism offers both, a worldview and an ethos. Referring to Lévi-Strauss, Erich Kolig writes: "[Lévi-Strauss] hints at the function of totemism in introducing order into an otherwise chaotic world, above all imposing order on human society through the use of principles assumed to be universal" (Kolig, 1988, p. 215). With respect to the classification schemes of totemic systems, Kolig maintains: "The purpose of devising classification schemes of a cosmic magnitude is not just to order the universe or society - order for order's sake as it were - nor is it done for intellectual pedantry or mnemonic ease. The purpose is obviously to gain power: the power which flows from knowing the principles of universal structure" (Kolig, 1988, p. 222). In or-

---

53 As a reminder, Geertz's definition of religion is quoted here again: "A religion is 1) a system of symbols which acts to 2) establish powerful, pervasive and long-lasting moods and motivations in men by 3) formulating conceptions of a general order of existence and 4) clothing these conceptions with such an aura of factuality that 5) the moods and motivations seem uniquely realistic." (Geertz, 1966/2010, p. 4).

der to maintain and exercise such power, an ethos, a set of required human behavioural schemes, is evolved:

> [In totemic systems], [s]ymbols in isolation have no meaning and are incapable of conveying power. The symbols of the [totemic] section and subsection systems are in themselves just pieces of nature, classes of people, etc. But in conjunction they express world order. Activated in ritual, they can work on the whole world through the intricate rules of sympathetic interaction. Seen in these terms, even the social rules of marriage, exogamy, incest, descent and sharing in accordance with the classification order, become symbolic statements capable of similar effects. (Kolig, 1988, p. 225)

In Australian aboriginal totemism, analogous to the aforementioned example, social rules guiding human behaviour, the ethos, are thus rooted in, and motivated by, the model of the world, the worldview.[54]

Having given an example of how worldview and ethos represent two moieties of one system of symbols, the question now is whether the same structure can be identified, emanating from a system of symbols, in the context of marketing. Moreover, with a view to the subsequent chapter, the question is whether marketing can create, through advertising, its main method, a system of symbols that is powerful enough to not only offer a worldview, but to also constitute an ethos, a blueprint for consumer behaviour?

3.2.2 Functional analogies

Religion, in the Geertzian sense, creates powerful, long-lasting moods and motivations in men and women that are perceived as uniquely realistic. The main difference here between moods and motivations is that the former are of a scalar nature and make sense with respect to their conditions of origin. The latter instead are directional, they are teleological and make sense with respect to the targets to which they are directed. Geertz says:

> "The major difference between moods and motivations is that where the latter are […] vectorial qualities, the former are merely scalar. [Motivations] have a directional cast, they describe a certain overall course,

54 For an introduction to totemism, see Lévi-Strauss (1971).

gravitate towards certain […] consummations. But moods vary only as to intensity: they go nowhere." (Geertz, 1966/2010, p. 11)

With respect to moods, as Geertz does not provide much insight as to how he uses the term, other than setting it off from motivations and stating that there are many different "sort[s] of mood[s]" (Geertz, 1966/2010, p. 11), this study works with a definition given by William N. Morris, which is compatible with Geertz's use of the term: "[Moods are] affective states that are capable of influencing a broad array of potential responses, many of which seem quite unrelated to the mood-precipitating event" (Morris, 1989, p. 3). Furthermore, concerning the connection between moods, irrespective of their origin and behaviour, Morris states: "The […] behaviours of people who are feeling good reflect their feelings"[55],[56] (Morris, 1989, p. 121). Transposed into Geertzian language, this would read: "The […] behaviours of people who are in a good mood reflect that mood." The cognisance that behaviour reflects the mood, however, still leaves the question with respect to the *driver* behind the behaviour – motivation – and its target unanswered.

Motivation, according to Geertz is "a persisting tendency, a chronic inclination to perform certain sorts of act and experience certain sorts of feeling in certain sorts of situation […]" (Geertz, 1966/2010, p. 10). It is important to note that Geertz does not differentiate between motivation and motives. With respect to motives, Geertz says: "Motives[57] are […] neither acts (i.e., intentional behaviours) nor feelings, but liabilities to perform particu-

---

55 The connection between *bad* moods and behaviour is less clear. For a further discussion of this topic, see Morris (1989).

56 Gilbert Ryle, whose work was a source of inspiration for Geertz, differentiates between "feelings" and "moods." Yet, in everyday language, the two terms are often used interchangeably. Ryle writes: "Mood words are commonly classified as the names of feelings" (Ryle, 1949/2009a, p. 85). In this sense, somebody "who feels good" is "in a good mood." However, that use of the verb "feel" does not describe a "feeling." Ryle writes: "Names of moods […] are not the names of feelings. But to be in a particular mood is to be in the mood, among other things, to feel certain sorts of feelings in certain sorts of situations" (Ryle, 1949/2009a, p. 88). Also: "In saying that he [or she] is in a certain mood we are saying something fairly general; […] that he [or she] is in the frame of mind to say, do and feel a wide variety of loosely affiliated things" (Ryle, 1949/2009a, p. 84). For a further discussion of how feelings relate to moods, see Ryle (1949/2009a).

57 Clearly, Geertz uses the terms "motivation" and "motives" with respect to their meaning as equivalents. This study, however, for notional clarity, limits itself to the use of the notion motivation. In this study, the term motive is only used in quotes.

lar classes of act or have particular classes of feeling" (Geertz, 1966/2010, p. 11). Yet, to understand why motives, or motivation for that matter, are *capable* of resulting in observable behaviour at all, another analytical building block is needed. Houston, Bee, and Rimm (1985) introduced the required addend to moods and motivation: Learning. They write: "[…] [L]earning resides within us and is invisible until it is converted into observable behaviour by motives. For example, we have all learned how to open a can of soup, but we don't go about opening soup cans constantly. We have to be motivated before this learning will be utilized. Motivation *is what translates learning on to observable behaviour*" (Houston, Bee, & Rimm, 1985, p. 222). A skill, once learnt, is a dormant competence. Now, if a mood is conducive to a certain behaviour and if, at the same time, motivation directed towards the attainment of a specific goal is there, so to speak as the driving force behind the action, it is the *learnt skill* that will determine the observable behaviour. As will be further elaborated upon in a subsequent chapter, learning of a blueprint for action is indeed an indispensable element in a marketing campaign's journey to success.

Having addressed the connection between moods and behaviour, and between motivation and behaviour, a look at the connection between a positive mood and learning is now warranted. A study on the effects of a positive or negative mood on cognition and motivation in a multimedia learning environment showed that

> [a] positive mood had a facilitation effect on cognition and motivation in a multimedia learning system, whereas negative mood had a detrimental effect on multimedia learning. These findings demonstrated that positive mood is desirable for learning in multimedia learning systems, while the presence of negative mood should be mitigated. (Liew & Tan, 2016, p. 113)

A positive mood facilitates learning and encourages behaviours reflective of and in accordance with the positive mood. Moreover, if what is learnt is a specific behaviour that promises to satisfy a specific desire, that desire will give the driving force behind the behaviour, that is, motivation, its specific direction.[58] In other words, if all of these preconditions are fulfilled and in alignment, the acting person is then motivated to act in a certain way, enacting the learnt behavioural patterns.

Referring again to Geertz's definition of religion, the establishment of powerful, pervasive and long-lasting moods and motivations that seem

58 For an in-depth discussion of different theories of motivation, see Madsen (1974).

uniquely realistic is the functional property of a religion. Such moods are specific to each religion and an integral part thereof. In Buddhism, for instance, the prevailing mood is perhaps best illustrated by the story of Siddharta Gautama leaving his father's palace: "After these encounters with old age, illness and death his [i.e., Siddharta's] strife for life had left him"[59] (Lehmann, 1986, p. 41). He is told that monks find bliss rooted in the non-decayable, following a path of solitude, living solely on alms. Recognising that this-worldly things are only illusionary, he awakens to the truth and decides to step out of the world of short-lived, worldly pleasures (Lehmann, 1986). According to Lehmann, this legend perhaps best captures the prevailing mood in Buddhism, which, can be described as dolefulness.

In Christianity, the prevailing mood instead is that of gratitude. "Let the word of Christ dwell in you richly, teaching and admonishing one another in all wisdom, singing psalms and hymns and spiritual songs, with thankfulness in your hearts to God" (Col. 3:16, English Standard Version). Besides, as writes Karl Barth: "It is deep reaching gratitude, the antecedent prevailing mood which, making the world as it truthfully is at last accessible, makes grand theology possible"[60] (Trowitzsch, 2012, p. 450).

The step from a prevailing mood of gratitude to the motivation to help others is illustrated by the following example. "Faith motivates people to help others – not only in Christianity" (Kirchenbund, 2013). The Evangelical Protestant Church of Grisons, Switzerland, for example, sees the motivation for diaconic commitment rooted in the life of Jesus Christ (Landeskirche, n.d.). Diaconic action as a form of behaviour is, in this case, modelled on Jesus Christ's deeds. Besides, it can be argued, extending help to others is also a type of behaviour that is in accordance with, and reflective of the aforementioned prevailing mood of gratitude. The faithful who wish to express their gratitude are then motivated to help others, following Christ's example. Furthermore, as it would be quite possible to imagine other ways of expressing gratitude, such behaviour must be seen as a specific type of learnt behaviour, learnt from Christ's example.

The question now is whether marketing could be equally capable of establishing moods and motivations in would-be consumers to the effect of issuing in a specific behaviour, that is, leading to the purchase of the marketed commodity. This study argues that the behavioural example given by the commercials' protagonists is learnt and acquired by viewers. They will,

59 Translation by the author, 2016.
60 Translation by the author, 2016.

if they wish to also enjoy, for instance, the pleasure of "feeling like a star" or the pleasure of consuming the advertised commodity – so deeply satisfying that it makes female consumers oblivious to the charms of the sexiest man alive – act according to the behavioural script learnt from watching the commercials. If that can be shown, then, in can be argued that there exists indeed, on the theoretical level, a functional analogy between religion and marketing.

3.3 Research question

As aforementioned, with respect to the overlap between religion on one hand and marketing and advertising on the other, peer research in the various fields of the study of religion, and of marketing, has addressed many issues connected with emotions, and motivation. Similarly, extensive research has been conducted on the role, and power, of images and of the media in general in the construction of a meaningful reality. Furthermore, research in marketing has looked into the role, and the performative power, of visual images in advertising, one of marketing's principal tools, or methods (Mc Cracken, 1986; Megehee & Woodside, 2010; Ko & Megehee, 2012). Yet, there is, to date, no available comprehensive audio-visual study of a marketing campaign that goes beyond a mere itemisation of sequentially ordered casuistries. A contribution by du Gay et al. (1997), focussing on the Sony Walkman as a cultural artefact, whilst scrutinising advertising as a representational practice, as a language that speaks "on *behalf* of the product" (p. 25), does not raise the question with respect to a possible structural premise of a marketing campaign as a needed, though perhaps not sufficient condition of its success. Perhaps commensurate with this condition, none of the currently prevailing marketing theories give an in-depth theoretical answer as to *why* and *precisely how* successful marketing campaigns function. As far back as 1986, Grant McCracken addressed the transfer of meaning from a culturally constructed world to the world of consumer goods in the context of advertising: "Meaning first resides in the culturally constituted world. To become resident in consumer goods, meaning must be disengaged from this world and transferred to goods. [...] Advertising works as a potential method of meaning transfer by bringing the consumer good and a representation of the culturally constituted world together within the frame of a particular advertisement" (McCracken, 1986, p. 74). According to McCracken, visual images play the dominant role in this transfer of meaning:

> Visual images and verbal material appear to assume a very particular relationship in this transfer process. It is chiefly the visual aspect of an advertisement that conjoins the world and the object [i.e., the consumer good] when a meaning transfer is sought. [...] Text provides instructions on how the visual part of the advertisement is to be read. (McCracken, 1986, p. 74)

However, what preconditions would have to be met for such a transfer to come about is not addressed by McCracken. He writes:

> Photographic and visual conventions will be exploited to give the viewer/reader the opportunity to glimpse an essential equivalence between the two elements of world and object. [...] [T]hese two elements [must be brought] into a conjunction that encourages a metaphoric identification of sameness by the would-be consumer. World and good must seem to enjoy a special harmony – must be seen to go together. When the viewer/reader glimpses this sameness [...], the process of transfer has taken place." (McCracken, 1986, p. 74)

Finally, with respect to the role of the viewer in the transfer of meaning, McCracken maintains, "it is worth emphasising that the viewer/reader is the final author in the process of transfer. [...] It is left to the viewer/reader to [...] effect the transfer of meaningful properties. To this extent, the viewer/reader is an essential participant in the process of meaning transfer [...]"[61] (McCracken, 1986, p. 74). McCracken therefore addresses the individual steps of the transfer, however, he does not address the structural and functional properties this meaning-making process needs to have in order to perform the task, that is, the transfer of meaning and, ultimately, the purchase of the advertised product by the viewer/reader. As was outlined in a previous chapter, it is the aim of this study to fill this gap.

Assuming the perspective pertinent to the study of religion, a look at the phenomenon of exceptionally high and sustained operating profit margins will potentially reveal that Nespresso's successful marketing campaigns not only exploits the desire-driven side of human nature, but that it goes farther. The campaign is structured in such a way that the advertised product is indeed merely a symbolic token, an element of a wider system of symbols. A purchase allows the consumer, through differentiation, to shape and construct a desired identity, while also allowing for the participation in a virtual world that has been jointly constructed by the consumer on

61 See Williamson (1978) for a further discussion of this topic.

one hand and the marketing campaign on the other. This complex process provokes real emotions in the consumer and leads to the fulfilment of desires perceived as real. The question arises whether a consumer's fantasy regarding the participation in the emotional reality presented through advertising motivates the consumer to purchase the advertised product. And if so, *how* does marketing accomplish such a feat? This question leads to the principal focus of this study: the alleged structural and functional analogy between religion and marketing. The principal research question of this study thus reads as follows: "Are there functional and structural analogies between religion and marketing?", addressing the desideratum of the aforementioned studies. As the question is approached through, and the analysis of this study's corpus is based on the Geertzian definition of religion, what is implied is a focus on Nespresso's marketing campaign's constitutive power to induce viewers to form a worldview with a corresponding ethos. As was addressed in chapter 2.1.2, and will be further discussed in chapter 5.2.1, the viewer's role in the creation of a worldview and ethos is of paramount importance. If the viewer were not the ultimate creator thereof, the corresponding moods and motivations would unlikely be perceived as "uniquely realistic" (Geertz, 1966/2010, p. 4).

4 Methodological Considerations

4.1 Approaching advertising in cultural studies

It is now necessary to return to the aforementioned challenge of transforming coffee into something consumers do not yet have – and, at the same time, of investing it with an aura of desirability. Once the commodity has, in the eyes of the potential consumer, acquired a fetish quality that he or she wishes to possess, desire, a guiding motivation, sets in and steers behaviour towards the purchase of the marketed commodity. In *Therapy of Desire*, Nussbaum presents a brilliant analysis of the Stoics' approach to desire (Nussbaum, 1994/2009). Put briefly, it can be said that Stoic philosophy advocated the extirpation of desire. Much later, in the European Enlightenment, the rational quality of human nature was favoured over its emotional, desire-driven side. And ultimately, the economic anthropology of the "homo economicus", at least for the purpose of analysis, totally stripped humans of all of their non-rational characteristics. As stated earlier, economists now question that anthropology, and new branch of economics, called behavioural economics, is beginning to address non-rational behaviour. These scholars have recently gained insight into aspects of human nature that marketing specialists have long known: that humans obviously have a strong desire-driven side to their nature. In short: "Desire is a modern theme in the daily lives of modern citizens" (Lades, 2015, p. 215).

Desire plays as important a part in the establishment of a link between advertising, the commercial's narrative, and the potential consumer of the advertised commodity, as do the imaginary and identification.

> [Advertising] must create an identification between the consumer and the product. Somehow, it must get us to see ourselves as – identify with or acquire the identity of – a potential buyer of the product: the 'sort of person who buys [...] this kind of thing'. No matter how much we like and admire the people in the advertisements, if we cannot see or *imagine* ourselves in that role, we will often be more reluctant to shell out the money required to purchase the commodity. (du Gay et al, 1997, p. 25)

Identification with at least some aspects of the narrative is a precondition for the success of advertising and, by the same token, of successful marketing. In that sense, identification is a necessary condition for a successful appropriation of the product's signified by the consumer who, in and through consumption, contributes to his, or her identity. For instance, if a product is constructed as part of the aesthetics of a narrative, identification and the subsequent purchase of the product enhances the consumer's identity through the consumer's absorption of the signifier's and referent's aesthetics.

Such absorption is subject to a process, which Williamson described as "alienation". Inspired, or triggered by the advertisement, the reader attaches certain attributes to the advertised object. In that sense, the reading of an advertisement by a potential consumer is a hermeneutical undertaking. Williamson then writes:

> Advertisements alienate our identity in constituting us as one of the objects in an exchange that we must ourselves make, thereby appropriating *from us*, an image which gives us back our own 'value'. [...] *you* [viewer] give the product its image/value [...] and then in buying the product you receive this image back. So, *this* alienation takes place via the product. However, the people in the [...] [advertisement] are also giving the product its value – creating its image, 'signifying' it, and also using it. Therefore, we are in the same relationship with the product as they are; it becomes the 'mirror' axis which unites them and us, although we are spatially separate. [...] [T]his is an identification which takes place across spatial distance. (Williamson, 1978/2002, p. 64)

The hermeneutical projection of a specific value, or characteristic, on to the advertised commodity, an act carried out by the viewer of the advertisement, charges and elevates its exchange-value way beyond its use-value. This, combined with the identification of the actions, portrayed by the people in the advertisement, inadvertently, leads to consumption, that is, to the buying of the advertised commodity, if the viewer wants to re-appropriate the value, or characteristics that he or she has projected on to the commodity. Such re-appropriation is then, with respect to the viewer's identity, a constitutive act.

Identity, and its construction, are also closely related to fantasy, and cinema as well as other audio-visual narratives, such as commercials can and do awaken the viewer's fantasy. Moreover, viewers may even imagine they are participating in the narrative according to the dynamics of their own fantasies (Cowie, 1990). "Identification [...] has been taken up within cultural studies, for example in film theory, to explain the powerful actualisation of unconscious wishes which can occur in relation to people or images, whereby we attribute qualities to ourselves and transfer associations making it possible to see ourselves in the image presented" (Woodward, 1997/2012, pp. 14-15). As such, these elements of fantasy and identification play a crucial role in advertising, allowing for the construction of an imaginary self by the viewer when he or she becomes a consumer. "The language of advertising – and representation in general – operates as much on fantasy and desire as it does on rational choices and so-called "real" needs. The people in the advertisements are therefore not a realistic representation of ourselves, but an *imaginary* one" (du Gay et al., 1997, pp. 25-26). The imaginary, the locus where the viewer's identity construction incubates, is a crucial moment in the viewer's journey from being a mere consumer of the message to a consumer of the product, thereby becoming the reification of the signified: its actual referent. Perhaps obviously, the characters portrayed in the audio-visual narrative are not the referent; they are part of the signifier. For the viewer, however, the real-world experience of the story shown in the commercial is potentially, just one step away. If the viewer identifies with the characters in the story and with their actions, or a part thereof, and moreover, if the imaginary comes into play and invites the viewer to participate in the action, moving the viewer's motivation to observable behaviour, the stage is then set for a potential re-enactment – through the viewer – of the action depicted in the narrative. "The imaginary does not satisfy the needs of sensibility and thought, but it realises itself in action" (Pezzoli-Olgiati, 2015, p. 24). Therefore, if, for instance, the narrative successfully changes the connotative meaning of a signifier, a cup of coffee in this case, thereby creating new signs and new codes, a viewer who is desirous of enjoying the benefits promised by the signifier's new meaning, will reiterate the actions portrayed by the commercial in the real world. Because the advertising firm will surely keep their products readily available, it will not be difficult for the viewer to find the signifier's referent in the real world. Thus, the viewer first consumes the meaning of the narrative, and then, subsequently, becomes a consumer of the advertised product. Ultimately, the viewer, when he or she becomes a consumer, also becomes the referent of the commercial's narrative. As the socio-empirical study will confirm, the signified becomes attached to the consumer, thereby completing the signifier's metamorphosis. Or, in other words, in the practice of consumption, the viewer, the quondam would-be consumer, becomes the real-world enactment of the meaning originally attributed to the signifier by the commercial's narrative. Arguing with Panofsky, the commercial's pre-iconographical meaning, that is, a man in a suit drinks a cup of coffee, changes through the commercial's narrative: George Clooney drinks a coffee for which there is no alternative. And precisely that meaning, drinking a coffee for which there is no alternative, is enacted, by the consumer's practice, in the real world. Expressed in the language of semiotics, the consumer has become the sign's referent, thereby confirming the worldview, albeit limited to the coffee world, put forth by the commercial.

Finally, it is important to note that when the viewer re-enacts the actions of the commercial, the motivation to do so must have, ex-ante, arisen prior to the action. Such motivation must furthermore be perceived as real and genuine, not artificial, but "uniquely realistic" (Geertz 1966/2010, p. 4), otherwise the viewer would be unlikely to repeatedly spend money on the advertised product. In this respect, learning plays a determining role. If learning is successfully completed by the consumer, then, he or she will not only have learnt that one should drink only Nespresso, the consumer will also have learnt what feelings are appropriate to have in connection with Nespresso consumption. Successful elicitation of those feelings through actual consumption does, ex-post, render the moods and motivations uniquely realistic. It is in consumption itself, through the ritual, that the ethos renders the moods and motivations uniquely realistic, thereby confirming the worldview. Or, as Geertz says, it is in the ritual where the model of, and for, the world meet:

> It is in [...][ritual,] some sort of ceremonial form [...] that the moods and motivations which sacred symbols induce in men and the general conceptions of the order of existence which they formulate for men meet and reinforce one another. In a ritual, the world as lived and the world as imagined, fused under the agency of a single set of symbolic forms, turn out to be the same world, producing thus that idiosyncratic transformation in one's sense of reality [...]. (Geertz 1966/2010, p. 28)

In the Nespresso marketing campaign, the making and tasting of a Nespresso is shown in great detail in most of the commercials, always involving the capsule, a Nespresso machine, and a Nespresso cup. Nespresso even launched a series of specially designed of cups called *Les Collections*. One of those series was designed by the world famous, late French designer Andrée Putman. Nespresso named those cups *The Ritual Collection* (Nestle-Nespresso, n.d.b).

Figure 3: The Ritual Collection (Nespresso Accessories Ritual Collection, 2015)

Nespresso refers to the drinking, the tasting of coffee as a ritual. On one of its websites, for instance, Nespresso writes: "For the festive season, *Nespresso* invites Club Members to enhance their coffee tasting ritual with *Les Collections* gift sets" (Nestle-Nespresso n.d.b). Clearly, the consumption of Nespresso is represented as a ritual. Moreover, through repeated coffee consumption, which requires that the consumer always performs the steps as portrayed in the commercial, those actions also become ritualised. In summary, the making as well as the drinking of Nespresso, production and consumption, become invested with the character of a ritual. In the words of Geertz, it is in the ritual where the model of the world and the model for the world, worldview and ethos, meet. The tasting of Nespresso not only reflects a model of the coffee world, it also represents an ethos, a model for the world, pointing towards future behaviour, future actions along the lines of "thou shalt drink Nespresso". Returning to the commercials and the protagonists' actions represented therein, the consumer's behaviour is, at the extreme if Nespresso is even tasted only once, from then on guided by that blueprint, or, in more generic terms, by the marketing campaign. And, from the firm's point of view, it can be realistically expected that this leads to high and sustained operating profit margins.

4.1.1 Encoding and decoding

In his paper *Encoding, Decoding*, first published in 1980, Hall develops a four-step theory of communication that makes an indispensable contribution to the theoretical framework used in the analysis of the audio-visual corpus of this study. According to Hall, the process of communication can be seen as a structure "produced and sustained through the articulation of linked but distinctive moments – production, circulation, distribution, consumption, reproduction" (Hall, 1993, p. 478). Hall subsequently expanded that four-step model to the circuit of culture, which also includes, as additional elements or loci of practice, representation, regulation and identity. In that context, for example, it is the representation of an event that attributes meaning to the event. Prior to being represented through a visual or audio-visual language – a system of symbols – events are simply that: events. Actions and occurrences only acquire meaning through representation. For instance, when water was privatised in Cochabamba, Bolivia, and the private supplier dramatically increased the price of fresh water, protesters in unauthorised demonstrations marched through the street (Assies, 2003). With respect to the representation of such an event in the media, it is up to news agencies whether protesters are presented as a bunch of law-breaking protesters or as courageous people standing up against a moral and human injustice. The event itself only acquires meaning through its representation, and the kind of meaning acquired depends on the manner in which this is done. This has to be kept in mind at all times, also in the analysis of the Nespresso commercials. In that sense, with respect to the commercials, the style of the representation will be given special attention. Furthermore, the production of meaning has implications for the viewer's (the receiver's) identity. In Woodward's words: "Representation includes the signifying practices and symbolic systems through which meanings are produced [...]" (Woodward, 1997/2012, p. 14). Then, through practices of consumption, the viewer ultimately completes the production of meaning, thus rendering the viewer an integral and indispensable agent in the process.

The element of production in Hall's circuit of culture as well as in his four-step model can be seen as a practice devoted to the production of meaning and messages in the form of sign vehicles, which themselves are organised "through the operation of codes within the syntagmatic chain of a discourse" (Hall, 1993, p. 478). Codes, in this sense, can literally be anything, a bodily movement, a look, or the sequence of different looks or bodily movements. Often, codes are specific to certain cultures: by establishing a fixed relationship between a sign and a concept, they stabilise meaning:

> Codes fix the relationships between concepts and signs. They stabilise meaning within different languages and cultures. They tell us which language to use to convey a specific idea. The reverse is also true. Codes tell us which concepts are being referred to when we hear or read which signs. [...] [C]odes make it possible for us to speak and to hear intelligibly, and establish the translatability between our concepts and our languages which enables meaning to pass from speaker to hearer and be effectively communicated within a culture. This translatability is not fixed by nature [...]. It is the result of a set of social conventions. It is fixed socially, fixed in culture. (Hall, 1997/2003a, pp. 21-22)

For reasons of notional clarity, it is important to note, that Saussure and Hall use the term "sign" in a different sense. For Saussure, a sign includes both the "signified" and the "signifier". Using Saussure's terminology, the quote above can be translated into: "Codes fix the relationship between the signified (i.e., the concept) and the signifier (i.e., the sign)". *This study then uses the term sign in the Saussurean sense, implying both the signified and the signifier*, or, in Hall's language, the concept and the sign.[62] In the case of symbolic signs, the attribution of a signified to a signifier is, as described above in subchapter 2.2.3, a matter of convention, and ultimately arbitrary. As quoted above, Hall uses the term "code" to describe what "fixes the relationships between concepts and signs" (Hall, 2003a/1997, p. 21). In Hall's terminology then, the "signifier" is the "sign", and the "signified" is the "concept". The term "code", in this study, will be used in Hall's sense, only instead of "concepts" this study uses the term "signified", and instead of "sign" in Hall's sense, this study uses the term "signifier". Therefore, the phrase "Codes fix the relationships between concepts and signs" will read: "Codes, in the case of symbolic signs, fix the relationship between the signified and the signifier".

In Hall's *Encoding, Decoding*, the four steps of the process of communication (i.e., production, circulation, distribution/consumption, reproduction) are, as aforementioned, linked to one-another in a four-step model. Therefore, the practice of production, cannot and should not, be seen in-

62 In subsequent quoted contributions made by Hall, the term "signifier" is substituted for the term "sign". The term "sign", henceforth, stands for the ensemble of "signifier" and "signified".

dependently of consumption. Whilst it might appear that production constructs the message in a fairly subjective or arbitrary process, assumptions about the audience play an important part in the production of messages and meanings. For instance, because the story or narrative told through audio-visual media will have to be, in the act of the story's consumption, read and therefore interpreted by the viewer, assumptions must be made about the viewer's gaze, his or her way of looking at the world and the interpretations made thereby. The salience of this issue increases also because there can be no guarantee that a viewer will read a message exactly as the producer has intended. In order to discuss the problems in connection with the stabilisation of meaning across whole processes of communication, another issue becomes relevant: the question of how the message, with its meaning, makes its way from production to the viewer, that is, the question of circulation and distribution. The answer can be succinctly put as: circulation and distribution of the meaning take place in a discursive form. The narrative, that is, the story is the carrier of the meaning/the message. However, the ultimate agent with respect to the meaning/the message is the viewer. And therefore, "reproduction" plays an important part. When the message/the meaning is produced, it must be moulded into a story in order to be circulated. The circulated story or narrative must moreover incorporate all the necessary codes, carrying the intended meaning. Thus, with the help of codes, meaning is melded into a story, meaning becomes a story – a kind of metamorphosis takes place. After the process of circulation and distribution to the viewer and would-be consumer is completed, in the process of its consumption, the story is re-translated back into *meaning*. To that end, the codes incorporated in the narrative must be read and interpreted by the viewer. This second metamorphosis or reproduction, however, is not entirely predictable. A viewer might extract a meaning from the narrative that deviates from the meaning intended by its producer. It is entirely feasible that a viewer's outlook and specific gaze causes him or her to read or interpret the codes in a manner that differs from, or is even contradictory to, the producer's intention. In order to minimise this risk, it is crucial that the viewer's gaze is taken into due consideration in the practice of production. Hall writes: "[…] [C]irculation and reception are, indeed, 'moments' of the production process […] and are reincorporated, via a number of skewed and structured 'feedbacks', into the production process itself" (Hall, 1993, p. 479). For instance, Nespresso gave George Clooney the leading part in its marketing campaign only after Nespresso Club Members had chosen him in 2004 as their Brand Ambassador (Nestle-Nespresso, 2016b), thus demonstrating the firm's attention to its target audience. After all, the consequences of a possible breakdown in the communication process caused by an illegibility of the codes by viewers and would-be consumers would be grave: if viewers do not extract meaning from the narrative, the communication process has failed. Hall writes: "If no 'meaning' is taken, there can be no 'consumption'. If the meaning is not articulated in practice, it has no effect" (Hall, 1993, p. 479). Hall further stresses the crucial interrelationship between recipient and producer when he writes:

> Before the message can have an 'effect' [...], it must first be appropriated as a meaningful discourse and be meaningfully decoded. It is this set of decoded meanings, which 'have an effect', influence, entertain, instruct or persuade, with very complex perceptual, cognitive, emotional, ideological or behavioural consequences. [...] [A]t [a] determinate moment the 'message' via its decodings, issues into the structure of social practices" (Hall, 1993, p. 479).

At the reception end of Hall's four-step model, the meanings signified in the discourse are transposed into practice or consciousness, thereby acquiring social use-value (Hall, 1993, p. 480). With reference to the Nespresso marketing campaign, this means that the would-be consumer must first consume the meaning carried in the message of the commercial in order to then consume the Nespresso capsule. Therefore, it is of paramount importance that the consumer's decoding of the narrative accords with the ideas and intentions of the producer. With respect to the communication process, coding and decoding of the message are determinate moments in which production of meaning is finalised by the viewer him- or herself, resulting in observable consumer behaviour, stabilised along the lines intended by the commercial's producer.

In order to understand why codes are an indispensable element in the production of meaning, that is clad in a narrative and subsequently circulated and distributed to consumers, a closer look must be taken as to how codes work. As discussed above, codes fix the relationship between a sign's signifier and signified – a connection that is generally arbitrary. Hall writes: "The articulation of an arbitrary sign [signifier] – whether visual or verbal – with the concept [signified] of a referent, [i.e., the actual object in the world that the sign is related to (Rose, 2012, p. 113)], is the product not of nature but of convention, and the conventionalism of discourses requires the intervention, the support, of codes" (Hall, 1993, p. 481). Codes themselves are the product of conventions, of the way certain things have become to be seen and interpreted by a given group. To fulfil the purpose of its circulation and distribution, meaning must be metamorphosed into a narrative, into a discursive form. To this end, the very conventionalism of discourses requires the use of codes that are themselves the product of convention. In the consumption of the narrative then, the viewer notices what happens in the story and hopefully will, assisted by the codes, draw the "right" conclusion regarding the intended meaning.

Now, codes as the articulation between a sign's signifier and the signified, can do both: denote or connote a meaning. For the purpose of this analysis, it is helpful to posit a theoretical differentiation between the denotative and connotative meanings of a sign. "The term 'denotation' is widely equated with the literal meaning of a sign" (Hall, 1993, p. 482). In a visual discourse, literal meanings of a sign are often shared universally. For instance, a bottle portrayed in a photograph is likely to be interpreted by most people as an object that can be used to store liquids. "'Connotation', on the other hand, is employed [...] to refer to less fixed and therefore more conventionalised and changeable, associative meanings, which clearly vary from instance to instance and therefore must depend on the intervention of codes" (Hall, 1993, p. 482). Therefore, at the connotative level of the meaning of a sign (i.e., of a signifier), it is quite possible to manipulate, alter and bend that meaning. This transformation of signification then allows for an already established code to acquire a new, transformed meaning. Hall describes the pivotal point where meaning is flexed and re-arranged as follows: "The level of connotation of the visual sign, of its contextual reference and positioning in different discursive fields of meaning and association, is the point where *already coded* signs intersect with the deep semantic codes of a culture and take on additional, more active ideological dimensions" (Hall, 1993, pp. 482-483). In this way, a sign's (i.e., signifier's) signified becomes attributed to a new signifier. Applied to the field marketing, it can be said that this is precisely the locus where marketing intervenes and operates, and where new meanings are attributed to a consumer product. Thereby, metonymic and synecdochal signs are created, that is, signs whose signifier becomes associated with something new, and signs that are "a part of something, standing in for a whole" (Rose, 2012, p. 121). The advertised product then stands for a way of life, or a belonging to a certain group. As the subsequent analysis of the commercials will show, this is the lever, with which reality as perceived by consumers, is turned.

4.1.2 The circuit of culture

The analysis of the audio-visual corpus is a multi-levelled undertaking whereby quite a few different perspectives are taken into account and brought into a meaningful relationship. Because such a process requires a careful structuring of the analysis, this study works with, as a structuring device, the circuit of culture, first published by du Gay et al. in 1997 in a study about the Sony Walkman.

To understand the circuit of culture in relation to Hall's semiotic paradigm outlined above, one must first look at Hall's definition, or concept, rather, of culture.[63] As was outlined above, signifiers, that is, words, images, and sounds, come imbued with meaning as they represent various signifieds, or concepts. Commonly held attribution of signifiers to their signified, or, in Hall's terminology, of signs to concepts and the conceptual relations between them, alongside with the corresponding codes, form a conceptual map (Hall, 1997/2003a). As previously mentioned, Hall defines culture in terms of shared conceptual maps: "One way to think about 'culture', then, is in terms of these shared conceptual maps, shared language systems and the *codes which govern the relationships of translation between them*" (Hall, 1997/2003a, p. 21). In accordance therewith, the circuit of culture encompasses the five aforementioned elements which correspond to five major cultural processes. They are: representation, identity, production, consumption and regulation. "These five processes [...], [t]aken together, [...] complete a sort of circuit – what we term the **circuit of culture** – through which any analysis of a cultural text or artefact must pass if it is to be adequately studied [...]" (du Gay et al., 1997, p. 3). These five elements represent dimensions, or perspectives that must be considered in the course of a serious analysis of shared cultural maps. This study's analysis of the corpus examines how and where, in the context of marketing and advertising, meaning is produced and consumed, as well as the pivotal role representation plays therein. Naturally, the analysis is extended to include

63 As discussed above, different scholars use different terminologies in their semiotic approaches. To date, no common terminology in semiotics exists. Collectively scholars do not use common terminology for common variables. For instance, Hall's use of the term "concept" is equivalent to Saussure's use of the term "signified". As Hall's approach to "culture" frequently uses the term "concept", this study, when quoting Hall, does not substitute the term "signified" for the term "concepts". Even though this might diminish, to some extent, notional clarity, the two terms "concept" and "signified", carrying the same meaning, are both used in this study.

the effects on the consumer's identity. The effect of regulation on identity and the production of meaning, and how they are related to representation and consumption are also analysed. In the context of this study, regulation is assumed to be controlled by market price. Hall writes: "[...][T]he market itself *regulates*. It allocates resources, rewards, efficiency and innovation, punishes inefficiency and lack of innovation, and above all [...], creates winners and losers" (Hall, 1997, p.229).

In order to see then, how regulation connects to identity, it is important to consider Paul Gilroy's contribution regarding identity. He writes:

> Uncertain, outward movement, from the anxious embodied self to the world, leads us towards [...][a] set of difficulties in the constellation of identity. This is the problem of sameness and therefore inter-subjectivity. Considering identity from this standpoint requires a recognition of the concept's role in calculations over precisely what counts as 'the same' and as 'different'. This, in turn, raises the difficult questions of recognition, and its refusal, in constituting identity and soliciting **identification**. The theme of identification as a social process rather than as the property of individual subjects enters here and adds further layers of complexity to deliberations about how selves – and their identities – are formed through relationships with others, of conflict and exclusion. (Gilroy, 1997/2012, p. 315)

Furthermore, Woodward argues that:

> [i]dentities are forged through the marking of difference. This marking of difference takes place both through *symbolic* systems of representation, and through forms of *social* exclusion. Identity, then, is not the opposite of, but *depends on*, difference. In social relations, these forms of symbolic and social difference are established, at least in part, through the operation of what are called classificatory system. A **classificatory system** applies a principle of difference to a population in such a way as to be able to divide them and all their characteristics into at least two, opposing groups – us/them [...]; self/other. (Woodward, 1997/2012, p. 29)

The market's price system can also function as a classificatory system, dividing members of a society into those who can and those who cannot afford a certain product – into insiders and outsiders. Regulation, through the market price, therefore, is also constitutive with respect to the insider's, that is, the consumer's identity. "Marketing promotions can construct new identities [...]" (Woodward, 1997/2012, p. 15). For this to function, "[a]dvertisements [...][must] provide images with which [...][consumers] can identify (Woodward, 1997/2012, p. 14). Advertising speaks to the viewer, the listener. "Advertising is the cultural language which speaks *on behalf* of the product" (du Gay et al., 1997, p. 25). The language spoken clearly need not be text-based only. A language can be visual, and, as in the case of commercials, audio-visual. On one hand, language, the melting pot of referents, signifiers and signifieds, or concepts, makes representation, as a signifying practice of the production of meaning, possible. On the other hand, the idea of culture seen as shared conceptual maps can also be applied to conceptual maps designed by marketing campaigns and communicated to potential consumers through advertising. In this sense, as the advertising clearly draws a line between the Nespresso Club and the outside world, allowing for exclusion, the meaning produced through the commercials' decoding is conducive to the formation of the consumer's identity.

Along these lines then, the analysis of the corpus is carried out, examining whether Nespresso's commercials are indeed geared towards the establishment of a specific cultural map, resulting in the creation of a meaning and a practice, which, in a Geertzian sense, mirror the functional and structural analogy between marketing and religion.

The production of meaning with visual, or audio-visual texts is, on the theoretical level, explored in detail because, according to Hall, an understanding of representation as the re-presentation of, say, a particular event, or a string of particular events and actions by images, thereby conveying an implied ontological meaning of those events would not only be a gross and complete misunderstanding of what representation does, but also of the nature of meaning and its production. According to Hall, an event can have many meanings. It is the producer of an event's representation, for instance by audio-visual means, that must and will, decide which meaning will be attributed to the event. The story of and about the event is then produced in such a way as to be conducive to the construction of the chosen, intended meaning. In this sense, the production of meaning is an arbitrary, subjective, and hegemonic practice. As is described in the subsequent paragraph, such hegemonic practice is a necessary condition, if, given largely saturated consumers, Nespresso's marketing campaign is to be a success.

As already discussed, the general backdrop of this study is a postmodern consumerist society with a comparatively high purchasing power. Therefore, the daily needs of the members of that society have in general been met, and the scarcity of goods, one of the fundamental tenets of economic theory, has become scarce itself. This may not be true for all goods, but it is most likely to be true for everyday consumer goods, including coffee. Therefore, from the point of view of a firm or firm wanting to introduce a new product to an already saturated market, offering a mere, perfect substitute nobody has been waiting for, the challenge is to sell something that nobody needs, (i.e., yet another perfect substitute). Operating on the assumption that selling something nobody really needs is nearly impossible, it becomes clear that the product must undergo a metamorphosis into something that is without alternatives, something that addresses a consumers' need that has, so far, not yet been catered for. In other words, a newly marketed commodity with a specific use-value that many other established products also possess must successfully be invested with a new meaning beyond its apparent use-value, thereby assuming, in the consumers' perspective, a special, commodity-specific exchange-value. In the following, an outline is proposed on how such a feat can be accomplished.

Hall differentiates between two systems of representation. The so-called system of mental representation attributes a concept, a signified, to a real-life event, an action or an object. These objects and actions are called, as already mentioned, the "referent". As concepts carry meaning, mirroring a particular standpoint, possibly including a worldview, the attribution of a concept to a real-world action allows for a meaningful perception and interpretation of such action.

Next, meaning also needs to be communicated, a process requiring a language and therefore necessitating signs. The attribution of a signifier to a signified, a concept, is needed to make the concept communicable. As signifiers can be attributed to various concepts and can be subsequently organised into language (Hall 2003a/1997), Hall terms this the system of linguistic representation. "Language is [...] the second system of representation involved in the overall process of constructing meaning." (Hall, 1997/2003a, p. 18) It is noteworthy that Hall uses the term "language" in a broad sense:

> The writing systems or the spoken system of a particular language are both obviously 'languages'. But so are visual images, whether produced by hand, mechanical, electronic, digital or some other means, when they are used to express meaning. And so are other things which aren't 'linguistic' in any ordinary sense: the language of facial expressions or of gesture, for example [...] Even music is a language. (Hall, 1997/2003a, pp. 18-19)

In the analysis of the corpus, this study uses the term language in the sense outlined by Hall. Advertising is approached as the "cultural language" (Hall, 1997/2003a, p. 25) that speaks, through words, syntagmatic actions, gestures, and facial expressions, on behalf of the product, carving out how meaning is encoded in, and attributed to, events and objects and subsequently decoded by viewers and would-be consumers.

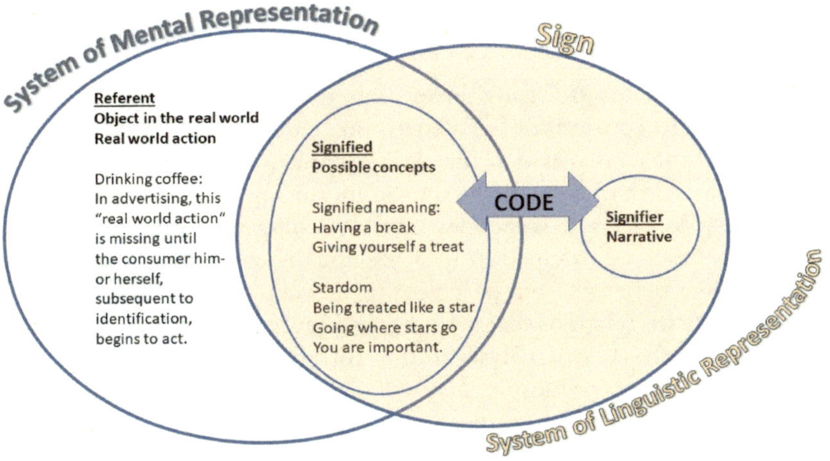

Figure 4: Systems of Representation (generated by the author with PowerPoint, 2016)

4.2 Contributions from microeconomics: the club theory

The theoretical body in this study is based upon a synthesis of visual culture theory as it is widely used in the remit of the study of religion and the economic theory of clubs. Given the general setting of this study, it is argued that the implied level of secularisation, in accordance with Bruce's line of argument, discussed in a previous chapter, warrants the use of economic theory in the analysis. This present subchapter introduces and presents James M. Buchanan's economic theory of clubs, which constitutes the microeconomic contribution to the theory applied in this study.[64]

64 For a discussion on the wide applicability of Buchanan's economic theory of clubs see Sandler (2013).

Iannaccone's study on religious behaviour (1992) paved the way for Buchanan's economic theory of clubs to enter the field of the study of religion. As to why an economic theory is of significance in an apparently unrelated discipline, Iannaccone argued as follows: "[...] [E]conomic theory has much to say about religious behaviour, particularly those aspects that appear least rational. [...] [In this paper] [r]eligion is modelled as a club good that displays positive returns to "participatory crowding" (Iannaccone, 1992, p. 272). A club good is characterised by a high excludability. Referring to a religiously active community, this means that only believers can join the group. In the case of Nespresso, this means that someone without a sufficient purchasing power is excluded from the regular, or frequent Nespresso consumption. Furthermore, club goods or products, have a low degree of rivalry, which means, referring to Nespresso, that someone's consumption of a cup of Nespresso in, for instance a Nespresso boutique, does not preclude someone else from doing the same, in the same way as a believer's participation in a religious ritual does not necessarily preclude other believers from participating as well.

In his study on religious divides published seventeen years later, Michael Makowsky also based his analysis on the club theory of religion, the application of Buchanan's economic theory of clubs to religion. He writes: "The economic theory of clubs has been used to study a variety of social phenomena (Cornes & Sandler, 1986; Buchanan, 1965). Within the economic study of religion, the club model has arguably been the most successful and frequently employed" (Makowsky, 2009, p. 9).

In an introductory paper to the economics of religion, Iannaccone acknowledges that many academic papers on the economics of religion take the club theory as their starting point (Iannaccone, 1998, p. 1482). "Club models are motivated by the observation that, despite its firm-like characteristics, the typical congregation functions as a mutual-benefit organisation, dedicated to the collective production of worship services, religious instruction, social activities, and other quasi-public 'club goods'" (Iannaccone, 1998, p. 1482).

Finally, and exemplary of many others, two additional studies serve as a reference. The first is a study of the economics of religious indulgences by Alberto Cassone and Carla Marchese (1999). These authors base their insightful analysis on a club model of the Catholic Church. Taking the economic theory of clubs as a basis, they explain various aspects of participation in the Church, for instance, access to and exclusion from the sacraments. The second study provides an analysis of the various levels of religious-giving by members of the Reformed Church in America. Three models were tested regarding their explanatory power (Luidens & Nemeth, 1994): a so-called "high-demand church model", the club model", and a "dues-paying model". In the study, the club model and the dues-paying model delivered very good results: they accounted for most of the explained variance (29 out of 35 percent), each explaining about the same amount of variance (Luidens & Nemeth, 1994, p. 212).

While Bruce maintains that, in general, economic theory can only be sensibly applied to the study of religion after some degree of secularisation has taken place, many scholars have successfully applied the economic theory of clubs to one or more aspects of the multifaceted field of religion. Whether this is because secularisation has indeed taken place, or whether Bruce's argument is perhaps incomplete, will not be further addressed. In this study, it is argued that in the appropriate context, microeconomic theory in general, and the club theory in particular, make a valid contribution to the study of religion. Microeconomic theory does so, because it provides a theoretical framework, which contributes to an understanding of the behaviour of the individual person, and the club theory, because it helps to analyse such behaviour with a view to the consumption of club goods, material or immaterial, such as "salvation", whose consumption may be shared by many, without compromising one another, yet, under certain circumstances, a specific individual might be excluded therefrom. With a view to this study's context, which is, as described in subchapter 2.1.2, a largely secularised, consumption-oriented society, the use of Buchanan's economic theory of clubs is warranted as it helps, on the theoretical level, to carve out and elaborate on the structural and functional analogies between religion and marketing hypothesised by this study.

Microeconomic theory differentiates between private goods, and public goods. Public goods are non-rival and non-excludable. A classic example is street lighting. Individual A's consumption of street lighting does not preclude individual B's consumption of the same street lighting at the same time. Therefore, street lighting is non-rival. Also, the consumption of street lighting by individual A does not allow for the exclusion of individual B from also consuming, simultaneously, that very same street lighting. Therefore, street lighting is also non-excludable. To further illustrate this, it is perhaps helpful to consider another example. Traditional subscription-TV is a service, which is non-rival, yet excludable: A practically unlimited number of clients can subscribe to the service without impeding one another's consumption. However, those clients who fail to pay the subscription fee will be excluded from consuming the service.

Private goods, on the contrary, are both: rival and excludable. Individual A's consumption of a cup of coffee precludes individual B's consumption of that same cup of coffee. Therefore, the consumption of a cup of coffee is rival. "With purely private goods, consumption by one individual automatically reduces potential consumption of other individuals by an equal amount. With purely public goods consumption by one individual implies equal consumption by all others" (Buchanan, 1965, p. 3). Furthermore, private goods are also excludable. The seller of coffee can easily exclude an individual, who is unwilling to pay the asking price, from consumption. Therefore, the consumption of coffee is also excludable.

Now, many goods that are consumed in everyday life do not strictly fall into either one of those two categories, lying somewhere in between those two extremes. Economic theory did not address them until, in 1965, James M. Buchanan presented his *Economic Theory of Clubs*. In that paper, he develops a theory explaining the characteristics of goods that are, to some degree at least, non-rival, and excludable. For instance, the visit to a public swimming pool is non-rival. Individuals A and B can both go swimming there at the same time. However, access to the pool is excludable. Usually an entrance fee is charged excluding those who are unwilling or unable to pay.

Similarly, Nespresso capsules, in a generic sense, are non-rival and excludable. When consumer A buys a capsule, clearly, consumer B cannot buy that very same capsule, making the capsules appear to be rival at first sight. However, consumer B can buy another, fully identical capsule, and the consumption of Nespresso capsules is therefore non-rival after all. But, like the public pool, Nespresso products are excludable, as consumers have to pay for the capsule. Potential consumers who are unwilling or unable to pay the requested price are excluded from consumption.

Henceforth, those goods, in accordance with Buchanan's theory, are now referred to as "club goods". Their distinctive features, as described above[65], are now further scrutinised along the tenets of Buchanan's contribution.

Remaining with the example of the public swimming pool, individual A's benefit from a visit depends on how many other people are visiting the

65 In the analysis of club goods the free rider problem is an issue. If exclusion cannot be enforced, some individuals might consume more than what they are entitled to. Even though the free rider problem is an issue that could be studied in the context of religion as well as of marketing along the tenets of the theory of economic clubs, this study does not focus on that issue.

public swimming pool at the same time. A few more other visitors do not really have a negative impact on A's personal experience, which might even be enhanced if other people are there as well. However, as it begins to get crowded and very noisy, A's benefit is reduced as a function of the increasing number of visitors. This situation is illustrated in figure 5 below.

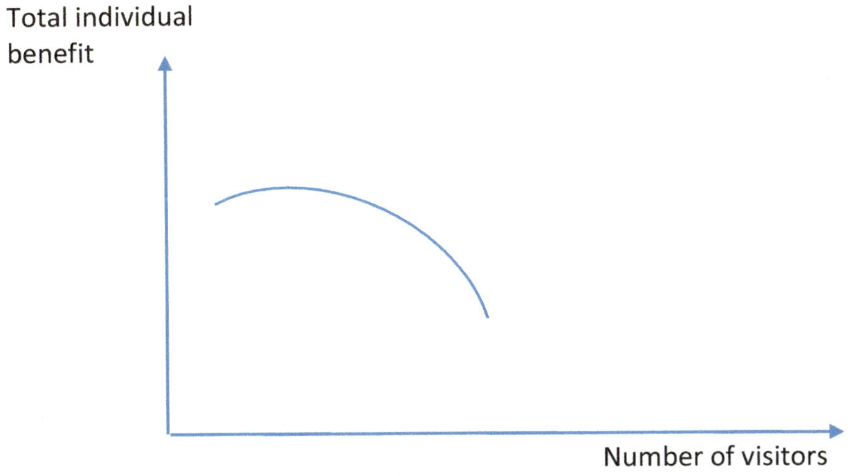

Figure 5 (generated by the author with Word, 2015)

For individual A, the increase in the number of visitors has, in addition to the effect illustrated in figure 5, one clearly positive effect. The more people frequent the public swimming pool, the lower the ticket price to get in. That situation is illustrated in figure 6 below:

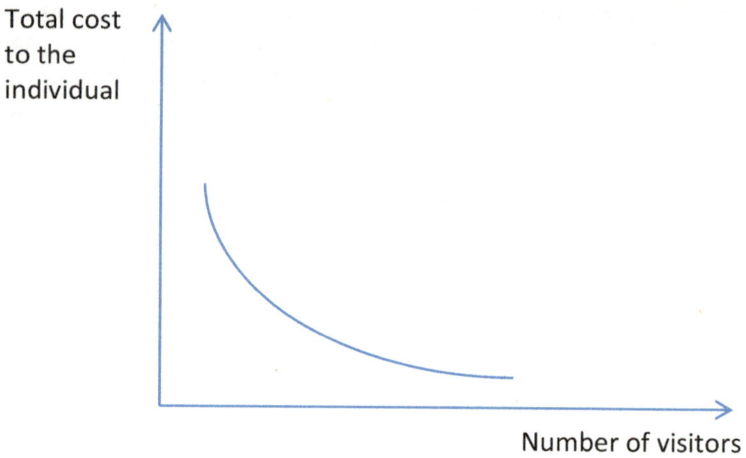

Figure 6 (generated by the author with Word, 2015)

As can be observed, for a relatively low number of visitors, the decrease in cost to individual A, that is, the rate of change of the cost, exceeds the reduction, that is, the rate of change, in benefit. Both diminish, but the cost diminishes by more than the benefit. Therefore, for low numbers of visitors, individual A is better off if the number of visitors to the swimming pool increases. The best situation for the individual occurs when the decrease in cost due to an increase in the number of visitors is exactly as large as the corresponding reduction in benefit. The merging of figure 5 and 6 into one diagram is illustrated by figure 7 below.

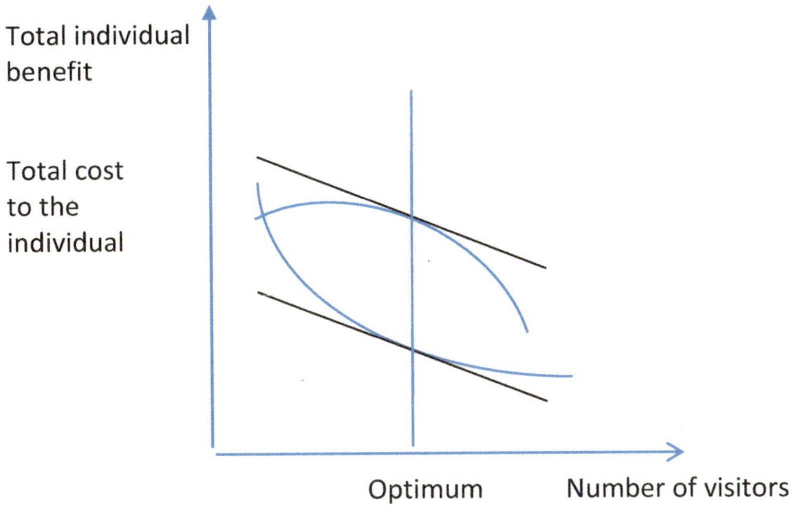

Figure 7 (generated by the author with Word, 2015)

Now, what happens if the swimming facility is expanded and another pool is built on the same premises? In economic terms, the "quantity of goods", or services available is increased. As a consequence, the price of an entrance ticket, for any given number of visitors, is now higher than before. However, due to the larger facility, it now requires many more visitors to overcrowd the facility. Both the benefit and the cost function shift upward, but the benefit function's slope only turns negative if there is a very high number of visitors. This is illustrated in figure 8.

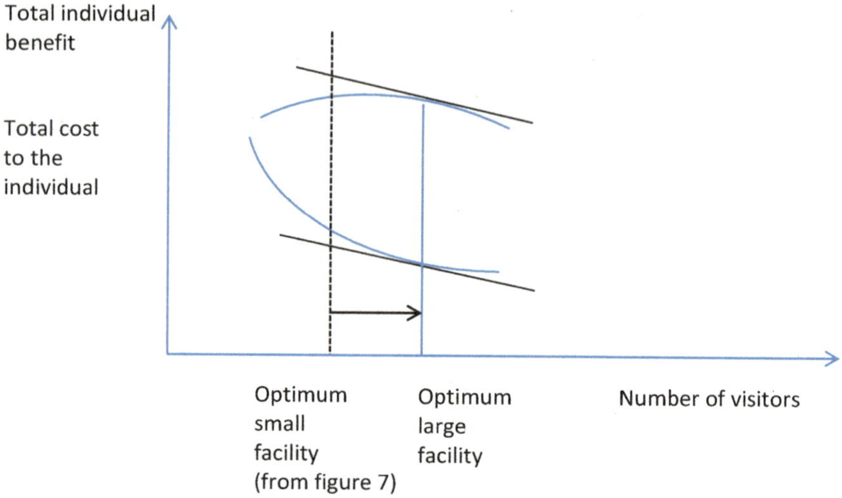

Figure 8 (generated by the author with Word, 2015)

What becomes apparent is that the individual's maximum benefit net of cost, in the case of a large facility or a large quantity of goods, goes with a comparatively high number of visitors. Or, in other words, clubs with a large membership (i.e., a high number of visitors) have to offer their members a large array of goods and services for an individual club member to be satisfied with the club.

These initial theoretical insights are now applied to the Nespresso case. Moreover, subsequent illustrations of the economic theory of clubs will be made using a vocabulary that has been adapted to the world of Nespresso. The number of visitors to the swimming facility becomes the number of Nespresso clients or club members, respectively. And the size of the swimming facility is referred to as the width of the product range and/or the diffusion of Nespresso's products and services, measured by the number of Nespresso shops worldwide.

Contrary to the behaviour of total cost to the individual club member described above, it is argued that the cost to the individual Nespresso client does not change with the size of the Nespresso community. This study neither addresses, whether or not Nestlé-Nespresso can possibly profit from economies of scale[66], nor whether Nestlé-Nespresso will pass on

66 Economies of scale are present if a company can reduce average total cost by increasing production capacities.

potentially lower average costs of production to clients. Abstracting from economies of scale and a possibly monotonic cost function, this study presupposes that the unit price is set exogenously by Nestlé-Nespresso. Graphically therefore, the cost to the individual Nespresso consumer is represented by a straight horizontal line. The individual benefit, however, remains consistent with the pattern in the previous example. From a global perspective, a widespread diffusion of Nespresso's products and services shifts the individual consumer's benefit function to the right. For example, access to a Nespresso machine in a hotel room far away from home yields, as verified by the empirical survey, consumer benefit. The point of individual consumer benefit maximisation is now consistent with a larger number of Nespresso clients, or club members, as it now takes a larger number of Nespresso clients to bring about the negative effect of brand dilution. The same is true for a wider product range. However, for any given level of diffusion or product range, a critical maximum number of Nespresso clients still exists, that should not be exceeded. This is, as mentioned above, because beyond that critical figure, the individual Nespresso client's benefit begins to diminish as the brand's appeal is becoming diluted. Of course, even if the number of Nespresso clients increases beyond the individual consumer's maximum benefit, until the individual's total benefits falls below the total cost to the individual, the individual consumer's benefit is still larger than the cost. However, the individual consumer no longer enjoys maximum benefit. For a given diffusion of Nespresso products or a given product range (illustrated by the respective cost and benefit functions), too many Nespresso clients or, in other words, too many club members cause the individual consumer's benefit to shrink, mostly due to brand dilution. Faced with that situation, from Nespresso's perspective, aiming to maximise profits and therefore aiming to keep consumer satisfaction at a maximum, it would make sense to simply put the prices up and thereby reduce the number of clients. This would of course also shift the individual's horizontal cost line upwards. However, whilst the difference between consumer cost and benefit would shrink, he or she would still be located in the area of *individual maximum benefit* and would not be exposed to the negative effects of brand dilution. Moreover, graphically not shown however, a price increase might also shift the individual consumer's benefit function upward as the product adopts a more exclusive character.

The above described situation is illustrated in figure 9 below.

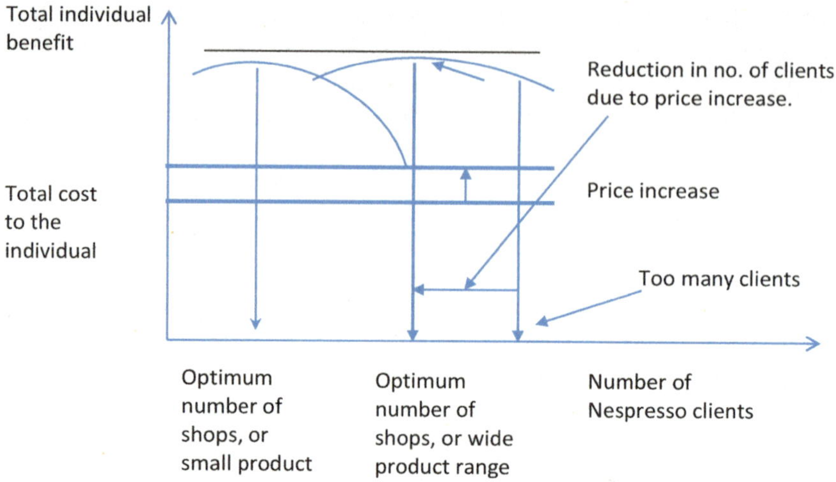

Figure 9 (generated by the author with Word, 2015)

As mentioned above, figure 9 shows that, for a given diffusion or product range, the benefit for Nespresso clients decreases beyond a certain number of club members. As a consequence, Nespresso must set sufficiently high prices to ward off an avalanche of potential consumers. Therefore, from the existing consumer's – an established club member's – point of view, the high prices fulfil a positive function: they keep the "riff-raff" away. And this keeps the individual consumer's benefit high.

In subchapter 4.1.2, the circuit of culture was introduced. One of its five elements is regulation. Here, the production of meaning with the cultural language of advertising is primarily *regulated through prices*. If the price of a capsule were so low that almost everybody could afford it, then the meaning carried by the concept of exclusivity (club) would most likely suffer. If the price were too high, the viewer's identification process with the actions portrayed in the commercials' narration would most likely not issue in an actual purchase of the capsule. In both situations, with prices too low or too high, the whole purpose of Nespresso's marketing – which is profit maximisation – would be defeated.

Now, given that the price of a Nespresso capsule is neither too low, nor too high, the combinations of the degree of diffusion of Nespresso's products and services as well as the width of the product range on one hand, and, on the other, the total number of Nespresso clients that represent an optimum for the individual client can be represented as a straight line:

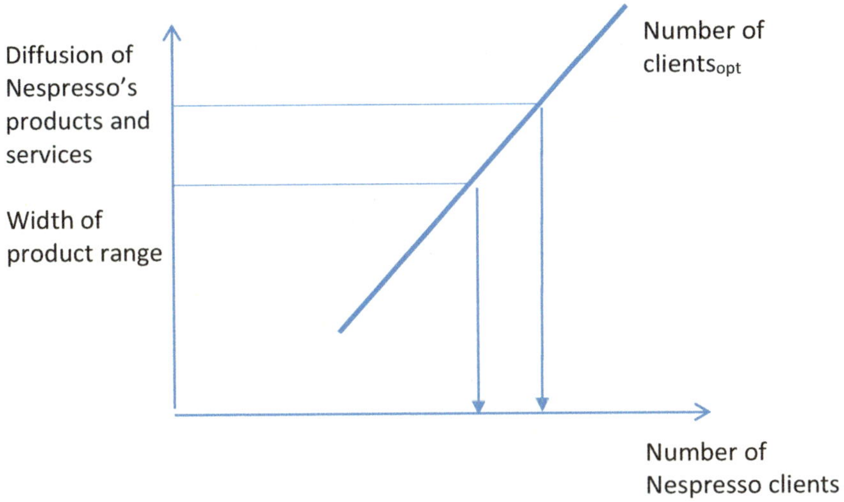

Figure 10 (generated by the author with Word, 2015)

Here, it is important to note that this straight line does represent a linear function of the form y = f(x), only that the independent variables (x) are shown on the ordinate (y-axis). In this sense, the optimal number of Nespresso clients is a function of the diffusion of Nespresso's products and services as well as of the width of the product range. The straight line illustrates the values of the optimal number of Nespresso clients for varying degrees of diffusion or width of product range under the condition that the individual client or club member's benefit be maximised.

In the next step, the number of Nespresso clients will first be held constant. On the abscissa, the degree of diffusion of Nespresso's products and services is measured, with the ordinate representing the individual consumer's total benefit and total cost. Figure 11 illustrates this situation, depicting a scenario with only very few Nespresso clients worldwide. The straight line represents the cost to the individual client. The concave curve shows the total individual benefit. For a given number of Nespresso clients, or club members, the curve shows firstly, an increase in total individual benefit resulting from a wider product range and a larger diffusion of Nespresso's products and services. Beyond a certain level, however, total individual benefit decreases with an increase in the product range and a larger diffusion of Nespresso's products and services. This is because for a given number of consumers, there would be so many Nespresso boutiques that each one appeared to be almost empty all the time, whilst abounding with a wide product range, giving the impression that the products are not in demand at all, thereby damaging the brand's reputation. Also, the cost to each individual client would be enormously high due to the small number of Nespresso clients and clearly, no optimum producing positive consumer benefit can be found.

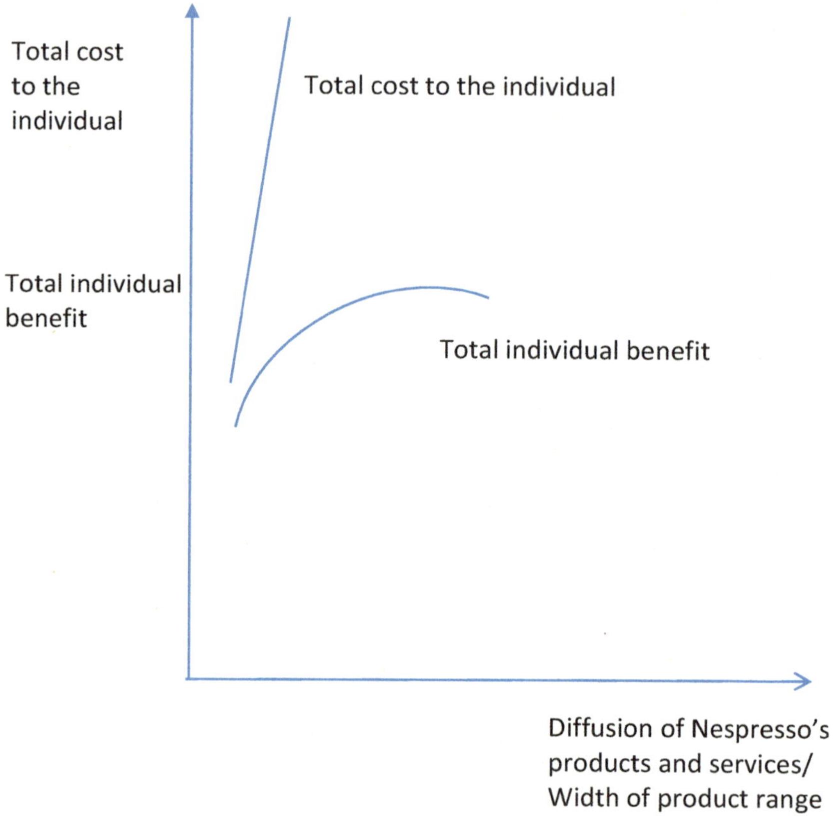

Figure 11 (generated by the author with Word, 2015)

If it is now assumed that the number of clients increases dramatically to a large number and is held there constantly, the total cost to the individual consumer can be illustrated, analogous to the situation described above, by a horizontal line. Due to brand dilution, the concave curve, representing the total individual benefit, tends to shift downward with the increase in the number of clients. Furthermore, compared to a scenario with only very few clients, the maximum of the individual consumer's benefit curve is reached in a point situated further to the right as the larger number of Nespresso clients manage to fill the boutiques, thereby contributing to a positive and uplifting atmosphere of sustained and on-going consumer demand. Figure 12 below illustrates this situation.

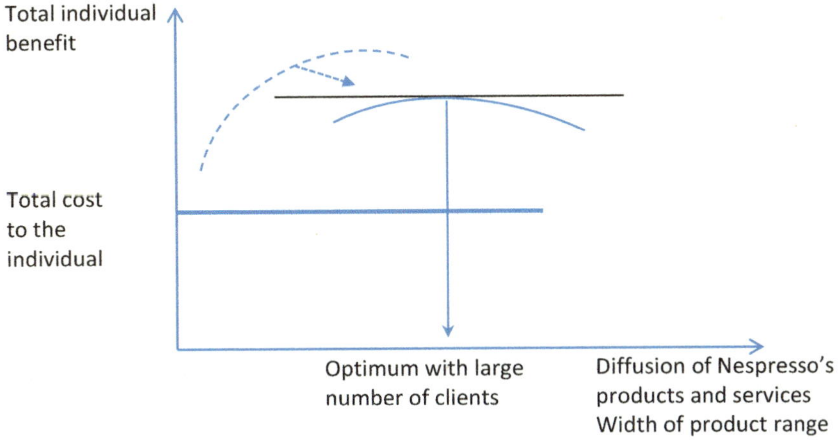

Figure 12 (generated by the author with Word, 2015)

Figure 10 determines the values of the optimal number of Nespresso clients for varying degrees of diffusion or width of product range. All points on the straight line constitute a combination that represents a maximum with respect to the individual consumer's benefit. Analogous thereto, under the condition that the individual client or club member's benefit be maximised, the optimal degree of diffusion of Nespresso's products and services, or width of the product range for varying given numbers of Nespresso clients or club members, respectively, can also be represented as a straight line:

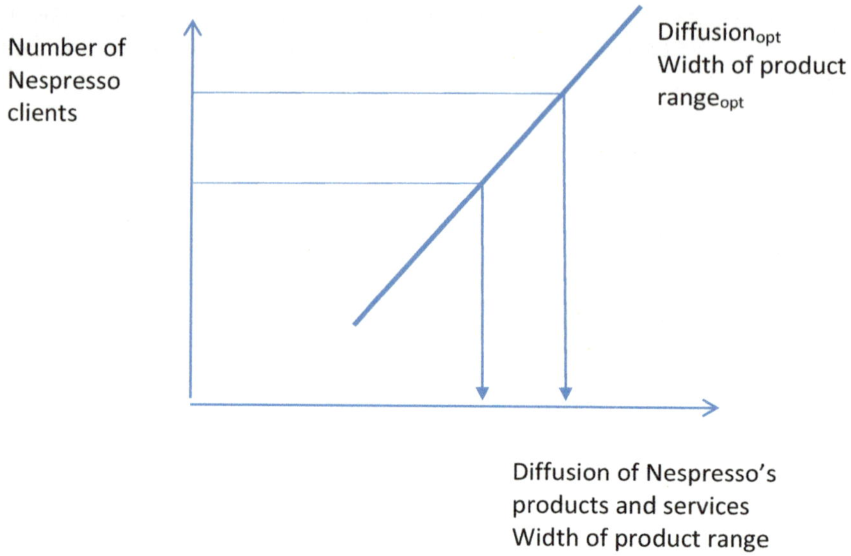

Figure 13 (generated by the author with Word, 2015)

Figures 10 and 13 can be simultaneously illustrated in only one chart. First, however, the axes in figure 13 have to be swapped. This is illustrated in Figure 14, showing the linear relationship between the number of Nespresso clients and the diffusion of Nespresso's products, with the former measured on the abscissa.

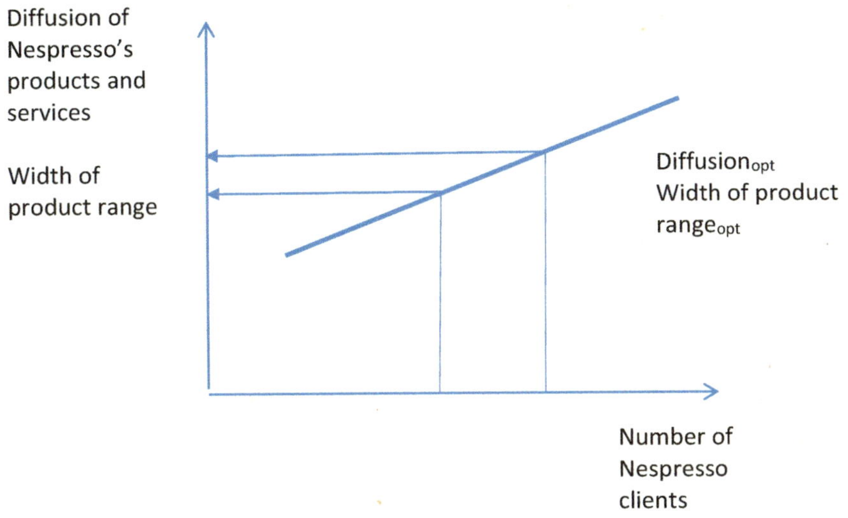

Figure 14 (generated by the author with Word, 2015)

Figure 15 below represents the two straight lines of optima from figures 10 and 14 in one single diagram.

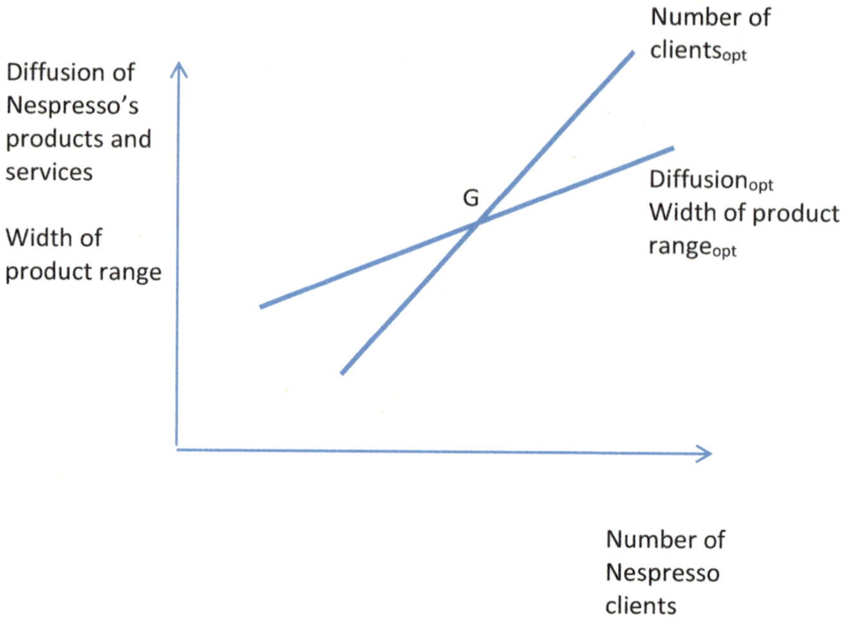

Figure 15 (generated by the author with Word, 2015)

Not only do these two straight lines represent a linear relationship between the two variables, number of Nespresso clients and diffusion of Nespresso's products or the width of the product range, respectively: they also determine the point of a general equilibrium, G, where the individual consumer maximises his or her benefit. "The individual is in equilibrium both with respect to [the diffusion of Nespresso's products, or the width of the product range, respectively], and to [the number of Nespresso clients], for the good, [Nespresso capsules], under consideration" (Buchanan, 1965, p. 9) In a manner of speaking, this is the peak of the consumer's pleasure mountain.

Moreover, as the following explanation illustrates, the point G also represents a *stable* general equilibrium. For instance, figure 16 below illustrates an example in which the actual number of Nespresso clients is N_K. This represents the starting point.

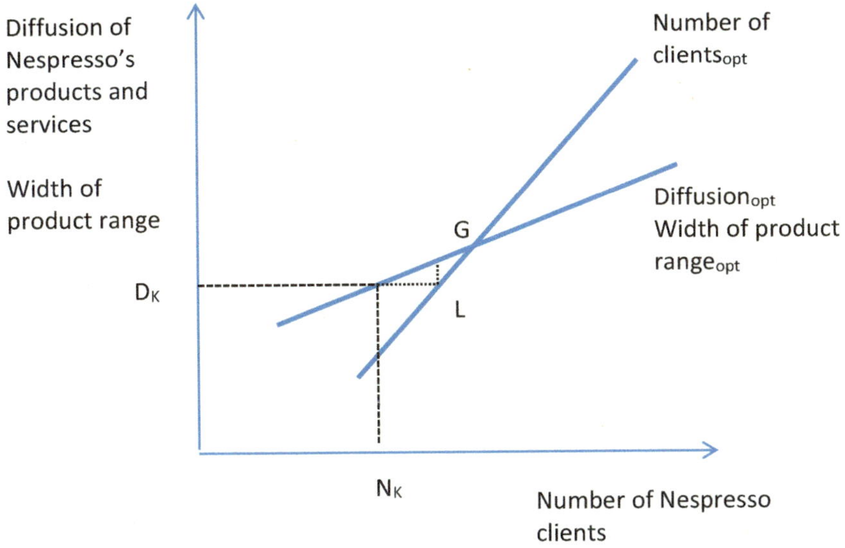

Figure 16 (generated by the author with Word, 2015)

Now, given N_K, point D_K represents the optimal diffusion that would go with point N_K under the condition that consumer benefit is maximised. However, given point D_K, an optimum with respect to the number of clients is reached at point L. Once the number of clients is increased, the individual consumer's benefit maximisation requires an increase in the diffusion of Nespresso's products, and/or a wider product range. This process continues until point G, the general equilibrium, is reached.

For a better understanding, the following figure 17 illustrates these steps once more, highlighted in colour. Now starting at point A, the optimal number of clients is identified to be B. Yet, given B, the optimal degree of diffusion is C. Yet, given C, the optimal number of clients or club members is D. This process continues, until the general equilibrium in G is reached.

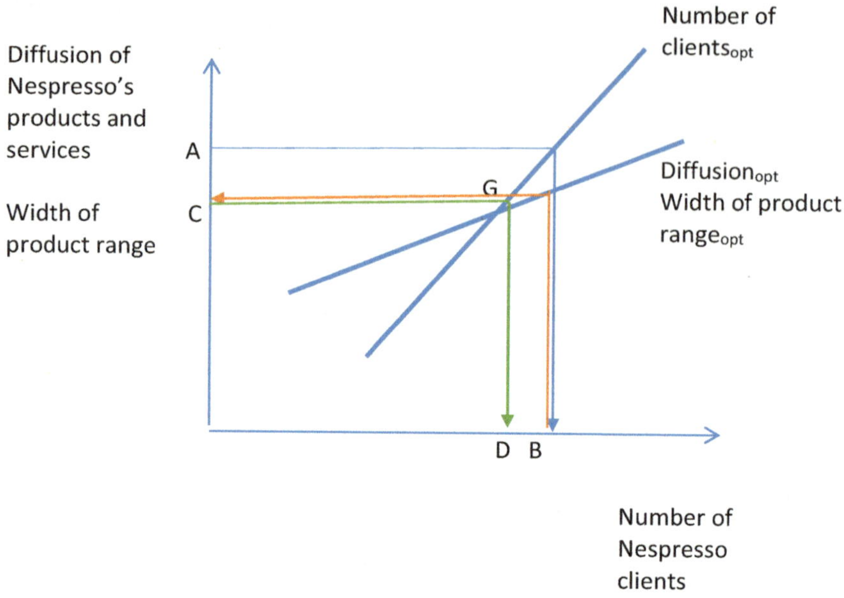

Figure 17 (generated by the author with Word, 2015)

Not only does Buchanan's economic theory of clubs allow for the identification of a linear relationship between the number of clients and the diffusion of Nespresso's products or the width of the product range, respectively, it also allows for the identification of a stable equilibrium regarding the maximum benefit of the individual consumer. This microeconomic theory makes, in the context of this study, an indispensable contribution. Hall's circuit of culture, including "regulation" as a determinant in the production of meaning, can, in a constructive and meaningful manner, be complemented by Buchanan's contribution.

4.3 An interdisciplinary approach

As the discussion of the state of actual research has shown, no theoretical body within marketing, that could satisfactorily explain Nespresso's remarkable success, exists. Therefore, with this study, another interdisciplinary approach is needed. Rooted in the remit of the study of religion, this study axiomatically, using contributions from microeconomic theory, from cultural studies, and from visual culture studies, attempts to analyse the said phenomenon. Furthermore, in the analysis of the audio-visual corpus, theoretical contributions from film studies will be used. This study is therefore of a most interdisciplinary-nature – a fact that, it is hoped, allows for the successful accomplishment of the study's goal, a fact, however, that also poses a challenge with respect to the establishment of a clear theoretical framework with which to carry out the analysis.

In this chapter, the theoretical contributions previously introduced are melded along an axis formed by the categories of analysis stipulated by Geertz's definition of religion; they are: (1) system of symbols, (2) moods and motivations, (3) worldview, and (4) ethos. The analysis of the corpus according to each of these four categories is then grouped into the five aspects provided by Hall's circuit of culture, which are: (1) representation, (2) production, (3) consumption, (4) identity, and (5) regulation. Consequently, that results in a total of 20 possible aspects according to which the corpus can be scrutinised. The contributions, made by the economic theory of clubs, of the neo-formalist film theory, of culture studies, and of visual cultural studies will then be, if appropriate, integrated into each one of these 20 possible aspects. For example, the aspect "worldview – production" is approached, amongst others, with a framework provided by neo-formalist film theory, explaining how "reality" is constructed, or produced, by the viewer.[67] In this manner, the entire corpus is then analysed according to the synthesis of theory presented below.

As the study of religion begins to widen its scope beyond the sole study of sacred texts, to include images and films, visual culture studies have made inroads into the study of religion. In this sense, films and commercials are naturally treated as a language, as texts, specifically: as audio-visual texts. Commensurate with this development, film studies enjoy a growing acceptance and importance within the study of religion.[68] "Regarding 'film

---

67 For example, Plate writes: "Reality, like religion and like cinema, is socially constructed, allowing its members to engage with it on deeply-felt personal levels. The role of cultural products such as film offers conduits of significance between the individual and the cosmic order of the universe" (Plate, 2008, p. 4). This contribution has methodological implications for this study inasmuch as, in the socio-empirical survey, questions are included to fathom whether or not a statistically significant difference between Nespresso clients and consumers of rival brands, with respect to the ontological quality of the chosen brand's supremacy over rival brands, exists. Naturally, as will be discussed, this "model of the world" only extends to the "coffee world" and is referred to only as a category of analysis to tease out, on the theoretical level, the functional and structural analogy between religion and marketing.

68 See also *Die Reise als Suche nach Orientierung*, Mäder (2012).

and religion', the study of religion has acknowledged 'film' as an important pool of discourses and themes which are crucial in the search for new understandings of, and insights into, religion as a cultural issue"[69] (Pezzoli-Olgiati 2008, p. 45). In particular, film studies in the context of culture studies make an indispensable contribution to the probing of systems of significant religious symbols. This point takes on particular salience because of Geertz's understanding of "culture": "The concept of culture I espouse [...] is essentially a semiotic one. Believing, with Max Weber, that man is an animal suspended in webs of significance he himself has spun, I take culture to be those webs, and the analysis of it to be therefore not an experimental science in search of law but an interpretative one in search of meaning" (Geertz, 1973, p. 5).[70] As outlined above, Hall, in his theory of representation, takes an identical approach to culture: "Meaning is intrinsic to our definition of culture" (du Gay et al., 1997, p. 10), and: "Because we interpret the world in roughly similar ways, we are able to build up a shared culture of meanings and thus construct a social world which we inhabit together. That is why 'culture' is sometimes defined in terms of 'shared meanings' [...]" (Hall 1997/2003b, p. 18).

Film then plays a leading role in this interpretative search for meaning as well as the construction thereof. John Lyden attributes to film the power to create meaning and worldviews. Applying Geertz's definition of religion to film, he writes: "If film does operate according to Geertz's definition, as I contend, then like religion it offers a connection between this world and the 'other' world imagined in offering both models of and for reality. These two aspects – worldview or mythology, and ethos – together express a vision of what the world really is and what it should be" (Lyden, 2003, pp. 53-54). In this realm, the realm of meaning and meaning-making, the parallels of film and religion are most apparent. In the words of Pezzoli-Olgiati: "Film and religion can thus be parallelised by virtue of their shared capability to produce myths, rituals, meaning, values, or worldviews"[71] (Pezzoli-Olgiati, 2008, p. 53). In this sense, films, or commercials, are an audio-visual language with the power to create both, a model of, and for the world.[72]

69 Original in German; Translation by the author, 2015.
70 See also Nehring, (2008), pp. 29-31.
71 Original in German; Translation by the author, 2015.
72 In case it went unnoticed, it should be stressed again that whilst, in the context of religion, the term "world" is often used in its broadest, most cosmic sense, in the context of this study, however, it is mostly used according to perhaps one of its most narrowed-down contents, meaning exclusively the "world with respect to

The synthesis of theory elaborated here attempts to explain the success of the cultural language of advertising in creating maximum consumer benefit, in creating maximum consumer motivation, and finally, in creating a positive attitude of the consumer towards the product, all of which results in very high operating profit margins. At the heart of this complex lies the successful production of meaning: the artistry of involving the consumer in the co-production of meaning so convincingly true, that the related motivation to buy the product seems "uniquely realistic". In other words, the individual consumer's desire, once awakened and interpreted for him or her through the language of advertising, observably results in a purposeful motivation to act. This motivation to act in conjunction with the intake and decoding of the message conveyed by the cultural language of advertising, and its subsequent enactment by the consumer, are crucial elements in the construction of commercial success. Besides, the real-life enactment of the meaning conveyed by advertising through consumers themselves further surrounds such meaning with an aura of factuality. It can be argued that the consumer's desire interpreted by advertising, in conjunction with the *practice* of factually buying the product, makes the accompanying moods and motivations indeed uniquely real in a literal sense.[73] For the consumer, things then truly *are* this way. For instance, using semiotic language, the moment the consumer acts as the referent, Nespresso obviously, in the "real" sense, *is* the "right choice". Alternatives are not favoured, or they are not even taken into consideration in the first place, as the choice has already been made for good: Nespresso *is* the right choice. Period. As the socio-empirical part of this study will reveal, Nespresso clients perceive this condition as a factual reality, a bit like gravity and the fact that the sun rises in the east.

The reader will recall that, with a view to the analysis of audio-visual corpus, this synthesis of theory is structured according to four categories of analysis rooted in the Geertzian definition (system of symbols, moods and motivations, worldview, and ethos). Furthermore, it is formulated with

---

the advertised product", that is, the advertised product and its context. By the same token, it must be repeated that the aim of this study is not at all to show or allege that drinking Nespresso *is* a religion. The aim is to identify, on the *theoretical* level, a structural and functional analogy between religion and marketing.

73 The words "real" and "reality", derived from the Latin word "res", meaning "thing" or "object", refer to the world as it can be perceived by a human's five senses, as opposed to the so-called "ideality", the world accessible through ideas and the imaginary. In this sense, "ideal" does not mean perfect. "Ideal" refers to something that only exists in the world of ideas.

special emphasis on the five elements of the circuit of culture. Now, before the synthesis of theory is elaborated, it is perhaps helpful to review Geertz's definition of religion in full:

> A religion is 1) a system of symbols which acts to 2) establish powerful, pervasive, and long-lasting moods and motivations in men by 3) formulating conceptions of a general order of existence and 4) clothing these conceptions with such an aura of factuality that 5) the moods and motivations seem uniquely realistic. (Geertz, 1966/2010, p. 4)

In the following, as the phenomenon under scrutiny, that is, Nespresso's continued and outstandingly high operating profit margin, is as much a financial/commercial as well as, with a view to the commercials (i.e., the advertisements), a cultural phenomenon, theoretical contributions from cultural studies, from visual culture studies, from neo-formalist film theory, and from micro-economic theory will, when appropriate and needed, be added to Geertz's definition to create a theoretical framework allowing for the detection of the definition's elements in a marketing context.

A religion is…
1)…a system of symbols which acts…

Geertz uses the term "symbol" in a broad sense. He writes:

> […][I]t is used for any object, act, event, quality, or relation which serves as a vehicle for a conception – the conception is the symbol's meaning […] The number 6, written, imagined […], or even punched into the program tapes of a computer is a symbol. But so also is […] the word 'reality', or even the morpheme '-ing'. […][T]hey are tangible formulations of notions, abstractions from experience fixed in perceptible forms, concrete embodiments of ideas, attitudes, judgements, longings, or beliefs. (Geertz, 1966/2010, p. 5)

With respect to marketing, the enormous width of Geertz's use of the term symbol has important implications. Marketing speaks through the cultural language of advertising. And language is a *system of symbols*. As described above, the term symbol includes a myriad of things, signs, gestures, and events. This list includes all the elements, stylistic and dramaturgical, of a commercial. And inasmuch as commercials are one form of advertising, it is feasible to see the language of advertising as a *system of symbols* – symbols that constitute the comprehensible forms of ideas, meanings and concepts with respect to the advertised product.

The production of a system of symbols implies "the manipulation of symbol structures so as to bring them [...] into parallel with the pre-established non-symbolic system [...]." (Geertz 1966/2010, p. 7). In that sense, a system of symbols constitutes a model *of* the world, offering, in a coded fashion, an interpretation of that world, or, with the words of Geertz, of the "pre-established non-symbolic system" (p. 7). In as much as the representation of such a system of symbols is limited to a very specific, clearly delineated aspect of reality, or club, the interpretation of that world, as coded in the production and decoded in the consumption of the commercial, leads to the production of a specific fabula, or meaning, by the viewer. In the case of advertising then, a commodity such as Nespresso coffee capsules, the pre-established non-symbolic system consists of the real-world Nespresso products[74] as well as the infrastructure providing access to them in Nespresso boutiques or online in the internet. Access to the capsules is limited or, in other words, regulated by both comparatively high unit prices and, seemingly, by the limited number of Nespresso boutiques. The Nespresso products can, of course, also be bought online. Online purchases require, however, that the customer be registered first. Registration with Nespresso turns the client, in Nespresso's words, into a Nespresso Club member, strengthening their products' club-good-character and potentially giving them, and their customers, a distinct identity. Using the model *of* the world as a category of analysis, clearly then, in a marketing context, the representation of the commercial's narrative, its production and the closely related coding of a message, the subsequent decoding, consumption, regulation and identity are all aspects that have to be included in the analysis of the system of symbols presented in the commercials.

Furthermore, a system of symbols is, in the words of Geertz, an "extrinsic source of information" (Geertz 1966/2010, p. 6 quoting Geertz, 1964). "Extrinsic", in this context, means that a system of symbols provides information which, unlike the information provided by a human's genes, is generated outside a human's physical body, thereby providing "a blueprint or template in terms of which processes external to themselves [to individuals] can be given a definite form" (Geertz 1964, p. 6, quoting Horowitz, 1956). In this sense, the production of a system of symbols must be viewed as the production of a blueprint, a template for human behaviour. Consequently, a system of symbols also acts as a model *for* the world, another cat-

74 Clearly, the wide range of Nespresso products includes not only a multitude of coffee flavours in differently coloured capsules, but also coffee machines, cups, and coffee spoons. This study, it must be noted, focuses on the capsules only.

egory of analysis of this theoretical framework. Geertz says that, inasmuch as a system of symbols constitutes a model for the world, "what is stressed is the manipulation of the non-symbolic systems in terms of the relationships expressed in the symbolic [system]" (Geertz 1966/2010, p. 7). Put bluntly, in marketing's terms, an individual would-be consumer's consumption pattern, if he or she is responsive to the marketing campaign, as intended by its producer (i.e., Nestlé Nespresso SA), will be influenced in the sense that he or she becomes a consumer of the advertised product. The consumer's behaviour then follows the ethos provided by the system of symbols, by the model *for* the world.[75] The extrinsic information, delivered by the commercial's narrative, carried by the codes, *acts* as the blueprint for the conceptualisation of social practices the viewer is hoped to assume, transforming the viewer and would-be consumer of the message into a consumer of the product. In this process, the decoding by the viewer and would-be consumer is crucial. The codes carried by the narrative lead to the construction, by the viewer, of a fabula (i.e., the story's chronological content[76]) according to the intended meaning. For this to happen, the viewer must establish a favourable relationship with the commercial's plot. In one way or another, the viewer must see himself, or herself as a part of the portrayed fantasy. This does not mean that the viewer must literally fantasise about assuming an active role in one of the commercials' plots, it suffices if the viewer does not mind if, for example, other people learn that he or she tried the advertised product.

A system of symbols, due to its symbolic nature, can act as both a model *of*, and *for*, the world. It is both, a seeming representation of the world and, as it carries in it the codes for a specific behavioural pattern, it is also a model for the world. Language is a system of symbols, and a system of representation. In this sense, an analysis of a system of symbols is always an analysis of its representation, that is, an analysis of the "production of meaning through language" (Hall 2003a/1997, p. 28), allowing for a pro-

75 As will be further discussed in this chapter, humans seem to apparently be most susceptible to models for the world as a determinant of their behaviour. This is perhaps best illustrated by Geertz's comments on the "innate, genetically programmed response capacities" (Geertz, 1966/2010, p. 13) of humans: "The extreme generality, diffuseness, and variability of man's innate (i.e., genetically programmed) response capacities means that without the assistance of cultural patterns he would be functionally incomplete […]. Man depends upon symbols and symbol systems with a dependence so great as to be decisive for his creatural viability […]" (Geertz, 1966/2010, p. 13).

76 The term "fabula" is further explained in subchapter 5.2.1.

found understanding of the processes involved in the coding of the model of the world and its decoding as a model for the world by a would-be consumer.

Finally, it must be remembered that advertising not only conveys meaning by using well-established signs and their codes; it can potentially convey meaning by actively changing and expanding the connotative meaning of signs, manipulating and transforming existing frameworks of meaning. As the viewer tries to make sense of the story according to his, or her schemata (i.e., organised clusters of a viewer's prior knowledge[77]), a commercial's plot can give cues to make the viewer set up new codes, attributing to a signifier a new signified. In this way, advertising and, by implication, marketing are potentially geared towards the manipulation of existing systems of symbols, producing of new-ones, thereby creating new models of and for the world.[78]

> ...to 2) establish powerful, pervasive, and long-lasting moods and motivations in men...

As previously described, moods are scalar; they can be weak or strong, or lie anywhere in between those two extremes. Moods are not directed towards an aim or an objective, they are non-teleological emotions. With respect to consumption, that is, with respect to marketing's success, moods play a decisive role. Learning, a crucial and indispensable part in the process of internalising the model for the world encoded in a commercial happens with greater ease if the commercial puts the viewer in a good mood. Therefore, the commercial's plot and the subsequent fabula construction by the viewer should be conducive to a good mood. Decoding by the viewer must support, must evoke a good mood in him, or her. For example, assuming that viewers might consider George Clooney's sex appeal superior to their own, their mood might be improved if the decoding of the plot moves along the lines of: "Who cares about sex appeal? What really matters is the coffee capsule! You can have it!" The syuzhet (i.e., the employment of narrative) must be conducive to that type of decoding. Similarly, a perceived accessibility to the club and to the thereby implied gratifications that it is likely to put the viewer in a good mood, facilitating the

77 The term "schemata" is further explained in subchapter 5.2.1.

78 It should be remembered that the use of the word "world" does not refer to its cosmic meaning but rather only to a narrowed-down meaning in reference to the advertised product with an emphasis on its denotative and connotative meanings.

viewer's identification with the plot – the precondition that has to be met if the language of advertising is to successfully create a process of learning by the viewer. In summary, good moods not only relate to consumption, they also facilitate identification, and are therefore conducive to the consumer's identity formation. And, to all viewers who consider their purchasing power to be sufficient, accessibility to the club is open, hence, regulation, the division of viewers into insiders and outsiders, works in their favour.

To make the step from moods to motivations, another element is needed. Motivation, in the words of Geertz, is "a persisting tendency, a chronic inclination to perform certain sorts of act and experience certain sorts of feeling in certain sorts of situation [...]" (Geertz 1966/2010, p. 10). Motivation is a propensity to act and feel in a *certain* way. Motivation obviously is of a vectorial, teleological nature, giving rise to action. Motivation does not come on its own, it comes with a complementary aspect, that of the targeted object, which is, in the case of marketing, the advertised product. Here, a consumer's desire and its interpretation, done for him or for her by marketing, come in. As previously mentioned, desire is connected to emotions. If a commercial is conducive to the viewer's good mood, and if identification is made, the viewer is likely to feel a desire to be, in some way or another, a part of the fabula. Moreover, as described by Bolz (2002), "Marketing interprets the consumer's desire[79]" (p. 97). As a consequence, the marketed product becomes the telos (i.e., goal) of the consumer's desire. Through the steps described here, moods and motivations lead to consumption, and possibly, with the help of the club's insider-outsider dichotomy, which itself is rooted in the product's regulation through its comparatively high unit price, to identity formation. For all of this to work, the representation of the commercial's syuzhet must be such that, in the process of viewing and decoding, the viewer's construction of the fabula elicits a good mood in him or her. Furthermore, a general desire to relate, in some way or another, to at least a part of the presented narrative must be evoked, otherwise identification with the narrative, or parts thereof, is unlikely to set in. That said, it is now the commercial's narrative, the portrayed actions and their codes, that assume the task of focusing and sharpening the viewer's general desire. Thereby the advertised product becomes the telos of the viewer's desire and motivation to act. Once this task is completed, he or she has then successfully learnt, or internalised, the behaviour, or ethos, depicted in the commercial.

---

79 Translation by the author, 2017.

Regarding production and representation, as the above described genealogy of the consumer's ethos shows, a successful wrapping of the needed codes into the commercial's plot at the stage of its production is a necessary, though not sufficient condition, for the commercial success of a marketing campaign. Decoding, the construction of the fabula according to the viewer's schemata must take place, in a manner, which is aligned with the marketing campaign's goals. To secure this, the producer must know who the viewers are. In the case of the Nespresso marketing campaign, as was previously discussed, a so-called postmodern consumer is presupposed, susceptible to depthlessness and to the annulment of the separation of thing and concept, allowing for a super-elevation of the marketed commodity. If learning is successfully accomplished and desire, guiding the viewer's motivation, is kindled, then the viewer's and would-be consumer's behaviour is most likely to follow the blueprint provided by the model for the world.

...by 3) formulating conceptions of a general order of existence...

It should perhaps be mentioned again that it is *not* the aim of this study to show, or allege, that drinking Nespresso *is* a religion. The aim is solely to show, on the theoretical level, that structural and functional analogies exist between Nespresso's marketing and religion. Therefore, the transcendent dimension contingently implied by the above-quoted, third element of Geertz's definition is not within the remit of this study. The "conceptions of a general order of existence" refer, in the context of this study, to a consumer's "world" of coffee consumption. The aim is to show whether marketing succeeds in establishing an order within the world of coffee brands that is no longer questioned by consumers, that is accepted as generic and unassailable. In the case of Nespresso, such an order includes the dichotomy of insiders, Nespresso consumers, and outsiders – belong or don't belong. According to the commercials' syuzhet then, belonging is rewarded, allegedly resulting in an experience of, so far, unimaginable pleasure.

In the Geertzian sense, as previously mentioned, humans are susceptible to models of, and for, the world as the intrinsic, genetic pool of information they are invested in is comparatively silent when it comes to "culturally right behaviour". As already quoted in footnote 74 above and repeated below for the reader's convenience, Geertz writes:

> The extreme generality, diffuseness, and variability of man's innate (i.e., genetically programmed) response capacities means that without the assistance of cultural patterns he would be functionally incom-

> plete, [...], a kind of formless monster with neither sense of direction, nor power of self-control, a chaos of spasmodic impulses and vague emotions (Geertz, 1962). Man depends upon [...] symbol systems with a dependence so great as to be decisive for his creatural viability [...]. (Geertz, 1966/2010, p. 13).

Not only are humans susceptible to cultural conditioning, humans need cultural conditioning to function properly. This is the gateway where marketing can hope to reach a would-be consumer with its message. Marketing orders the chaos of the nearly countless number of brands supplied in the marketplace. It offers the consumer, with respect to the advertised product, a model of and for the world, communicated through the cultural language of advertising.

The meaning encoded in the representation of the commercial's narrative must, when decoded by the viewer, make it quite clear that the advertised brand is superior to all other brands. The commercial's production must include codes carrying that meaning. Equally, the narrative shown in the commercials should allow for only one meaningful decoding. The authoritarian weight of the meaning encoded in the commercial must be such, that decoding in a corresponding manner is inevitable. Such decoding then issues in a construction of meaning to the effect that the advertised brand's superiority acquires a close to ontological quality. Subsequently then, in the words of Williams, the consumer can, after attributing an image and a set of values to Nespresso, re-appropriate those values through consumption. As it is indeed the viewer who, through decoding, ultimately invests the product with the image, such image is, in other words, appropriated from the viewer, a process which Williamson (2002) calls alienation (p. 64). Then, to receive that image back, the viewer must buy the product. This process, insofar as it is reiterated, results in the continued consumption of the marketed product.

Such decoding is subject to a representation of the exclusive nature of the advertised product. What is best, is not commonplace. Therefore, regulation to the effect of limiting access to the product is an important feature of the formulation of such an order. If the number of potential Nespresso clients included almost everybody, a decoding affirming Nespresso's supremeness would be unlikely. Besides, limited access is likely to strengthen elitist identity-building on the part of the consumer. Feeling part of an exclusive group naturally presupposes exclusion. In this sense, the viewer's fabula construction is tantamount to the construction of a general order with respect to the world of coffee brands in which Nespresso reigns supreme.

A final point to consider, with respect to the hoped-for decoding, is the required diffusion of the advertised product. As was discussed in subchapter 4.2, Buchanan's economic theory of clubs specifies a stable equilibrium where consumers maximise their benefit. That equilibrium is determined by a certain number of club members, that is, clients, and a corresponding degree of diffusion of the product. In order to maximise the operating profit margin, a firm must first maximise consumer benefit. High consumer benefit is tantamount to a comparatively high willingness to pay, allowing for the capturing of consumer benefit by the firm through comparatively high unit prices. In anticipation of the discussion of the socio-empirical survey's findings, it can perhaps be said that Nespresso appears to have found that point of equilibrium. One participant, for instance, expressed his delight (i.e., high consumer benefit) at finding a Nespresso coffee machine in his hotel room in a remote place in Thailand (i.e., obviously Nespresso is ideally diffused across the planet) (FG 1,, 30:28).

...and 4) clothing these conceptions with such an aura of factuality...

Now, the clou is *not* that viewers are expected to just believe the narrative if only they see it a sufficient number of times. Instead, truth and, related to it, factuality are constructed. Factuality is established through two avenues: through its connection to truth and beauty, and through the consumer's becoming the system's referent, him- or herself.

With respect to truth and beauty, Martin Seel says:

> [According to] the Platonic conception – influential for the entire tradition of aesthetics [...], beauty is an appearing of the good and – but this is *my* qualification – *sometimes* of what is true in a cognitive sense *as well*. To be sure, this philosophical link of beauty and the good and the true has often been mocked [...]; however, I believe it touches the heart of the matter. (Seel, 2015, p. 1678)

As a socio-empirical, exploratory study carried out in connection with this study shows, consumers establish a link between the perceived visual beauty of a product, (i.e., the capsules, their colour, the shape and the material of the Nespresso cups), and the seeming factuality of the product's, (i.e., Nespresso's) supreme and unrivalled quality with respect to taste (Ulrich, 2017). The personal, individual consumer's experience of "beauty" with respect, for instance, to the capsule's colour, morphs, in the consumer's judgement, into an experience of supreme taste with respect to the coffee. The clothing of the conceptions (i.e., the notion that Nespresso's supremeness is unassailable) with an aura of factuality is actually brought to life by the consumer, yet the consumer has no conscious awareness of such a process taking place: The consumer's judgement with respect to the aesthetic surface of the product extends itself, unnoticed by the consumer, to include an explicit judgement regarding the product's taste and quality. The aura of factuality of the product's supremeness is established through its beauty. What looks good *is* good.

"Representation is the production of meaning through language" (Hall, 2003a/1997, p. 28). The signs used by the language of advertising include spoken words, gestures, looks, body movements as well as iconic, indexical and symbolic signs. With respect to bestowing the aura of factuality upon the conceptions of a general order, it is imperative that the signs transported by advertising are, when decoded by the viewer, perceived and experienced as, and judged to be visually appealing. The aesthetic surface of the representation is, so to speak, the locus where the consumer experiences the conceptions' factuality in what could perhaps be likened to a Kierkegaardian leap, an experience of a sudden and striking awakening, subsequently reinforced and reproduced by continued consumption.

The aura of factuality then also rests on a second pillar. In the enactment of learnt behaviour, that is, in consumption, the consumer becomes the referent of the signs and symbols portrayed in the commercial's narrative. The production of meaning, successfully coded and decoded, is now reflected in the act of consumption. Put differently, through consumption, the commercial's system of symbols obtains its referent. The enactment of coffee consumption, a ritualised, signifying practice, is part of the system's referent. Therein meaning is reproduced and perpetuated, consolidating the factuality of the established conception of the general order, that is, investing Nespresso's claim to supremacy with an ontological touch.

This places the focus of the analysis on the referent of the system of symbols, focussing not only on the consumer as an important part thereof, but also including the more than 450, materially existent Nespresso boutiques worldwide (Nestle-Nespresso, n.d.a), Nespresso's online boutique, visited, according to Nespresso, by "340,000 *unique* customers [...] every day" (Nestle-Nespresso, n.d.a), as well as the products, capsules and accessories, offered by Nespresso, enabling the consumer to act as and become the system's referent.

Inasmuch as access to the system's referent-world is regulated, or limited by price, only consumers with the required purchasing-power can enter the system. Consumption is therefore related to a specific group, or class of consumers. That helps promote a sense of identity on the part of the consumer, or referent, as consumption implies the placing of oneself in that particular group. The production of meaning, ultimately finalised and perpetuated in consumption is, in this sense, also part of a genealogy of consumer identity. Actual, factual consumption amounts to a continued consolidation of consumer identity. This does not, however, imply that consumers are consciously of such processes. Moreover, should they be aware, they might not wish to admit to it.

Returning to the "conceptions with an aura of factuality", it is, from an analytical point of view, helpful to focus on the advertised commodity and inquire about its identity, its qualities. Value judgements made by consumers with respect to Nespresso shed light on what, in their eyes, Nespresso *is*. The question is not whether such value judgements mirror a factual reality or "only" an imagined-one. The question is whether they are perceived, by consumers, as mirroring a factual reality.

> ...that (5) the moods and motivations seem uniquely realistic.

With respect to that fifth point, Geertz says:

> It is [...] [the] placing of proximate acts in ultimate contexts that [...] alters [...] the whole landscape presented to common sense, alters it in such a way that the moods and motivations [...] seem themselves supremely practical, the only sensible ones to adopt given the way things 'really' are. (Geertz, 1966/2010, p. 38)

This "placing of proximate acts in ultimate contexts", transposed to the "world of coffee", means that 'drinking a cup of Nespresso' is not about "drinking a cup of coffee", instead, it is about "drinking the best coffee" or "drinking the coffee that trumps George Clooney". With a view to consumers that have successfully learnt and internalised the meaning of the commercials' narrative, one is even inclined to substitute the term "magic potion" for Nespresso.

Moods, as the reader will recall, are affective states that can encourage a specific behaviour, and motivations are a tendency to act and feel in a certain way. The act of consumption itself does not, of course, allow for a compelling inference in the sense that a consumer's mood must have been conducive to the act of consumption. Yet, it mirrors the fact the consumer's mood at least was not obstructive to the purchase of the advertised product. With respect to motivation, it can be said that the act of consumption is by itself a confirmation of a prior, corresponding motivation.

With respect to the connection between film and fantasy, as quoted in a previous chapter, Rose, paraphrasing Cowie (1990) says: "Cowie's (1990) key point about fantasy is that the subject [i.e., the viewer of a film] need not only be the audience of a fantasy. The subject may also imagine that [...][he or she] participates in the fantasy as well [...]" (Rose, 2012, p. 178). "Fantasy is an imagined scene in which the subject is a protagonist, and which always represents the fulfilment of a wish [...]" (Cowie, 1990, p. 153). Regarding the fantasy represented in Nespresso's commercials, the part of the *viewer's* fantasy, should it involve the tasting of Nespresso can, given the required purchasing power, easily be fulfilled. Given the viewer's decoding of the commercial's narrative attributes to Nespresso the status of the best coffee, through the tasting of Nespresso then, with the consumer as its protagonist, the meanings of the model of the world are reproduced. Decoding and the commensurate grading of Nespresso have already happened by the time Nespresso is consumed for the first time. Moreover, through the tasting, the consumer not only fulfils, as mentioned above, his, or her personal wish, the personal nature of the wish makes the accompanying moods and motivations seem uniquely realistic along the lines of: Given Nespresso is the best coffee (a view established in the decoding), the consumer cannot but perceive (positive) moods and motivations, which appear to be, again given Nespresso's supreme quality, uniquely realistic.

With respect to a possible perpetuation of the established moods and motivations, ritualised behaviour plays a constitutive role. As mentioned in chapter 4.1, Nespresso itself refers to the tasting of a Nespresso as a ritual (Nestle-Nespresso, n.d.b). And, as the findings of the focus group talks show, so do many consumers. In as much as the tasting of a Nespresso is both, a learnt behaviour and a ritual, the viewer, once metamorphosed into a consumer, is likely to engrave such learnt behaviour deeper and deeper in his or her every-day behavioural pattern. As described previously, it is in the ritual where both, the model of and for the world meet. In the ritual, as a signifying practice, the model for the world becomes the model of the world, and vice versa. In this manner, in the ritual, the two models reinforce one-another, perpetually solidifying and strengthening their explanatory and normative power.

In this context, furthermore, it is also important to remember Hall's contribution: "Representation is the production of meaning through language. [...] Languages can use signs[80] to symbolise, stand for or reference

80 Here, Hall uses the term "sign" in a way that is compatible with the Saussurean sense.

objects, people and events in the so-called 'real' world. But they can also reference imaginary things and fantasy worlds [...]" (Hall, 1997/2003a, p. 28). And, referring to the two representational systems introduced in a previous chapter, Hall says:

> We use signs, organised into languages, [...] to communicate meaningfully [...]. [However], [l]anguage does not work like a mirror. Meaning is produced within language, in and through various representational systems which, for convenience, we call 'languages.' Meaning is produced by the practice, the 'work,' of representation. It is constructed through signifying – i.e., meaning-producing – practices. (Hall, 1997/2003a, p. 28)

In this sense, a *ritual* is also a signifying, meaning-producing practice. If the decoding of the commercials' meaning makes the seemingly ontological truth unfold that Nespresso is indeed the best coffee, through the ritual, the consumer receives the living, reified "proof" that the model of the world is correct, affirming the meaning conveyed by the model *of* the world. In summary, the ritual as an enactment of both, the model of and for the world has a constitutive role. As was addressed in subchapter 2.2.2 above, "[...] men attain their faith as they portray it" (Geertz, 1966/2010, p. 29). The consumer, through the ritual, becomes involved not only in the perpetuation of the model of, and for the world, he or she also undergoes confirmation of their trueness. It is in this melding of the two, that the meaning, carried and conveyed by the system of symbols and supported by moods and motivations is perpetually reproduced and upheld. In this sense then, the moods and motivations preceding and accompanying the tasting of Nespresso, seem uniquely realistic. And obviously, going through the ritual, shaping his or her behaviour as prescribed by the model for the world, the consumer enacts precisely the behaviour that was hoped for in the production, in the coding of the commercial's meaning. Obviously, a continued re-enactment of the ritual presupposes a continued purchase of the advertised product. High and satisfactory sales figures are thereby secured. In other words, in the ritual, the consumer, following the model for the world, not only continuously reproduces and validates the meaning of the model *of* the world, but, at the same time, he or she becomes part of the living bonanza feeding Nespresso's sustained and high operating profit margins

Finally, there is yet another reason why the moods and motivations seem uniquely realistic. As was outlined above, consumption amounts to the reification of the system's meaning, and, in the enactment of the ritual (i.e., the tasting of Nespresso), the models of and for the world are both, in the reified sense, reproduced. The ritual is commensurate to the anchoring of the model (i.e., the conceptions of the general order as well as the corresponding ethos) in the consumer's tangible, everyday reality. Now, given the comparatively high price of a Nespresso capsule, and given the perhaps exaggerated claim made by the commercials' narrative, the consumer might feel the need to explain his, or her actions to him- or herself. That explanation then is afforded by judging the accompanying moods and motivations to be uniquely realistic, that is, the only ones that make sense vis-à-vis the advertised brand.

If Nespresso is tasted once, through the tasting's ritual-character, the models of and for the world become both, confirmed and reified. Therefore, consumption is likely to happen again. In what looks like a perpetual motion machine, the aura of factuality with respect to the model of the world, and the perception of the corresponding moods and motivations as "uniquely realistic" endlessly reinforce one another through the ritual. In other words, once consumption has set in, it is, conceptually speaking, nearly impossible for the consumer to break out of the models' dynamics.

4.4 A mixed-method single case study

A single case study is, according to Robert K. Yin, an appropriate design if "the case represents an *extreme* case or an *unusual* case, deviating from [...] everyday occurrences" (Yin, 2014, p. 52). As already mentioned, Nespresso's commercial success, especially its operating profit margin, is both, exceptional and, with respect to theory, so far unaccounted for. An explanatory single case study then, aiming to explain how the phenomenon under scrutiny occurred, is ideally suited to the purpose of this study. Moreover, it can reveal insights that provide a basis for causal inferences that are conducive to theory-building, and thereby explain the phenomenon under scrutiny.

There is yet another reason why a single case study is ideally suited to the purpose of this study: Case studies leave room for an individual design that fits the phenomenon under scrutiny, for example combining more than one method. Yin writes: "[...][M]ixed methods research can enable you to address broader or more complicated research questions [...]" (Yin, 2014, p. 67). This study aims to contribute to theory; it aims to go beyond the mere building of hypotheses by trying to validate the results of the audio-visual analysis. Therefore, a mixed-method approach is taken. That is the reason why in this study, the audio-visual analysis is complemented by a socio-empirical analysis. It is hoped, that the findings of the socio-empirical analysis support and confirm the findings of the audio-visual analysis, thereby substantiating the theoretical contribution of this study.

The audio-visual analysis takes a hermeneutical approach, based on the theoretical framework synthesised in this study. The complementary socio-empirical survey is carried out to a) test for the *statistical*[81] significance of the results of the hermeneutical analysis and b) to thereby underpin the building of theory. The socio-empirical survey then is itself structured into two parts: A quantitative survey of Nespresso clients and a corresponding control group, based on a questionnaire, and a qualitative Nespresso survey based on three focus groups whose participants had all been included in the quantitative survey. The questions of the questionnaire are phrased in such a way that the answers given by the interviewees allow to either support, or rebut, the findings of the analysis based on the categories stipulated by the Geertzian definition of religion. In this way, through a statistical generalisation[82], the results of the quantitative survey allow to support the internal and external validity of the conclusions drawn from the findings of the hermeneutical visual analysis – two methodologically different, yet complementary procedures.

The results of the three focus groups (qualitative survey) then are also hermeneutically analysed according to the categories of analysis discussed in chapter 4.3. That analysis serves the purpose of identifying whether there is, hidden in the socio-empirical data, a normative meaning and if so, to tease it out and make it visible. This method, in a sense comparable to grounded theory[83], allows for the building of theory based on the collected data. Furthermore, the construction of theory is possible since the categories used in the analysis represent analytical generalisations of the issues discussed in the focus groups. Of course, there are limits to the degree generalisation is possible. For example, it must be remembered that the social

81 Statistical significance allows for the generalisation from a sample to a population, that is, the population of Nespresso clients. It is important, however, to keep in mind that statistical test do not serve as evidence in the mathematical sense, nor does, in the case of this study, statistical significance imply anything regarding societal significance, that is, the results of the survey do not warrant conclusions regarding the survey's social context.

82 For a discussion of these topics, see Field, (2013).

83 With respect to grounded theory and the construction of theory, Michael Burawoy writes: "Grounded theory works with a particular image of science in which theories are induced from data" (Burawoy, 1991, p. 274).

context of the survey, and its participants, is given and imposes limits to an abstraction from time and space: Generalisations across the results of the socio-empirical survey are meaningful only within the boundaries of the survey's given context.

This explanatory, single case study's complex pluralism of methods allows for an added benefit: The inclusion of a control group in the socio-empirical survey carries with it one important beneficial effect usually characteristic only of multiple case studies: It makes comparison possible, thereby fulfilling a precondition for statistical generalisations[84] which, in turn, helps to support the results of the hermeneutical analysis. Given the wide context, and the complexity of the phenomenon under scrutiny, the mixed-method approach of this study is essential in meeting the study's objective.

Finally, the benefit of this study's mixed-method, interdisciplinary approach can perhaps be best described by the notion of "crystallisation". In the words of Laure Ellingson,

> [c]rystallisation combines multiple forms of analysis [...] into a coherent text or series of related texts, building a rich and openly partial account of a phenomenon that problematises its own construction, highlights researchers' vulnerabilities and positionality, makes claims about socially constructed meanings, and reveals the indeterminacy of knowledge claims even as it makes them. (Ellingson, 2011, p. 4)

This approach, obviously, precludes the establishment of seemingly objective results, results that could be replicated under what might be compared to laboratory conditions. Yet, this clearly is not the aim of this study. As outlined in chapter 1.3, the aim is to shed light, from different angles, on a multi-layered commercial phenomenon to better understand its structural and functional parallels with religion. Laurel Richardson writes:

> In post-modernists, mixed-genre texts, we do not triangulate, we *crystallise* [...]. I propose that the central image for "validity" for postmodern texts is not the triangle – a rigid, fixed, two-dimensional object. Rather, the central imaginary is the crystal, which combines symmetry and substance with an infinite variety of shapes, substances, transmutations, multi-dimensionalities, and angles of approach [...] Crystals are

84 It must be remembered that statistical methods cannot shed light on the cause of an observed effect. Causality lies beyond the reach of statistical methods. However, they can support an argument made in the course of an analytical generalisation.

> prisms that reflect externalities and refract within themselves, creating different [...] patterns [...] casting off in different directions. [...] Crystallisation provides us with a deepened, complex, thoroughly partial, understanding of the topic. Paradoxically, we know more and doubt what we know. Ingeniously, we know there is always more to know. (Richardson, 2000, p. 934)

According to Ellingson, the various qualitative methods used in this approach represent a continuum, ranging from mixed-method research (i.e., research combining qualitative and quantitative methods), random sampling, and structured interviews to interactive interviewing and autoethnography (Ellingson, 2009). That continuum is "part of a larger continuum of methods that includes quantitative methods – freeing [...] researchers from the unproductive strictures of a fixed and definitive set of practices in favour of a continually changing map of the territory" (Ellingson, 2009, p. 53).

The combination of quantitative and qualitative methods allows for the illumination of important aspects of the phenomenon under scrutiny. The implied paradigm pluralism, that is, "[t]he combination of multiple methodological practices [...] in a single study is best understood as a strategy that adds rigor, breadth complexity, richness, and depth to any inquiry (see Flick, 2002/2007)" (Denzin, 2012).

5 The Audio-visual Analysis

5.1 Corpus and production context

Since 2005, George Clooney has been the Nespresso brand ambassador, after being chosen by Nespresso Club members (Nestle-Nespresso, n.d.a). In 2006, Nespresso released the first commercial, featuring George Clooney. Subsequently, every year, at least one new commercial has been released, all featuring George Clooney. Some of them contain visual references to religious symbolism, as is the case in the commercials featuring, alongside George Clooney, John Malkovich in the role of Saint Peter (Daily Mail reporter, 2010). However, as was outlined above, this study does not focus on overtly religious symbolism, or, by the same token, on commercials using clearly religious symbols. Rather, it aims to carve out functional and structural analogies to religion present in a marketing campaign that are not, at first sight, appearing to borrow from religious symbolism. That is the reason why, for the purpose of this study, three Nespresso commercials were chosen, that clearly do not contain or use any religious symbols. Instead, they all, as their strong semiotic overlap illustrate, work with codes whose rearrangement, provoked by their narratives, issue in structural and functional analogies to religion. Moreover, as will be demonstrated in subchapter 7.1 below, the selection of the three commercials, which constitute the audio-visual corpus of this study, was motivated by the hidden, yet powerful meaning-making effects of their release's chronological order: if they are analysed in the chronological order of their release, a telling, syntagmatic semiotic progression can be identified.

The analysis of the corpus starts with the first Nespresso commercial featuring George Clooney, which was released in 2006 (Spitzenpfeil, 2010). The narrative closing with "What else?" introduces this punch line as Nespresso's principal pun. Its soundtrack, composed by Benjamin Raffaelli and Frédéric Doll, titled *The Boutique* became the music for all subsequent Nespresso commercials to date. This first commercial is a very good example of how, through the language of advertising, a signifier's signified can be transferred to another, metonymic new signifier. As mentioned, in 2006, George Clooney was chosen by *People*, a weekly US magazine, for the second time since 1997, to be the sexiest man alive. Given the cultural context of this study's backdrop, it can reasonably be expected that a man of

George Clooney's standing, exhibiting the characteristics legitimising his election, would naturally induce heterosexual women to at least take note of him, or, if given the possibility, to try to make his acquaintance. These characteristics, qualifying his election, are all addressed in that first commercial, yet, they are not attributed to George Clooney, they are instead, attributed to Nespresso.

The second commercial in the corpus was released in November 2012. That commercial was released in two versions, a full-length version and a slightly shorter-one. In the shorter version, two scenes are omitted: the opening shot, showing George Clooney leaving a luxury hotel, as well as a shot charged with sexual allusions, showing the boutique's hostess pulling out a Nespresso sleeve from a shelf, closing her eyes. George Clooney, in that shot, is seen in the background, from behind, making the Nespresso of his choice.

In this study, overtly sexual allusions do not constitute a category of analysis. Therefore, only the shorter version is included in the corpus. In that commercial, George Clooney, is treated like a star. Closing hours are ignored, the Nespresso hostess, who obviously recognises George Clooney addressing him as Mr. Clooney, joyfully works overtime. However, as then becoming obvious, that treatment is not owed to his stardom, which actually is completely denied throughout the commercial's narrative. That treatment is owed to being a Nespresso client. In Nespresso boutiques, Mr. and Ms. Everybody are treated like Hollywood stars, and naturally then, they feel accordingly – like a star.

The third and final commercial included in the corpus, and released in November 2013, shows a beautiful young woman, Miss Switzerland of 2005, faced with the choice of becoming acquainted with George Clooney or accepting his offer, to fetch another Nespresso for her. She opts for the latter, and as George Clooney heads for the tasting area where the coffee machines are located, she sets all the women present in the club on him. As these women besiege George Clooney, the beautiful young woman drinks George Clooney's Nespresso, which he had left behind. The message is, that, in the order of things, a Nespresso clearly ranks above George Clooney. Drinking a Nespresso, is preferable, to being with George Clooney.

That commercial was also released in a short, and an extended version, including an epilogue with Hollywood actor Matt Damon. However, that extended version is not included in the corpus as the epilogue does not provide new material, which would be relevant for the analysis.

The commercials were all shown on Nespresso's website. Moreover, according to the interviewees who participated in the socio-empirical survey, they were also shown on television and in cinemas. However, as Nestlé S.A. declined to contribute to this research[85], it is not possible to make precise indications with respect to where, when and for how long the commercials had been displayed. Meanwhile, the commercials included in the corpus have all been deleted from Nespresso's website. They were, however, still accessible on YouTube. Moreover, it could not be established how often their website is contacted, and whether the number of times a commercial is viewed by a user correlates with that user's overall order amount. By the same token, the production context of the commercials could not be studied in detail, for example, it was not possible to identify in which countries the commercials were produced. This posed clear limits to the analysis of the commercial's production. Fortunately, however, Nestlé-Nespresso S.A.'s decision not to support this study did not have any negative repercussions regarding the study's audio-visual analysis.

5.2 Approaching commercials

Drawing an analogy between ancient Greek drama and present-day films, Margaret Miles says: "[...][F]ilm represents the particular class, behaviour, and loyalties of its characters. [...] It is not [...] a far-fetched claim that popular films can also be seen as implicitly, if not explicitly, addressing the question of how human beings should live" (Miles, 1996, p. 7). So, popular films make an ethical claim. They present a model for the world.

As was discussed above, the learning of a specific behaviour, by the commercial's viewer, is an indispensable step[86] in his, or her internalisation of the model for the world. In this perspective, focussing on the question of how one should live, the commercials included in the corpus are seen as having an effect similar to the effect of many fictional, or narrative films.

85 Nestlé-Nespresso S.A., Vevey, Switzerland, after an initial promise to support this study with their resources withdrew their support in 2012. In 2016, Nestlé-Nespresso S.A. was approached again. However, as I was requested to hand over all the material in connection with this study, a request which I declined, a collaboration was not possible.

86 A step that is, as writes Miles, facilitated by the largely visual nature of the medium itself: "The power of vision to encourage imitation has been recognised since Plato" (Miles, 1996, p. 26).

Naturally, there are many features setting commercials off from films[87], the most obvious would be (the usual) duration, distribution and purpose. Feature films, for example, aim to entertain a paying audience, and documentaries aim to present specific issues and thereby teach and enlighten the viewer, whereas the prime objective of a commercial is the viewer's inducement to buy the advertised commodity, or service, respectively. Yet, all the different categories of film, from the feature film to the commercial, aim to bring across their message invested with the claim to truth. In accordance therewith, the analysis of the commercials zeroes in on the development of knowledge, of alleged truths. With respect to such development of knowledge, in connection to classical film, David Bordwell writes:

> The mystery film, with its resolved enigma at the end, is only the most apparent instance of the tendency of the classical syuzhet [i.e., a film's plot] to develop toward full and adequate knowledge. Whether a protagonist learns a moral lesson or only the spectator knows the whole story, the classical film moves steadily toward a growing awareness of absolute truth. (Bordwell, 1985/1997, pp. 158-159)

With respect to commercials, the hypothesis is that they, speaking on behalf of the product, also attempt to establish a truth with respect to the product and its context, establishing a worldview and an ethos, both invested with an aura of factuality. And such establishment is effectuated, in the case of a commercial, using the same language, based on the same grammar as is used by feature films and documentaries: the language of film. The analytical tools used to approach a commercial are, therefore, the same as those used in the analysis of films in general. The representation of a commercial, and its reception by the viewer, and, connected thereto, the production of meaning, can be scrutinised by the same theoretical framework as would be used in the analysis of film. In that sense then, as will be outlined in the following subchapter, this study works with Bordwell's neo-formalist approach to film.

Bordwell says that the viewer of a film is also the constructor of the fabula, that is, the film's meaning. Cued by the film's narration, the viewer, decoding the codes carried by the commercials, aims to establish a narrative logic. In that process, expressed in the Saussurian terms of signified and signifier, the viewer can bring out the transfer of a signified to a new signi-

87 One feature that does *not* qualify to set commercials off from films is the number of shots, or scenes. Films with only one shot, lasting over an hour, exist. Some of them are, like VICTORIA in 2015, recipients of great acclaim (Sternborg, 2015).

fier. Because of this compatibility with both, Saussurian semiotics and Hall's cultural theory regarding the production of meaning, the filmic analysis, readying the material for the subsequent steps, is carried out according to David Bordwell's neo-formalist film theory. Before the commercials are analysed according to Hall's cultural theory and Buchanan's economic theory of clubs (presented and discussed in the previous chapter), they are thus analysed, or pre-processed, according to a theory of film that accords with Hall's and Buchanan's contributions. It is important to notice, however, that this does not imply two separate analyses. What it means, rather, is that the analysis of the corpus according to a theory of film is a step, which is *conceptually* prepended to the analysis according to Hall's and Buchanan's contributions. What his theory says, and why it is ideally suited to this study, is further explained in the following subchapter.

5.2.1 A neo-formalist approach to film

As previously stated, in a first step, so to speak in a pre-processing of the commercials, the analysis draws on the tenets of David Bordwell's neo-formalist film theory. According to that theory, film viewers construct their own story, or, more precisely, the story's chronological content, cued by two formal systems, syuzhet and style[88], present in a film. Bordwell writes: "According to constructivist theory, perceiving and thinking are active, goal-oriented processes" (Bordwell, 1985/1997, p. 31). "The [film's] sensory stimuli alone cannot determine a percept, since they are incomplete and ambiguous" (Bordwell, 1985/1997, p. 31). According to Bordwell, the perceiver "*constructs* a perceptual judgement on the basis of non-conscious *inferences*" (Bordwell, 1985/1997, p. 31). His theory places the perceiver, that is, the viewer, in a constitutive role with respect to the construction of the story's chronological content, the so-called fabula. That fabula, embodying "the action as a chronological cause-and-effect chain of events occurring within a given duration and special field" (p. 49) is constructed by the viewer who is engaged in the decoding of the cues and codes carried by the film's, by the commercial's, narrative. Such decoding follows the path of hypothesis testing by the viewer. Bordwell writes: "In all these [perceptual] activities [...], organised clusters of [prior] knowledge guide our hypothesis making. These [organised clusters of prior knowledge] are called

88 These two notions, "syuzhet" and "style", are discussed and explained later in this chapter.

schemata. The mental image of a bird [for instance] is a schema for visual recognition" (Bordwell, 1985/1997, p. 31).[89] Quoting Reid Hastie, Bordwell continues: "Schemata may be of various kinds – prototypes (the bird image, for instance), or templates (like filing systems, [helping to fill in missing information]), or procedural patterns (a skilled behaviour, such as knowing how to ride a bicycle)" (Bordwell, 1985/1997, p. 31 quoting Hastie, 1981, pp. 40-41).

Based on the perceived cues, the viewer, with the help of those schemata, then infers perceptual hypotheses with respect to the meaning of the fabula, along the lines of: "If this and this happens, then that must be true." Or: "If this and this happens, then that is most likely to happen next." With respect to the falsification, or confirmation of those hypotheses by the viewer, Bordwell writes: "Like all inferences, perceptual experience tends to be a little risky, capable of being challenged by fresh environmental situations and new schemata. After some interval, a perceptual hypothesis is confirmed or disconfirmed; if necessary, the [...][viewer] shifts hypotheses or schemata" (Bordwell, 1985/1997, p. 31). The construction of the fabula by the viewer is thus an inferential activity. Conclusions are drawn according to the perceptual input, and yet, they are guided and influenced by both, the schemata the viewer has internalised prior to seeing a film, and the schemata that are newly formed as a consequence of the viewer's attempt to make sense of the perceptual input.

The fabula, as a set of inferences made by the viewer, is not "materially present on the screen or soundtrack" (Bordwell, 1985/1997, p. 49). What is, instead, materially, phenomenally present, are two formal systems, which Bordwell calls "syuzhet" and "style", the former embodying the "film as a "dramaturgical" process" (Bordwell, 1985/1997, p. 50), the latter "as a "technical" one" (Bordwell, 1985/1997, p. 50). Through their interaction, they provoke and steer the viewer's hypotheses and inferences.

The syuzhet includes the sequential order of the narrative's main dramaturgical events and moments. That order presented in the syuzhet, that is, the plot, need not correspond to the fabula's chronological order. Some events, for instance, might be missing altogether, others might be included as a flashback. Bordwell writes: "The *syuzhet* (usually translated as "plot") is the actual arrangement and presentation of the fabula in the film. It is not the text in toto. [...] It is [...] the patterning of the story [...]" (Bordwell,

89 In Hall's terms, this refers to the system of mental representation. In that sense, Bordwell's theory accords well with Hall's model of communication (cf. Hall 1993 and 2003b).

1985/1997, p. 50). Because a film's syuzhet is organised "according to specific principles" (Bordwell, 1985/1997, p. 50), Bordwell, as already mentioned, refers to the syuzhet as a system. The organising principles are: (1) Narrative logic, (2) time, and (3) space. "In classical fabula construction, causality is the prime unifying principle" (Bordwell, 1985/1997, p. 157). Consequently, narrative logic often depends on causal linear relations along the lines of the following syllogism: If A leads to B and C is like A, then C must lead to B, too. Fabula construction through the viewer is encouraged by such causal relations and the hypotheses, and inferences that are drawn therefrom. A voluntary violation of the principle of cause and effect, for instance, can actually induce the viewer to draw different hypotheses or alter his or her schemata, or both. Similarly, the way time is represented within the syuzhet also has an impact on the viewer's fabula construction. For instance, "[t]he syuzhet can signal fabula events as taking place any number of times (*frequency*)" (Bordwell, 1985/1997, p. 51). Consequently, the viewer is likely to infer that such specific fabula events, that is, events that the viewer, cued by the syuzhet, has placed into his or her constructed fabula, happen with great regularity and can, therefore, be *expected* to happen in that way; fabula events, therefore, can assume an aura of factual regularity. Space, as the third organising principle, provides the spatial frame with respect to fabula construction. Any fabula must take place within a spatial frame of reference, "however vague or abstract" (Bordwell, 1985/1997, p. 51). Through that frame of reference, the viewer receives cues encouraging specific hypotheses, also correlating fabula space to fabula action. Moreover, in the construction of fabula, the viewer, responding to the syuzhet's cues, might also infer a *causal* relation between fabula space and fabula action. In summary, it can be said that the viewer's

> schematising and hypothesising activities are guided by the syuzhet's cues about causality, time, and space. [...] The syuzhet aims not to let [...][the viewer] construct the fabula in some logically pristine state, but rather to guide [...][the viewer] to construct the fabula in a specific way, by arousing in [...][the viewer] particular expectations at this or that point, eliciting [...] curiosity or suspense, and pulling surprises along the way. (Bordwell, 1985/1997, pp. 51-52)

Finally, in Bordwell's theory, style is also regarded as a system, albeit mostly dominated by the syuzhet. Style, in this context, simply refers to a "film's systematic use of cinematic devices" (Bordwell, 1985/1997, p. 50), like camera position and movement, or different shot sizes. In this context, it is important to note that viewers also deploy stylistic schemata, favouring specific hypotheses in function of a film's stylistic cues. Often, the style supports the syuzhet and provides, with respect to fabula construction, corresponding cues. Style, the second system encouraging a specific fabula construction, plays a constitutive role in cueing the viewer's cognitive activity.

A film's cues, present in syuzhet and style[90], alongside the viewer's held schemata are the principal determinants of fabula construction. In order to understand how and why a film is successful in guiding, encouraging and restraining the viewer's activity toward the construction of one specific fabula, a close look at the film's syuzhet and style, as well as the viewer's schemata is needed. Schemata are, in the words of Bordwell, "[...] organised clusters of knowledge [that] guide [...][the viewer's] hypothesis making. The mental image of a bird is a schema for visual recognition. And the concept of a well-formed sentence functions as a schema in speech perception [...]" (Bordwell, 1985/1997, p. 31).

To understand, why a commercial's narrative is decoded in a specific manner, and how its specific meaning is constructed, it usually does not suffice to look at a film's aesthetic surface only. What is needed, is a close, in-depth look that takes into account all the different, interwoven layers of interaction between a film's syuzhet and style, that is, the film's narration, and the viewer's manifold schemata.[91] In this sense, the following subchapter introduces a method known as "thick description", which takes these concerns into account.

5.2.2 Thick description

Advertising is a signifying practice, and commercials are one of the media used by the language of advertising. They are, in the context of this study, the crucial element in the production of meaning. This study's analysis of a commercial's meaning uses a method that has been termed "thick description". The term was introduced by the English philosopher Gilbert Ryle, (Ryle, 1971/2009b). With respect to meaning, Ryle says: "[...] [T]he meaning of an expression is not an entity denoted by it, but a style of operation performed with it, not a nominee, but a role [...]" (Ryle, 1949/2009a, p.

90 With the syuzhet addressing the question of *what* is being presented, and the style addressing the question of *how* it is done.

91 Bordwell defines the term "narration" as follows: "In the fiction film, narration is *the process whereby the film's syuzhet and style interact in the course of cueing and channelling the spectator's construction of the fabula*" (Bordwell, 1985/1997, p. 53).

384). And to understand that role, that is, the meaning of an expression, what is needed, according to Ryle, is thick description. Ryle's explanation of thick description is perhaps a bit cumbersome and verbose. However, it is well worth including it here because paraphrasing it comes with the risk of losing some of its detailed aspects, all of which are indispensable to a thorough understanding.

In his explanation of thick description, Ryle tells a story of two boys contracting their right eyelids:

> Two boys fairly swiftly contract the eyelids of their right eyes. In the first boy, this is only an involuntary twitch; but the other is winking conspiratorially to an accomplice. At the lowest or thinnest level of description the two contractions of the eyelids may be exactly alike. From a cinematograph-film of the two faces there might be no telling which contraction, if either, was a wink, or which, if either, was a mere twitch. Yet there remains the immense but unphotographable difference between a twitch and a wink. For to wink is to try to signal to someone in particular, without the cognisance of others, a definite message according to an already understood code. It has very complex success-*versus*-failure conditions. The wink is a failure if its intended recipient [...] misconstrues it [...]. A mere twitch, on the other hand, is neither a failure nor a success; [...] it carries no message. (Ryle, 1971/2009b, p. 495)

Contrasting the voluntary wink with the perhaps involuntary twitch, Ryle continues:

> The [...] [winker] himself, while acknowledging that he had not had an involuntary twitch but (1) had deliberately winked, (2) to someone in particular, (3) in order to impart a particular message, (4) according to an understood code, (5) without the cognisance of the rest of the company, will rightly deny that he had thereby done [...] five separately do-able things. He had not *both* tried to contract his eyelids *and also* tried to a second, synchronous thing or several synchronous things. [...] [H]e had not both contracted his eyelids and also done a piece of synchronous signalling to his accomplice. True, he had contracted them [...] on purpose, but this feature of being on purpose is not an extra deed; he had contracted them at the moment when his accomplice was looking in his direction, but its being at this chosen moment is not an extra deed; he had contracted them in accordance with an understood code, but this accordance is not an extra deed. He had tried to do much more than contract his eyelids, but he had not tried to do

> more things. He had done one thing [only] the report of which embodies a lot of subordinate clauses. (Ryle, 1971/2009b, p. 495)

Ryle then elaborates the story further, introducing a third boy that wants to make fun of the boy who winked, hoping to amuse his friends. That parody of the winker, the third boy's wink, is one single deed only, yet it has three innate layers to it: That third boy tried to (1) imitate the boy who winked, (2) trying to signal to that boy's accomplice by (3) contracting his eyelids. To make his point, Ryle evolves the story further, introducing yet another layer: Given the boy who parodies the winker wants to do that parody well, that boy may choose to practise first. By practising, he is

> trying (1) to get [...][himself] ready to try (2) to amuse [...] [his] cronies by grimacing like [...][the winker] trying (3) to signal covertly to his accomplice by trying (4) to contract his eyelids. [...] So now our parodist, in practising his parody [...], would have to be described with the help of [...][four] verbs of trying – and still there is only one thing he is trying to do, [...] there is only one contraction of the eyelid that, at a given moment, the cinematograph film records. The thinnest description, of what the rehearsing parodist is doing is, roughly the same as for the involuntary eyelid twitch; but its thick description is a many-layered sandwich, of which only the bottom slice is catered for by that thinnest description. (Ryle, 1971/2009b, p. 496)

Advertising, in the sense of a signifying practice, might carry many meanings. Therefore, thick description, as described above, is used in the hermeneutical analysis of the commercials, as thin description will reveal only the most obvious, in the literal sense superficial meaning. The purpose of this study is to dig deeper, unwinding the convolute of the many layers of a commercial's narrative. Thick description, it is hoped, looking at each slice of the sandwich carefully, will help to reveal the cause of Nespresso's unrivalled success.

Next, the three commercials are analysed. To carry out the analytical steps introduced above, in a very first step, a protocol for each commercial consisting of one scene was made, systematically analysing the commercial's aesthetic surface as well as, in broad lines, the main elements of the narration. The protocols are listed in annexe I.

5.3 Analysis of What Else

The opening shot shows George Clooney walking, in a relaxed, but purposeful way, down the street in a developed, fairly elegant urban area. The viewer is invited to formulate first hypotheses: "It's George Clooney, there might be romance in the air. Where is he going? He might be meeting a woman." As he turns to his right, the tracking camera reveals where he is going: to a Nespresso boutique. The syuzhet's spatial logic places the fabula's action inside the boutique. This inside/outside dichotomy is also supported by the lighting: compared to the bright lights of the first shot showing George Clooney outside in the streets, the lighting of the subsequent shots, showing George Clooney inside the boutique is, by comparison, softer and more low key, creating an atmosphere of intimacy.

As he enters the boutique, the male shop assistant who is busy with another customer, greets him with a nod. A possible hypothesis is, that the shop assistant will immediately come over to George Clooney and attend to the celebrity's needs. Yet that hypothesis has to be rejected. With a smile and a greeting gesture of his arm, George Clooney walks past the shop assistant who continues to attend to the needs of that other client. A possible inference is that George Clooney is a regular in that boutique. Then, a long shot of the inside of the boutique shows two women sitting at a round table. This introduction of two new characters is likely to prompt new hypotheses: "They might be thrilled seeing George Clooney. Perhaps one of them, or both, fall for George Clooney." They clearly register George Clooney's presence; however, they show no reaction to him. They only seem to register that some man, any man, has entered the boutique. George Clooney's charms are completely denied by the narrative. Obviously, a hypothesis that they would immediately react with delight to George Clooney's presence must be rejected. They are, facing one another, both just continuing to drink their Nespresso. The two story lines are now evolving separately, on one hand there is George Clooney walking over to the coffee counter, preparing the Nespresso of his choice, and on the other there are the two women, absorbed in conversation. So far, no words have been spoken, only, as from the outset, the Nespresso melody is being played. Shot 7 shows George Clooney from the front, in a medium close-up at the coffee counter. In the background, the inside of the boutique is visible. This special logic, supported by the Nespresso melody, is conducive to a fabula construction that links fabula action to fabula space, which is the Nespresso boutique.

Figure 18: What else, shot 7, 00:11

The next shot, an insert with the capsule, shows how George Clooney is putting a Nespresso capsule into the coffee machine. The colour of the capsule is golden, clearly setting it off from the black of the coffee machine and the darker, brownish colours of the background. The capsule is placed in the upper centre of the frame, leaving enough space in the frame to also partially show the coffee machine and George Clooney's fingers, first holding, then letting go of the capsule, showing all of the minutest of details of how a capsule is inserted into the coffee machine, thereby emphasising that action, or, in other words, George Clooney's behaviour.

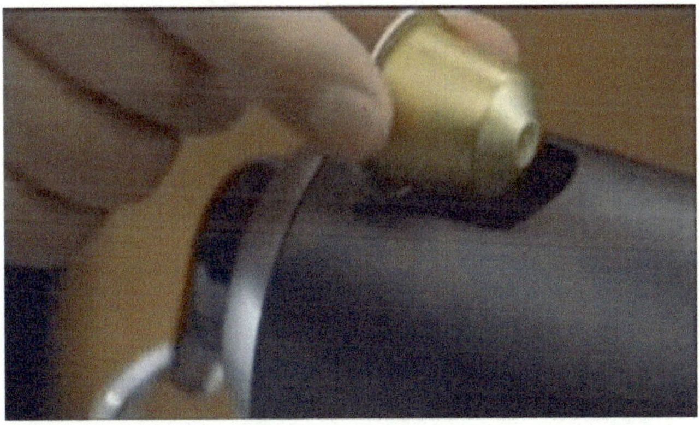

Figure 19: What else, shot 8, 00:12

Then, with George Clooney still at the coffee counter, one of the two women says in a subdued, sensual manner: "Dark" (WHAT ELSE, 00:12).

Following the other woman's agreement, she continues: "Very intense" (WHAT ELSE, 00:14). Then, the other woman adds: "Balanced" (WHAT ELSE, 00:17). The list of characteristics the two women list, is getting longer and longer: "Unique, mysterious, an intense body, delicate and smooth, with a strong character, rich, very rich, Latin American, deep and sensual, [with] a delicious aftertaste" (WHAT ELSE, 00:18-00:37). Simultaneously, the camera's eye is showing a close-up of one or both of the women drinking Nespresso, of George Clooney preparing his Nespresso overhearing the women's conversation, and of the coffee cup being filled with Nespresso.

These sequences act as potentially metonymic signs. Metonymic signs operate through association and contiguity, that is, the spectator is cued to associate a certain signified with a new signifier, for example, the signified "object of desire" is then no longer associated with George Clooney, but with a cup of Nespresso instead. The commercial's syuzhet, so far, leaves it open, to which signifier, that is, George Clooney or Nespresso, the characteristics (i.e., the signified) listed by the two women apply. The viewer might feel prompted to construct a contiguity to George Clooney, the seeming archetype of the Latin lover. Yet, with Nespresso present in the syuzhet, there is another "actor" involved apart from George Clooney and the two young women.

The commercial stages the cup filled with Nespresso as one of the narrative's leading characters. Irrespective of whether the camera shows George Clooney or one or both of the cups of the two women, the cup as such, repeatedly shown in a paradigmatic choice of sequence of individual shots, is positioned between two so-far parallel story lines: George Clooney preparing his Nespresso and the two women's conversation. This choice of sequence is an opening for the attribution of the signified to a new signifier. The sensual voices of the two women, listing all the characteristics from "sensual" to "intense body", serve as the backdrop to the carving out of the cup, filled with Nespresso, as a paradigmatic sign, investing it with its new connotative meaning appropriated from George Clooney, the former signifier.

As mentioned, the viewer is prompted to formulate a hypothesis that the two women are most likely talking about George Clooney. "Perhaps George Clooney and the two women will begin to flirt with one-another." George Clooney, still overhearing the women's chat, is obviously also pondering a hypothesis that the two women might be talking about him. The close-ups, revealing his facial expression, provide the commensurate cues. This is even more so as it would correspond to a possible narrative logic that only George Clooney, the sexiest man alive, can be the cause of the content of the women's conversation. After all, there is no one else present there; except for the cups all filled with Nespresso, but which might not yet be subject of a viewer's hypothesis.

Figure 20: What else, shot 13, 00:18

Shot 14 shows, with respect to the cup in an insert shot, George Clooney's hand, pushing "the button" of the coffee machine, triggering the genesis of a Nespresso. Shot 14 is one of the shots that show, without any gaps, the complete sequence of steps involved in the making of a Nespresso. This is important regarding the viewer's learning. Learning does not only happen with respect to a new order of things, learning also extends to a specific behaviour, that is, the making and tasting of a Nespresso.

Figure 21: What else, shot 14, 00:19

Shot 15 again shows a big close-up of one of the two women, saying: "mysterious". And then, in shot 16, showing George Clooney, she continues: "An intense body". This is all overheard by George Clooney. Here, the viewer is again invited to underscore the hypothesis that the two women are indeed talking about George Clooney. Then, however, in shot 18, the fourth character, apart from George Clooney and the two women, is shown in a close-up: the Nespresso cup.

Figure 22: What else, shot 18, 00:24

In this way, the syuzhet prepares the viewer for another hypothesis, and, by the same token, for another metonymy: The contiguity of the all characteristics mentioned by the two women, that is, "dark, very intense, balanced, unique, mysterious, an intense body, delicate and smooth, with a strong character, rich, very rich, and finally Latin American temperament" could well apply to a man with the looks of George Clooney, or even George Clooney himself. Yet, the syntagmatic character of the shots' sequence prepares the viewer for another metonymy, for a second hypothesis. That second hypothesis then states that the two women might actually be talking about Nespresso; Nespresso could actually trump George Clooney. In this way, by the syntagmatic, and paradigmatic nature of the sequence of these shots, the viewer is prepared for the construction of a contiguity to Nespresso, instead of George Clooney. What matters here is not only the sequence of the shots, but also the choice of the visual content of those shots. Thereby, the viewer is prepared for a transfer of all the characteristics named by the two women from George Clooney to Nespresso.

When the cup is filled, and the making of the Nespresso is completed, George Clooney takes his cup and walks over to the two young women. Here the two storylines intersect, the story is about to climax. The camera, showing George Clooney in a close-up from the front, zooms out to also include the two young women in the frame. George Clooney then begs to know whether they are talking about Nespresso – and, alas for him, the women's response leaves no doubt that they are.

Figure 23: What else, shot 27, 00:37

Obviously, one of the hypotheses was that they would be talking about him. Yet, the two women react with restrained, yet bewildered disbelief, wondering about that seemingly odd question. The viewer is prompted to reject the hypothesis that the women had been talking about George Clooney, and accept the alternative hypothesis, that the women had been talking about Nespresso all along. Now the contiguity to Nespresso is clearly established. The rejection of the first hypothesis, and the attributing of all the characteristics to Nespresso instead of George Clooney, completely divests George Clooney of all those characteristics. In this way, the transfer of the signified to the new signifier, Nespresso, takes place. Here, by the rejection of the first hypothesis, the template and the prototype schemata are altered to uphold the logic in the narrative schema. Cause and effect play an important role therein. The observed effect must have a cause. To keep the narrative logic going, there must be a reason for the women's indifference to George Clooney and their infatuation with Nespresso. And the reason, compellingly, can only be that Nespresso, with respect to the listed characteristics, outscores George Clooney by a wide margin, so wide that George Clooney's qualities are not even noticed. Here, the sexiest man alive is stripped of his qualities, with them being transferred to a cup of coffee. Here, a commodity like coffee assumes an exchange value that, by a wide margin, outstrips its use-value.

In a long shot of the Nespresso boutique, the final frame shows George Clooney, having moved off to the side, watching the two women from a distance, peeking around the edge of a screen inside the Nespresso boutique. Apparently, George Clooney cannot himself believe what has just happened: his displacement by a cup of coffee. And, in case the viewer might not have yet registered who the winner is, Nespresso's logo, the capital N, is clearly visible (as can be seen in figure 24 below), right next to George Clooney.

Figure 24: What else, final frame, 00:48

This final shot makes narrative sense only if the procedural schema places Nespresso in the position of the object of desire. A successful decoding, honouring generic syllogisms of cause and effect, compellingly elects Nespresso the object of desire, totally eclipsing the sexiest man alive. In this way, a viewer and would-be consumer's desire is interpreted for him, or for her.

The commercial's narration suggests that a cup of Nespresso clearly beats George Clooney with respect to the points where he is supposed to score highest; evidently, a Nespresso has something going for it that outscores George Clooney's charms. A transfer of signifiers, from George Clooney to Nespresso takes place, giving Nespresso a ranking clearly ahead of George Clooney. That transfer is brought about by the syntagmatic, paradigmatic, and metonymic nature of the signs used. One single sign can be of a syntagmatic, paradigmatic and metonymic nature. The different terms only help to emphasise the different ways in which the desired effect is achieved. Syntagmatic signs "gain their meaning from the signs that surround them […], or come before or after them in sequence in a moving image" (Rose, 2012, p. 119). Paradigmatic signs, instead, gain their meaning by what is included in one particular shot, and what is left out. Such a choice induces the viewer, who aims to uphold a narrative logic, to construct a certain meaning, to reject a certain hypothesis and accept another-one instead. Finally, metonymic signs, as stated above, operate through association and contiguity, cueing the spectator to associate a certain signified with a new signifier: Nespresso is not contrasted with competing coffee brands, but with the sexiest man alive. As Nespresso clearly comes out the winner, the signified formerly attributed to George Clooney then moves on to Nespresso. Furthermore, the commercial's syuzhet places Nespresso, besides being George Clooney's choice of coffee – a handsome, and appealing, wealthy man is most likely to choose the best coffee brand – even ahead of George Clooney: Two young women, fully absorbed by and immersed in their coffee-tasting are, vis-à-vis Nespresso's qualities, totally oblivious to George Clooney's appeal. As thick description suggests, the import of that message can only be grasped if it is understood who, in Hollywood's star system, George Clooney is, and what role bodily attractiveness plays in present-day Western society. The commercial favours a fabula construction that powerfully shifts the characteristics attributed to George Clooney over to Nespresso. Codes are rearranged, a signifier's meaning travels on to another, new signifier. The narrative's codes are wrapped in such a way that, when unwrapped and decoded by the viewer, the procedural schemata applied in fabula construction only make sense if viewers readjust their prototype and template schemata. Or, in other words, the narrative makes sense only if it is recognised that the characteristics, a prototype schema would attribute to George Clooney, are also attributable Nespresso and that, in the case of Nespresso, these characteristics are infinitely stronger; so much so, actually, that George Clooney's allure is, by comparison, eroded to complete insignificance. A decoding following a logic of cause and effect needs to, in order to make sense, conclude that in a hierarchy, with respect to the characteristics named in the narrative, Nespresso clearly is the winner, George Clooney, instead, is insignificant. This order is mirrored by the two young women's behaviour who, devoting their entire attention to their Nespresso-tasting, react with bewildered consternation to George Clooney who is begging to know, whether they are actually talking about Nespresso. If, in addition to all of that, the role consumption plays in identity formation is also taken into consideration, it becomes visible that the story does not end here. It is finally completed by the viewer and consumer who, through consumption, re-appropriates the qualities and characteristics that he, or she, in the fabula construction, has attributed to Nespresso.

5.4 Analysis of Like a Star

Whilst the commercial WHAT ELSE strips George Clooney of his allure as the sexiest man alive, LIKE A STAR divests him of his stardom. In both commercials, George Clooney, as a symbolic sign – a sex symbol and a star – is eviscerated. In semiotic language, the signified that would, according to a viewer's prototype schema, be attributed to George Clooney as a signifier, is transferred to a new signifier: Nespresso. That transfer is, in the narrative's spatial logic, taking place inside a Nespresso boutique, implying a spatial causality aimed to rail in and limit the many possible decodings to only just one. Fabula construction, by the viewer, follows a narrative logic, honouring logical laws of causation.[92] For this narrative logic to be upheld, a metamorphosis in the viewer's prototype and template schemata is needed, which means, in this commercial's context, that the object of desire is not George Clooney, but Nespresso. As will be shown below, in that meta-

92 What appears to be "logical" is, in the context of this study, determined by cultural and *zeitgeist*-related factors. This study's backdrop assumes a postmodern, largely secularised society with a significant number of consumers with above-average spending power. In the logic of a postmodern Zeitgeist, determined above all by depthlessness, it would appear logical that a film star and sex symbol like George Clooney would be the centre of attention wherever he goes.

morphosis, the aforementioned transfer of the signified to a new signifier, that is, Nespresso, is carried out.

The opening shot, a tracking shot, zooming out from a medium close-up to a medium-long shot, shows a figure, from behind, walking across a zebra crossing. Because of the suit that figure is wearing, it can be concluded that the figure is most likely a man. A car passes right in front of him. It is dark, evening perhaps, and it is raining heavily. The Nespresso music *The Boutique* is being played.

The man is moving fast, obviously trying to get out of the rain as quickly as possible. In shot 3 then, in a medium close-up, the identity of the man is revealed. It is George Clooney. He is obviously looking at something specific from underneath his umbrella. The viewer is invited to formulate a hypothesis with respect to what exactly George Clooney might be looking at. The answer to that hypothesis is delivered by the next shot. In a long shot, the surrounding area is shown: George Clooney is standing in front of the entrance to a Nespresso boutique. Obviously, as the shutters are already coming down, he arrived late.

Figure 25: Like a Star, shot 3, 00:03

Figure 26: Like a Star, shot 4, 00:03

George Clooney is clearly placed outside the Nespresso boutique in a unpleasant environment. The lit Nespresso lettering as well as the logo, two lit-up capital Ns, are clearly visible, shining into the inhospitable night. Everybody in the picture is moving fast, underlining the hostile character of the world outside the Nespresso boutique. A prelude to the tune *The Boutique*, the Nespresso music, is playing as George Clooney turns away, facing the dark, rainy night, adding to the contrast of the inside with the outside. The viewer is encouraged to ask what George Clooney might be doing next. "Is he going to walk away?" Then, a female voice says: "Please, please, come on in!" (LIKE A STAR, 00:08).

Figure 27: Like a Star, shot 7, 00:09

Figure 28: Like a Star, shot 9, 00:11

A young beautiful woman, obviously a Nespresso hostess, is calling out to George Clooney, waving him in. Their eyes meet, George Clooney makes successful contact with the inside, with the club. The contrast of inside and outside is heightened by the young woman's delightful smile. And with respect to style, in shot 9, her smiling lips are neatly parallel to the gradient line of Nespresso's logo, the capital N, clearly visible in the lower left part of the frame. She is obviously very happy to tend to George Clooney's needs, even after hours. A viewer might formulate a hypothesis that this is probably because George Clooney is a world-famous Hollywood star. Such a hypothesis corresponds with the aforementioned, presupposed postmodern logic of both, the procedural and prototype schemata, and it is confirmed by the woman, adding: "... but only because it's you, Mr. Clooney" (LIKE A STAR, 00:10).

Inside the boutique, the hostess asks George Clooney: "Ristretto as usual?" This question indicates that George Clooney's behaviour, that is, his visit to the Nespresso boutique, is of a regular nature, a regular behaviour. Then, in shot 11, George Clooney is shown from behind, in a medium close-up zooming in, approaching the counter with the Nespresso machines. Step by step, all the individual steps of the making of a Nespresso are shown in inserts, underlined by the Nespresso music *The Boutique*. In shot 13, the rebounding drop of Nespresso, towering almost phallus-like above the creamy coffee, prepares the viewer for the formulation of a hypothesis whose eventual rejection will facilitate the transfer of meanings as intended by the commercial's producer.

Figure 29: Like a Star, shot 13, 00:16

Figure 30: Like a Star, shot 13, 00:17

This representation of the making of a Nespresso facilitates learning, the learning of a behaviour, which obviously is, to tell by the way the shop assistant welcomed George Clooney as a regular client, a regular behaviour for him.

So far, all the narrative's codes correspond to the pre-established logic of the prototype and template schemata. Fabula construction is somewhat straightforward in the sense that it seems natural, that a Hollywood star like George Clooney is let into the Nespresso boutique after closing time. After all, these are the fringe benefits of stardom. According to the template schema, most likely held by viewers as they are presupposed in this study, it can be inferred that the boutique hostess only let him in because he is a star. Even though she literally only said "... because it's you", the template schema allows to infer that what she meant was: "... because you are a star, Mr. Clooney". This is even more so as a fabula construction along these lines is also supported by the syuzhet and the prototype schema, suggesting that any female shop assistant would be more than delighted to serve George Clooney, especially if it is *after* closing time.

In a medium close-up, George Clooney is shown how he is about to taste his Nespresso. Then, a male voice from the background upsets the narrative logic so far established: "Please come in, ... but only because it's you Mrs. Martin" (LIKE A STAR, 00:17). Following a big close-up of George Clooney's head seen from the side at an angle, the camera makes a slight turn, focussing on the background, showing the viewer, what George

Clooney is seeing: A male shop assistant letting a certain Mrs. Martin into the boutique. Here, the narrative logic so far created collapses. Mrs. Martin stands for Mrs. Everybody.

Figure 31: Like a Star, shot 15, 00:20

At this point, the Nespresso music stops. Then, the shop assistant continues: "Volluto, as usual?" (LIKE A STAR, 00:20), implying that Mrs. Martin is a regular customer.

The next shot shows George Clooney, in a medium-long shot, still at the counter with the coffee machines, as he turns around, watching the scene, with the cup of Nespresso in his right hand.

George Clooney gently shakes his head, and a clear tinkle resounds, marking that something has happened now. The hypothesis that George Clooney was let in because he is a star has to be rejected. His stardom as the cause of the represented story has to be questioned. The explanations offered by both, the template and the prototype schemata are rendered invalid. Obviously, fabula construction suffers a rupture here, and that rupture is underscored with a tinkle. The effect of this rupture is that the viewer, rejecting the above-mentioned hypothesis, is prompted to ponder another fabula construction. This prepares the viewer for the transfer of meaning, the signified, from one signifier to another.

In the next shot, a mid-shot taken from the front, George Clooney, having walked over to Mrs. Martin, sipping the Nespresso he has made for himself, looks over to Mrs. Martin as she is being served her Volluto. The representation of George Clooney bringing the cup filled with Nespresso, which he holds in his right hand, to his mouth whilst looking at Mrs. Martin, who, in turn, is looking at the Nespresso she is being served, moves that cup of Volluto, even though placed at the bottom right-hand corner of the frame, to the centre of the viewer's gaze. Here, the syuzhet places two story lines at an intersection, preparing the viewer for a climax.

Figure 32: Like a Star, shot 17, 00:23

Mrs. Everybody, alias Mrs. Martin, is served her cup of Nespresso, whilst Hollywood star George Clooney had to make his coffee himself. His stardom obviously fails to afford him the treatment that one would expect. It also fails to provide a reason why he was let into the boutique after closing time. Despite her ordinariness, Mrs. Martin was also let in, actually even after George Clooney, and, contrary to him, she is waited upon, being served her cup of Nespresso. Obviously, she gets better treatment than George Clooney. George Clooney's stardom fails to provide any advantages. The viewer's hypothesis-making is steered toward the presumption that in this context, Clooney's stardom does not matter at all. What matters, possibly, is that they are both regulars at that Nespresso boutique. When they were asked which coffee flavour they desire, the boutique hostess, as well as the male shop assistant, both used the expression "as usual" indicating that both, Mrs. Martin and George Clooney, regularly visit that Nespresso boutique. This is important with respect to the viewer's learning of a specific behavioural pattern. And it is also important for the maintenance of the narrative's logic. Both are regulars at the boutique. That could, according to a possible hypothesis, be the reason why they were let in after closing hours. Moreover, generalising the constructed fabula action, it can be hypothesised that the male staff of the boutique display chivalrous behaviour towards female clients.

Shot 19 confirms these hypotheses. In a medium close-up both, Mrs. Martin and George Clooney are seen from the front. Then, Mrs. Martin, looking at George Clooney, says: "When I come here, I always feel like a star, don't you?" (LIKE A STAR, 00:25).

Figure 33: Like a Star, shot 19, 00:26

Those hypotheses are further consolidated by George Clooney's answer. In a close-up, over the shoulder shot he says, contritely: "More or less" (LIKE A STAR, 00:29). Then a tinkle resounds, whilst George Clooney slightly twitches his head. Here, in religious terminology, one could say that the "transfiguration" is taking place. In the syuzhet's decoding, that is, in the fabula construction by the viewer, the prototype and the template schemata are readjusted, transferring the signified of the star to a new signifier: the regular Nespresso customer, or, in other words, the Nespresso Club member. This, for instance, allows for a connection of consumption, identity, moods, and motivations. It also outlines a clear ethos, based on an established model of the "coffee world" wherein the Nespresso Club member is afforded treatment that obviously does not come with just being a star. It comes with being a Club member. A viewer that would also like to feel like a star is, consequently, motivated to enact the portrayed behaviour, that is, become a regular at a Nespresso boutique. This, by implication, also addresses the issue of regulation: With respect to that treatment, a clear dichotomy exists between members and non-members. The benefits of stardom have found a new constituency: Nespresso Club members.

As the hostess hands George Clooney the shopping bag, presumably containing the sleeves with the coffee capsules of his preferred flavour, Mrs. Martin seals the transfer of the signified to a new signifier by saying: "You see? What did I tell you?" (LIKE A STAR, 00:34). The meaning is clear: Everyone gets treated like a star here, you too. One must remember that it is entirely unclear whether or not Mrs. Martin has recognised George Clooney – maybe she has not. In that case, with George Clooney's stardom completely denied by the syuzhet, a fabula construction that links the favourable treatment afforded to Mrs. Martin and George Clooney in the Nespresso boutique to being a Nespresso Club member rather than stardom, is encouraged.

Figure 34: Like a Star, shot 23, 00:34

Her rhetorical question is clearly heard and registered by George Clooney. His ear, though not in focus, is clearly visible, underlying with the frame's composition, the transfer of the message. A fabula construction that solidifies the attribution of the signified to a new signifier is encouraged. A viewer that decides to become a Nespresso Club regular, can trust that he or she will be treated as represented in the commercial. At this point, the

Nespresso music kicks in again. Upon receiving the Nespresso bag with her commission, Mrs. Martin leaves the boutique, walking out of the picture. The final shot shows George Clooney, in a medium close-up, zooming in, standing there, pensive, apparently puzzled by the disendowment he has just been subjected to.

5.5 Analysis of *In the Name of Pleasure*

This commercial, working with nearly uninterrupted erotic insinuations, establishes Nespresso as a source of pleasure that trumps rivalling George Clooney. The commercial's female protagonist, a former Miss Switzerland, when faced with the choice of spending time with courteous George Clooney or drinking another cup of Nespresso on her own, opts for the latter. George Clooney's allure is entirely eclipsed by Nespresso. The commercial conveys that pleasure, as a signified, goes with Nespresso as its signifier, and not, as might be mistakenly assumed, with George Clooney.

The opening shot shows, in a long shot with the camera in circular motion, the inside of an elegant restaurant, or coffee bar opening to a roof garden. The premise is clearly situated on a rooftop in a developed urban area. The Nespresso music *The Boutique* is being played. A viewer familiar with that music is encouraged to formulate the hypothesis that fabula action takes place inside a Nespresso boutique. The next shot, a medium-long shot zooming in to a mid-shot, shows George Clooney leaving a lift. To his left, the Nespresso lettering is clearly visible. The aforementioned hypothesis regarding the place shown in the syuzhet being a Nespresso boutique is strengthened.

Figure 35: In the Name of Pleasure, shot 2, (00:02)

This hypothesis is further encouraged by the subsequent shot, showing an array of Nespresso capsules, all neatly arranged in a capsule holder with the Nespresso lettering written on its rim. A hand, presumably George Clooney's hand, picks one of the capsules. Here, the viewer becomes aware of the width of the product range offered by Nespresso. This is important because, as stated by the economic theory of clubs, the equilibrium where consumer benefit is maximised is characterised by a specific number of club members on one hand, and a corresponding width and diffusion of Nespresso's product range on the other.

Figure 36: In the Name of Pleasure, shot 3, (00:04)

Fabula construction by the viewer is clearly encouraged to place the commercial's narrative in a Nespresso boutique. This is supported by the subsequent three shots illustrating all the steps of the making of a Nespresso. This not only facilitates learning by the viewers, it also moves the cup filled with Nespresso to the centre of attention.

Figure 37: In the Name of Pleasure, shot 6, (00:08)

Figure 38: In the Name of Pleasure, shot 6, (00:09)

In those shots, Nespresso is the protagonist. The syuzhet is immaculately clean, the colours all beautifully harmonise with one another, and in shot 6, the rebounding column of coffee, leaving a drop dancing in the air, alludes to perfect aesthetic beauty. Perhaps shot 6 also alludes to the erection of a pillar of coffee, ejaculating a drop of Nespresso, hovering freely above the cup. The music, that is, *The Boutique* has subsided and the Nespresso column with the dancing drop above it is underscored with a bright tinkle.

Then, a female voice says: "Experience the quality of Nespresso, and you'll let no one compromise your pleasure" (In the Name of Pleasure, 00:06 – 00:12). Those last words, "[…] no one compromise your pleasure" fall on to shot 7, showing, in a medium close-up, zooming out to a mid shot, allowing a glimpse in George Clooney's surroundings. It is, with respect to the fabula construction, left in suspense whether or not George Clooney is part of the pleasure. The template as well as the prototype[93] schemata would surely see him as a part of it, yet the wording of the message allows for the implication that George Clooney might be the one that is about to compromise somebody's pleasure. The viewer is encouraged to ask: "What might that pleasure be?" or: "What pleasure is there that could surpass a pleasure in connection to George Clooney?"

George Clooney then walks on to the terrace, looking for a free seat. In shot 8, with the city's skyline in the misty background, the roof garden's shaded glass fence is clearly visible, separating the inside from the outside. The medium-long shot supports a fabula construction on that basis. Whatever is going to happen, happens inside the Nespresso boutique.

In shot 9, the two protagonists meet. One should actually say, the three protagonists meet, as the third protagonist, which is actually the key player, is also right there, included in the frame: a cup of Nespresso.

93 This study's backdrop assumes, as mentioned, a postmodern, largely secularised society. The viewer of the commercial, living in a postmodern Zeitgeist, which is, above all determined by depthlessness, is not unlikely to have internalised cultural templates, the so-called prototype schemata, that interpret the possible company of George Clooney as something pleasurable.

Figure 39: In the Name of Pleasure, shot 9, (00:14)

George Clooney asks: “May I?” and gets the response: “Please!” (In the Name of Pleasure, 00:16 – 00:17). George Clooney and the beautiful young woman have now started their interaction. This is supported by a narration, that is, the interaction of the syuzhet and style, “cueing and channelling the spectator’s construction of the fabula” (Bordwell, 1985/1997, 52) that, in a succession of alternating over the shoulder shots, joins George Clooney and the woman’s perspectives.

Figure 40: In the Name of Pleasure, shot 10, (00:16)

Shot 10, in a medium-long shot of the young woman, underlines, once more, the inside-outside dichotomy present throughout the whole scene. Behind the young woman, sitting on a lounge chair, the enclosure of the roof garden is clearly discernible, separating the inside, the Nespresso boutique from the outside, the city, whose skyline is clearly visible in the distant background. George Clooney's and the young woman's encounter not only takes place inside a Nespresso boutique, it also takes place high above ground level.

George Clooney sits down. The prototype schema would now propose that he begins a conversation, and indeed, he does: "It's a Volluto?" (In the Name of Pleasure, 00:19). As he is saying this, he is looking down at his crotch whilst pointing his erect index finger at the beautiful young woman.

Figure 41: In the Name of Pleasure, shot 12, (00:19)

These erotic insinuations explicitly guide the viewer's hypothesis-making, encouraging an expectation that this encounter is possibly going to issue in an erotic climax. The woman then responds: "It was," indicating that she has already emptied her cup (IN THE NAME OF PLEASURE, 00:21). Then, George Clooney says: "Uhm … do you want me to …?" proposing to fetch another coffee for her (IN THE NAME OF PLEASURE, 00:12). He underlies his proposal with a masterly dance of his left hand, with the erect index finger at a telling angle. Here, the narration leaves room for a different fabula construction wherein George Clooney's question leaves room for erotic allusions.

Figure 42: In the Name of Pleasure, shot 14, (00:23)

Figure 43: In the Name of Pleasure, shot 14, (00:24)

Figure 44: In the Name of Pleasure, shot 14, (00:24)

The woman, accepting his offer, asks for his name: "Mr?" (IN THE NAME OF PLEASURE, 00:24). The viewer is led to believe that she possibly does not know that her vis-à-vis is the world-famous George Clooney, as mentioned, twice elected the sexiest man alive and thereby, by implication, the object of erotic fantasies. So far, the viewer's fabula construction is in line with the prototype and template schemata. After all, why shouldn't the sexiest man alive, vis-à-vis a beautiful young woman, play his best trump card? In shot 17, showing how George Clooney gets up from his seat, the visual erotic insinuations are led to a climax: The woman is situated in the central axis of the frame. Her posture allows for a look underneath her skirt, a look whose imagined prolongation leads directly to her crotch. Even though George Clooney neither looks at her crotch, nor does he kiss her, the representation of the action, if the third dimension is neglected, suggests precisely that he does. As he is getting up from his seat, his lips, seen in a two-dimensional way only, meet hers (IN THE NAME OF PLEASURE, shot 17, 00:29), and her skirt, loosely draped around her crossed thighs, partly reveals the underside of her right thigh, allowing, through the dark opening of her skirt, for a gaze in the direction of her crotch. Moreover, in that shot's final frame, George Clooney's now bent index finger is pointing directly to his genital area with the dark opening in the woman's skirt right next to it.

Figure 45: In the Name of Pleasure, shot 17, (00:28)

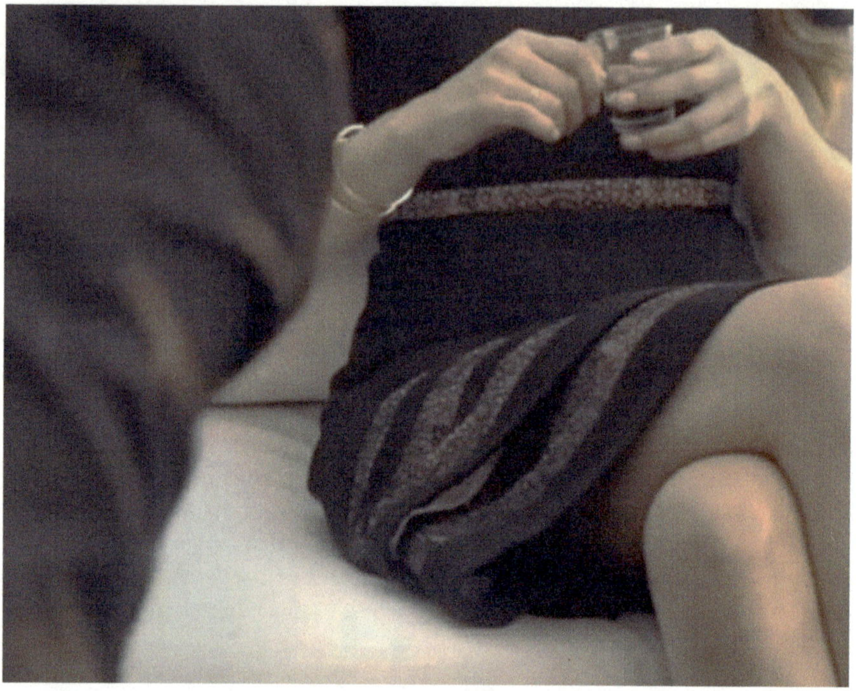

Figure 46: In the Name of Pleasure, enlarged detail of shot 17, (00:28)

Figure 47: In the Name of Pleasure, shot 17, (00:28)

Figure 48: In the Name of Pleasure, shot 17, (00:28)

Figure 49: In the Name of Pleasure, shot 17, (00:29)

Figure 50: In the Name of Pleasure, shot 17, (00:29)

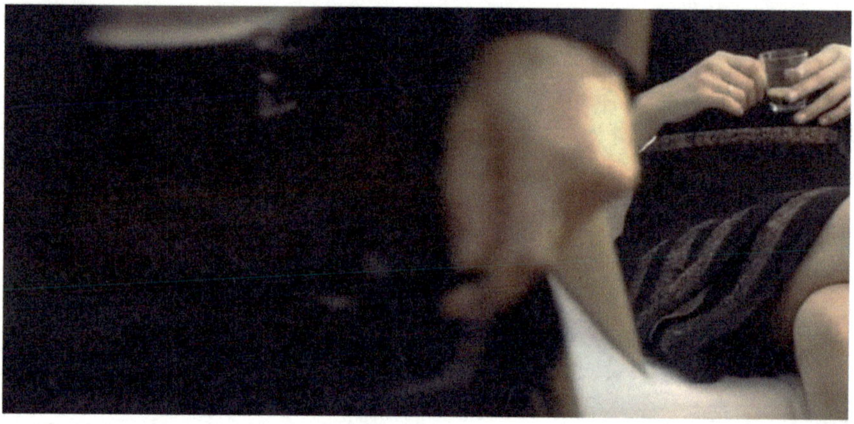

Figure 51: In the Name of Pleasure, enlarged detail of shot 17, (00:29)

These insinuations are continued in the subsequent two shots, strengthening the viewer's hypothesis with respect to a potential erotic ending of the story. In shot 18, George Clooney is heading for the counter with the coffee machines. He is looking back at the woman, confirming the connection they have just established between themselves. Tellingly, the area George Clooney is heading for is called "tasting area" - allowing for a connotation other than the mere tasting of coffee.

Figure 52: In the Name of Pleasure, enlarged detail of shot 18, (00:31)

In shot 19, a dramatic turn in the narrative is heralded. The shot's first frame shows the roof garden's enclosure clearly visible behind the woman, reminding the viewer that the narrative is taking place inside the Nespresso boutique. The woman's left hand is pointing to her crotch, hidden behind the dark opening of her skirt, potentially alluding to, expressed in a choice of words perhaps commensurate to the erotic charge of the narrative's representation, another "tasting area".

Figure 53: In the Name of Pleasure, shot 19, (00:31)

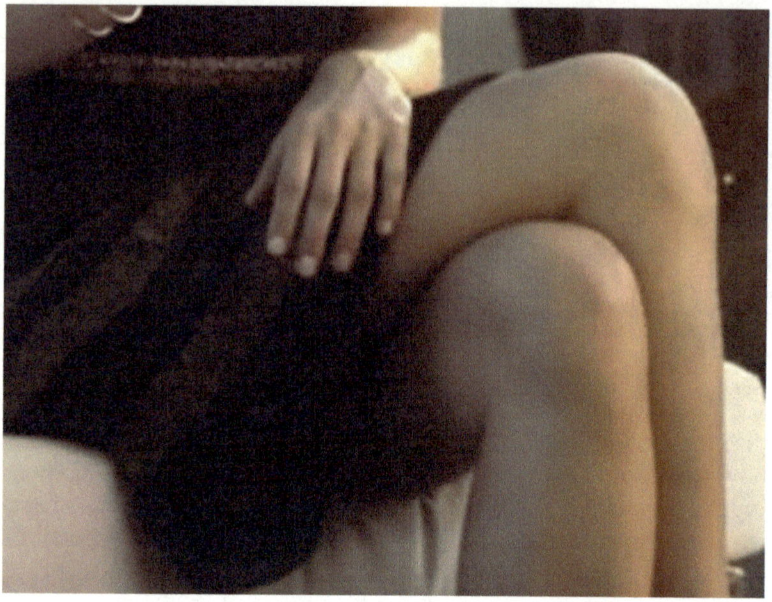

Figure 54: In the Name of Pleasure, enlarged detail of shot 19, (00:31)

Moreover, throughout the preceding shots 17 and 18, the Nespresso music was being played. Then, in shot 19, the music stops and a bright tinkle sounds, announcing the narrative's logic turn, or "transfiguration".

The woman, looking down at the coffee table in front of her, puts her empty cup on the table and quickly reaches for the filled cup George Clooney has just left there. The woman does not hesitate a bit. The exchange of the cups is an intended and decisive action on her part.

Figure 55: In the Name of Pleasure, shot 19, (00:33)

Figure 56: In the Name of Pleasure, shot 20, (00:33)

Figure 57: In the Name of Pleasure, shot 20, (00:33)

Figure 58: In the Name of Pleasure, shot 20, (00:34)

Figure 59: In the Name of Pleasure, shot 20, (00:34)

Here, in the blink of an eye, the procedural, the prototype and the template schemata all have to be adjusted. Obviously, the action is going in a different direction than hypothesised. The original hypothesis has to be rejected. The prototype schema fails to explain the narrative's development and, consequently, the template schema gives wrong cues. Obviously, the beautiful young woman, first and foremost, wants to taste another Nespresso. Erotic tastes are not important, or they can wait. This is further strengthened by the narrative's development: In the next shot, the woman jumps up from her seat and, pointing with her right arm outstretched to the tasting area, calls out to the other guests present in the boutique, shouting: "George Clooney is inside!" (In the Name of Pleasure, 00:34 - 00:35). So, obviously, she had recognised him right from the start, and has now cleverly taken her chance to get rid of him and his, obviously, unwanted advances.

In a long shot then the other female guests are shown as they, electrified by the news, stare at one another in awesome disbelief. They are screaming at the top of their voices, jumping up from their seats all at once, and, in a massive shrieking stampede, run towards the tasting area. They, in contrast to the female protagonist, obviously prefer the tasting of George Clooney to Nespresso.

Next, in a medium close-up zooming in, George Clooney is shown, standing at the counter making a Nespresso, turning around in disbelief, noticing, with a stern look, the onslaught of female admirers. The young female protagonist, shown in the final shot, again visibly positioned inside the boutique, takes a sip of the conquered Nespresso, and closes her eyes as she is leaning back in her seat. It will be a while before George Clooney, if at all, makes it back to her. The setting sun in the background envelops its light around her, and she appears as if she had been carried off to another sphere beyond the screechy fascination of George Clooney's fans – a sphere where ultimate pleasure resides – a sphere where only Nespresso can take you.

Figure 60: In the Name of Pleasure, shot 25, (00:40)

Figure 61: In the Name of Pleasure, shot 25, (00:41)

One of George Clooney's signified, being the fulfiller of desire and the allegedly ultimate pleasure-bringer, is successfully transferred to a new signifier: Nespresso. Some lesser people, as shown in the stampede, might not yet have caught on to that, yet, the narrative's female protagonist knows: If you seek pleasure so intense it takes you close to celestial realms, then there is one behaviour that can take you to it: the consumption of Nespresso.

5.6 Summary

In all three of these commercials, the narrative takes place inside a Nespresso boutique. Along the inside-outside divide, a specific world, a world of coffee consumption is represented. That world, as represented, has its own rules and canons. In three different scenarios, the representation in the commercials portrays the advertised brand as king of the roost. Decisions are made by the commercials' protagonist that only make sense, if it is presupposed that a cup of Nespresso trumps George Clooney's charms. In fact, in all three commercials, George Clooney is running against Nespresso, and comes out the loser. Nespresso beats him on every count, beats him with respect to each of the qualities widely attributed, according to the prototype schema, to him. Through repeated metonymy, along a syntagmatic and paradigmatic logic, George Clooney's signified becomes attributed to a new signifier, Nespresso. George Clooney, seen as a symbolic sign, is divested of all of the meanings attributed to him. In what could even be labelled an evisceration, all his signifieds are transferred to Nespresso, the new signifier replacing George Clooney.

As is shown by Mrs. Martin, who always feels like a star whenever she visits a Nespresso boutique, the signified attributed to Nespresso by the commercials' narration is also transferrable to the consumer. The "feeling like a star", that is, the signified, is transferred from George Clooney, through Nespresso, to the ordinary consumer. The reader might recall that, prior to making that comment, Mrs. Martin was served, by the male shop assistant, a cup of her favourite Nespresso. And, when she makes that remark, the Nespresso cup, which she holds in her hand, is clearly visible in the foreground. The syuzhet induces the viewer to connect the meaning "feeling like a star" to the drinking of a Nespresso. In this manner then, a consumer item as profane as one of many coffee brands in the marketplace, devoid of any exceptional use-value, first assumes, through metonymy, a truly elevated exchange-value, which is then, through momentous decoding and commensurate fabula construction, transferred to the consumer.

As mentioned above, the commercials' narratives are all clearly positioned inside a Nespresso boutique where access is limited to those with a sufficient purchasing power. This categorisation of inside-outside issues in the formation of a world of its own, encouraging a fabula construction according to the dichotomy of an inside, Nespresso's world, and an outside, favouring the formation of a model of the world by and through the viewer. And in that world, as mentioned, Nespresso is the beverage that outshines George Clooney with respect to all of the characteristics attributed to him. In this way, the commercials' representation carves out a specific model with respect to coffee consumption. This model of the world, is paralleled by a model, for the world. The representation's cues invariably imply that the commercials' protagonists regularly drink Nespresso, and, in the case of LIKE A STAR, regularly visit a Nespresso boutique. This consistency with respect to the protagonists' choice with its implicit value judgement regarding Nespresso not only induces the viewer to construct a fabula, a meaning, that attributes all of the aforementioned characteristics to Nespresso, it also facilitates learning by the viewer. Learning is further facilitated by the representation's aesthetic surface. Targeting a would-be clientele with a certain purchasing power, the immaculate design of the represented Nespresso boutiques, as well as the design of all Nespresso artefacts, from the coffee machine to the capsule, facilitate identification by the viewer. For identification by the viewer to take place, the viewer needs to, in some way or another, share at least parts of the fantasy represented by the commercial. For instance, the viewer might place him- or herself into the narrative and become motivated to see for him-, or herself whether Nespresso really tastes so good. In other words: before a viewer becomes a real-life consumer him- or herself, he or she must have an idea, a fantasy depicting him, or her, as the protagonist consumer. Identification in this sense is encouraged by the commercials' narration, that is, the commercials' combination of style and syuzhet. The plot of the shown stories, as well as the style they are represented in, provokes a shift in the viewer's prototype and template schemata. In other words, the narrative logic can only be upheld, if the signified, formerly attributed to George Clooney, obtains a new signifier: Nespresso. And the bet is, that a viewer might want to test that for him-, or herself. If so, identification takes place and learning regarding the implicit value judgements about Nespresso sets in, facilitated by the portrayed intent of the represented protagonist, coded in the commercials and decoded by the viewer.

Regarding the viewer's motivation to taste Nespresso, there is one important aspect that should not be overlooked. The commercials' female protagonists are all in a good mood and highly motivated to taste their Nespresso. As motivations are of a teleological nature, the viewer, aiming to make sense of the female protagonists' represented behaviour regarding the consumption of Nespresso, is steered towards the construction of a fabula wherein Nespresso must obviously, given the protagonists' behaviour, be the fabula's telos, that is, the one dominant object of desire. In this way, through the narration's repeated representation, inviting learning by the viewer, the viewer learns what his or her desire is. Thereby, the viewer's desire is interpreted for him or for her, to the effect that the viewer, next to the model of the world, through a corresponding fabula construction and the commensurate unfolding of the viewer's desire, also becomes invested with a model for the world, an ethos.

Finally, the signified of the new sign, Nespresso in all its shapes, forms and behavioural patterns, not only includes all the characteristics formerly attributed to George Clooney: As the syuzhet, in all commercials, clearly places the consumption of Nespresso inside the boundaries of a Nespresso boutique, setting it apart from other, more profane spheres of life, the signified also includes the touch of belonging to a select group. This facilitates identity formation by the viewer and consumer as identity depends on a feeling of being different from and exclusion of the perceived other, in this case, the outsider who does not drink Nespresso.

6 The Socio-empirical Survey: Data Collection and the Methodological Framework

6.1 *Collecting quantitative and qualitative primary data: Questionnaires and focus groups*

Between December 2013 and August 2015, well more than 700 people were asked to fill in the questionnaire, which enquired about their coffee consumption. One hundred and ninety-seven were willing to participate in this quantitative socio-empirical survey, 153 of them have a Western cultural background, mostly living in German-speaking Switzerland and Germany, 44 are Chinese citizens, living in Shanghai, the People's Republic of China.[94] Finally, one participant lives in the United Kingdom, and another one lives in Denver, in the United States of America. The participants were selected according to the principles of convenience sampling. "Convenience sampling is a non-probability sampling technique where subjects are selected because of their convenient accessibility and proximity to the researcher" (Explorable, n.d.).

> [...][It] is a specific type of non-probability sampling method that relies on data collection from population members who are conveniently available to participate in a study. Facebook polls or questions can be mentioned as a popular example for convenience sampling.
> Convenience sampling is a type of sampling where the first available primary data source will be used for the research without additional requirements. In other words, this sampling method involves getting participants wherever you can find them and typically wherever is convenient. In convenience sampling no inclusion criteria identified prior to the selection of subjects. All subjects are invited to participate.
> In business studies this method can be applied in order to gain initial primary data regarding specific issues such as perception of image of a particular brand or collecting opinions of perspective customers in relation to a new design of a product.
> In its basic form, convenience sampling method can be applied by stopping random people on the street and asking questionnaire ques-

94 The questionnaire in Mandarin (for Nespresso clients) is included in appendix II.

> tions. 'Pepsi Challenge' marketing campaign can be referred to as a relevant example for this sampling method. 'Pepsi Challenge' is occasionally held in large shopping centres and other crowded locations and all members of population are invited to participate in the contest without any discrimination. (Research Methodology, n.d.)

In public places in Zurich, Lucerne, and Shanghai, chosen according to convenience of access, passing pedestrians were asked, for the purpose of data collection, whether they were willing to participate in a survey or not. Four interviewers helped me to find, through convenience sampling, coffee drinkers willing to participate in the survey. A noteworthy incident happened in Shanghai. There, the interviewer went directly to the Nespresso boutique aiming to interview Nespresso clients. After a couple of successfully completed interviews, she was asked by the manager to leave the premise. He told her she had to obtain official permission from Nespresso to continue the interviews.[95] As Nespresso had, by then, already ceased its communication with me, no attempt was made to obtain such permission.

95 The following is the message of the email (in full length) sent to me by the Chinese interviewer, describing the incident:
It is a small shop with three walls and one entrance. One wall for all kinds of capsules with two cashier desks, one wall for the coffee machines and the other wall for a mini-bar, where customers can taste the various coffee flavours. Also, there is another table displaying some coffee machines in the middle of the room. Not much space left...
Therefore, the shop assistants saw me once I entered the shop. Shop assistant A greeted me, so I told him the background of this survey (it's for a doctoral thesis in Switzerland, etc.) and asked him if I could do it in the shop. He declined without any hesitation and explained two reasons: 1st, they were very busy that day because of the Spring Festival. 2nd, it is forbidden to do any non-official survey, which is not assigned by their own company. Quickly, he left me and went to help other customers.
Then I tried my luck with shop assistant B, who was friendlier and offered to hand in the questionnaire to their manager in the back office for his approval. However, shop assistant A noticed that and stopped him, saying that's not necessary because the answer must be "no". There were indeed many customers at that time, so they both went to help them and left me alone.
Then I started to ask around quietly. The 9 answer sheets included:
- 3 customers at the cashier. They had just paid.
- 3 couples at the mini bar. The first couple was waiting for their parents, the second had their trial coffee and bought one machine, the third were just sitting there for a break.
The shop assistants might be too busy to take care of me. Shop assistant C must have seen me while serving the second couple, but she didn't interrupt me. When I was with the third couple, the manage arrived. He had listened for a while, be-

All the participants of the quantitative survey were classified into two groups: Nespresso clients and, as the control group, coffee drinkers who prefer other brands or, for some reason or another, do not drink Nespresso. Members of the control group were asked the same 32 questions as Nespresso drinkers, only that the questions, obviously, did not refer to Nespresso, but to the coffee brand of their choice.[96] The aim was to see, whether the two groups would, in a statistical sense, exhibit a different pattern in their responses.

In a second step, the interviewees who had participated in the quantitative survey and had also been willing to give their contact details were approached and asked whether they would be willing to participate in a qualitative survey, involving focus groups. As the results of the quantitative survey had clearly established that the response patterns are indeed *not* independent of group affiliation, the focus groups were limited to Nespresso clients, no focus control-group was set up.

As outlined above, convenience sampling, as a method, does not choose "subjects that are representative of the entire population" (Explorable, n.d.). Therefore, a later generalisation of the study's conclusions including all Nespresso clients might appear unsound. However, a look at the map below, indicating the location of Nespresso boutiques worldwide, shows that Nespresso is neither present in African, nor in Central Asian countries. It is highly concentrated in European and South East Asian countries. Furthermore, it is present in China, Japan, the USA, and three Latin American countries. It is argued that the interviewees, regarding the general postmodern backdrop of this study, constitute a selection that is representative of Nespresso consumers. Furthermore, the data of the socio-empirical survey, due to the inclusion of Chinese participants, could avoid a European or Western bias.

---

fore cutting in: "Sorry, I'd like to clarify that this questionnaire is not from our company. You can decline to answer if it is disturbing you." They told him that they were already informed about the background and they were answering the questions with pleasure. After we completed the whole questionnaire, the manager ushered me to a corner. He was polite but determined. He insisted that his company doesn't allow any non-official survey to be carried out within the boutiques worldwide. He was also concerned that the survey could be considered as a marketing event. After knowing it was for a doctoral thesis, he gave me his business card and offered to help submit the digital version of the questionnaire to his marketing colleagues for an official approval.

96 The Nespresso questionnaire is included in annexe II.

Figure 62: Nespresso's global presence (Nestlé-Nespresso, n.d.c)

A final remark regarding the collection of the primary data is warranted. The responses and contributions made by the participants of the socio-empirical survey were all based on their personal recall, so to speak, retrieved from their personal memory. Possibly, their recollection of what had actually happened is distorted and bears the mark of a personal bias. In this sense, strictly speaking, the data is of a secondary nature and it would require the collection of either primary data under laboratory conditions or in an embedded field study in order to generate, in the strictest sense of the notion, primary data. Still, in the context of this study, the data collected is referred to as primary data.

6.1.1 How to spot and gauge moods and motivations: A quantitative survey collecting first-hand[97] data

As some of the most important questions in the quantitative survey involved emotionally-based value judgements of, to some degree, a personal nature, the issue was not addressed upfront or head-on. The aim was to get

97 Inasmuch as the questionnaire included questions requiring participants to draw on their memory, it could be argued that the data generated through those questions is, strictly speaking, not primary, but secondary data – data stored in the participants' memory. In this study however, for notional clarity and reading comfort, all the data generated by the socio-empirical survey is referred to as "primary data".

access to the interviewee's intimate views regarding his or her preferred brand. To avoid an emotional closure on the part of the interviewee, these issues were not approached head-on. The questionnaire therefore contains several introductory questions, aiming to first create a comfortable atmosphere. Some of the subsequent questions then contain a lead to specific issues.[98] Those questions were phrased in that manner to make the interviewee give a response to the particular issues under scrutiny. Moreover, with all the questions in the questionnaire being closed questions, the possible answers cover the entire range from complete consent to total disagreement. Finally, as the survey aims to carve out a possible statistically significant difference between the response of the Nespresso clients and the members of the control group, all interviewees were asked identical questions, with the reference to Nespresso being replaced by a reference to a generic coffee brand for the control group.

Eleven out of a total of 32 closed questions are of prime importance with respect to this study. With respect to the questionnaire presented to the participants who declared themselves to be Nespresso clients, these core questions and the possible answers thereto are listed below:

2. Which-one of the following statements do you most agree with?

- ☐ I prefer my coffee brand to other brands. This is the brand of my choice, and I would not like to change brands. In a way, it has become a little bit part of my world.
- ☐ My current coffee brand tastes good, I like it. However, there certainly are other, good coffee brands. Why not try them sometime?
- ☐ My current coffee brand is a random choice. I can't really say I prefer it to other coffee brands.

3. Is Nespresso your preferred coffee brand?

☐ yes ☐ no

98 As Maggie Bruck and Stephen J. Ceci showed in a study (Bruck & Ceci, 1999), there seem to be "age-related differences in suggestibility, with preschool children being particularly susceptible to misleading suggestions. […] Newer studies that have addressed these criticisms, however, have largely confirmed the earlier conclusions." (419) In this context, it is important to note that all interviewees that participated in the survey were either young adults or older.

Questions 2 and 3 aim to find out whether there is a difference between Nespresso drinkers and members of the control group regarding the formulation of a clear preference.

> 10. Do you believe, with the wink of an eye, that in a way, Nespresso is partof a way of life?
>
> ☐ yes ☐ no

Inasmuch as a way of life not only includes certain attitudes, but also certain behavioural patterns, this question aims to identify whether the consumption of Nespresso reflects the presence of an ethos.

> 15. Imagine you are preparing, for yourself, the Nespresso of your choice. You have the peace of mind, and the time to deeply enjoy this moment.
> Is this moment a little bit special, more than just the simple making of a coffee?
>
> ☐ yes, most definitely so ☐ not really
> ☐ yes, in a way ☐ no, definitely not

This question aims to identify whether Nespresso clients perceive the moment of coffee consumption as a moment set apart from other moments, alluding to the potentially ritual-like character of coffee consumption. It is, so to speak, to opening question to question 16.

> 16. Would you agree to the following statement?
> "The making of my coffee is a pleasure in itself, I enjoy it almost as much as the coffee itself. In a special way, it has become a little ritual."
>
> ☐ yes most definitely so ☐ not really
> ☐ yes, in a way ☐ no, definitely not

Question 16 aims to identify whether Nespresso clients are aware of their ritualised behaviour. The phrasing of the question invests the ritual with a positive connotation, implying a consumer's mood that is conducive to an enactment of the ritual.[99]

17. Do you believe, with the wink of an eye, that people who drink Nespresso are a little bit more special than other people?

☐ yes most definitely so ☐ not really
☐ yes, in a way ☐ no, definitely not

This question addresses a consumer's identity, and, with respect to the consumption of Nespresso, identity-formation.

25. Is Nespresso the "right choice"?
☐ yes, always the right choice
☐ yes, most of the time the right choice
☐ yes, sometimes the right choice
☐ no, it isn't

Question 25 addresses a consumer's worldview with respect to coffee (model of the world). It aims to find out, whether marketing was successful in the categorisation of the "coffee world". Furthermore, the question also addresses an ethos as "choice" implies action, and in this case, consumption.

26.Are there other coffee brands which you prefer to Nespresso sometimes?

☐ yes ☐ no

This question addresses both, the ethos, the model for the world as well as the model for the world. Furthermore, it aims to fathom whether or not the learnt behaviour, the ethos, is firmly established.

99 Moods, inasmuch as they are an emotional state, can be conducive regarding certain actions. For a further discussion of the connection between emotions and actions, see Nussbaum (2001/2008).

27. Are you presently presuming you could be replacing Nespresso with another coffee brand soon?

☐ yes, most definitely so ☐ not really
☐ yes, in a way ☐ no, definitely not

Similar to question 26, this question aims to reaffirm and consolidate the answer given to question 26. It gives, so to speak, the interviewee a final chance to opt out of the model of, and the model for the world.

30. Could you imagine definitely replacing Nespresso with another coffee and to immerse yourself in the same experience of pleasure and gusto as before?

☐ yes ☐ no

Question 30 tries to find out whether a consumer has reason to feel his or her motivation and the corresponding moods are uniquely realistic. If a consumer perceives the commodity of his or her choice as being devoid of any alternative, he or she is, by implication, more inclined to judge the moods and motivations in connection to consumption as uniquely realistic.

31. Has Nespresso become a pleasant constant in your life?

☐ Yes it has. ☐ well, not really
☐ well, in a way ☐ no, definitely not

This question, again, addresses the worldview and the ethos, and, by implication, the accompanying moods. Once the consumption of a specific commodity, or brand, has become a constant in the individual consumer's life, then so has the behavioural pattern related thereto. Effective learning of the behavioural patterns represented in the commercials has then issued in the establishment of a firm ethos, ultimately issuing, in the firm's perspective, in a sustained and comparatively very high, operating profit margin.

6.1.2 Listening to the voice of Nespresso enthusiasts: A qualitative survey withfocus groups

The standardised nature of a quantitative research based on closed questions does not allow the capturing of an individual consumer's special relationship with a commodity. Even though participants of the quantitative survey often shared personal detailed information with the interviewer regarding their consumption pattern or their emotional, affective relationship with the product, those contributions, given the rigid structure of the survey questionnaire, do not flow into the quantitative analysis. As it is, of course, important to include them in this study as well, the quantitative survey was complemented by a qualitative survey with focus groups.

In focus groups, a comparatively small number of participants are encouraged to share their views regarding a specific topic. A high level of trust and mutual respect is needed amongst the participants and the interviewer, otherwise participants are unlikely to open up and share their most intimate views with others. In this survey, the aim was to get the participants to share their innermost views on Nespresso with others. The role of the interviewer therein was to introduce the topics that would be explored and to make sure that all the members had a chance to voice their views and make their contributions heard. Out of the 197 participants of the quantitative survey, nine people were ultimately willing to actively participate in a focus group. In order to make sure the participants felt welcome and at home in their group, three homogeneous groups were formed with three participants in each. That group size is representing a minimum number of participants required. The benefit of such a small group size is that, if the participants are chosen appropriately, it secures, amongst the group members, a maximum degree of trust and of feeling protected. As the Nespresso campaign, based on "one of the sexiest men alive", is not free of erotic insinuations, female and male consumers, when discussing with each other, might possibly feel slightly uncomfortable facing these issues, in case they come up in a focus group. In order to exclude the possibility of such a situation, the groups were formed according to gender: one group with only women in Zurich, and two groups with only men, one in Zurich and one in Munich. The meetings lasted one and a half hours, and all the contributions were electronically recorded. In Zurich, the interviewer and a recording secretary were present. In Munich, there was no recording secretary available. Therefore, the interviewer was also responsible for the recording. The recordings of all focus groups were transcribed at a later date.

In those three separate focus groups, the participants were asked the trigger-questions listed below, inviting them to enter into a discussion and to share their views and personal experience with the other participants and the interviewer:

- o What makes coffee so irresistible?
- o What is special about Nespresso?
- o Please tell us how you got your first Nespresso machine.
- o Would you ever want to be without it again?
- o Did Nespresso change your mornings/your days?
- o Please, for a moment, ponder the idea of having to make it without Nespresso. What does that feel like?
- o What does it feel like to imagine, I no longer allow myself to drink Nespresso?
- o Do I even want to imagine a world without Nespresso?
- o Has Nespresso become a part of my world? A ritual?
- o Did Nespresso revive our coffee culture?
- o Does Nespresso show me how beautiful everyday life could be?
- o What is it, that makes Nespresso so special?
- o How far would I go for a Nespresso?
- o Do I feel more secure with Nespresso? Or better?
- o Is it a serene feeling to be part of the Nespresso world?
- o Do I trust that Nespresso will always give me a good cup of coffee?
- o Does it make me happy to be part of the Nespresso world? Does it have to do with self-love and/or self-respect?
- o With respect to coffee, I have made my choice. Would you agree with that? Does that feel good?

6.2 Analysis of the socio-empirical data

6.2.1 A quantitative analysis based on the methods of inferential statistics

The primary data collected through the quantitative survey consists of categorical data with respect to outcome and with respect to the predictors. The predictors are grouped into two independent categories: a participant who does not consider him- or herself a Nespresso client falls into the control group. No participant is registered in both groups. Also, the possible answers are of an exclusively categorical nature, for instance, the answer to many questions must either be a "yes" or a "no".

The aim is to test whether or not a statistically significant association between the predictors and the outcome exists. If such an association exists, it can be said that if, for instance, a consumer is a Nespresso client, he or she can be expected to act in a different way to members of the control group. To identify a possible association between the predictors and the outcome, a so-called non-parametric Chi-square test based on the Chi-square statistic, which was developed by Karl Pearson, is performed. That Chi-square test of independence is a statistical method testing the independence of two categorical variables, in the case of this study, group association (i.e., whether a participant is a Nespresso consumer or a member of the control group) and the response given. This test is based "on the [...] idea of comparing the frequencies you observe in certain categories to the frequencies you might expect to get in those categories by chance" (Field, 2013, p, 772). For this purpose, the test calculates the expected frequency, that is, the number of people responding in a certain way, if the response is given by chance. For the test results to be valid, that number should, for a test involving two groups and two possible answers, not be below 5 (see Field, 2013, pp. 734-735). Often, if the sample size is small, this problem does arise. However, with a sample size of nearly 200, this problem does not arise in this study. Then, the term "non-parametric" implies that the data for such a test does not have a meaningful average. And this, in the case of the primary data generated by the quantitative survey, is clearly the case: For instance, if the answer "Yes" is given by ten participants, and "No" by another ten participants, then, of course, one cannot say that, on average, the answer was "Yes".

The statistical significance is identified with the help of the so-called p-value, often labelled "Sig." by statistical computer programs. The p-value indicates, either in percentages or in decimal figures, the likelihood that, given the null-hypothesis of no association is true, another sample[100] taken from the same population, would yield identical or more extreme results.

In a Chi-square test, a null-hypothesis if formulated, postulating independence and no association between predictors and outcome. The alternative hypothesis then states that such an association does indeed exist. For the purpose of this study, the null-hypothesis is falsified, that is, rejected, if

100 It is understood that, if additional samples are taken, they are of the same sample size, that is, that they included the same number of participants.

the p-value of the calculated Chi-square statistic[101] is below .05 (= 0.05), or 5 percent. If that is the case, that is, if the null-hypothesis is rejected, then the alternative hypothesis is considered to be supported by the data.

If a null-hypothesis can be rejected, and the association between the predictors and the outcome is statistically significant, then the strength of that association must be identified. In order to do that, IBM SPSS calculates two statistics, one is called "Cramer's V", and the other-one, is referred to as "Phi". IBM SPSS always calculates both statistics. In the case of a Chi-square test with respect to two groups (Nespresso clients and the control group), and a question with just two possible answers, that is, "Yes" or "No", the value of the Phi-statistic is relevant. A value of 0.3 is considered a medium effect, and a value of 0.5 is considered a large effect (Zaiontz, n.d.). In the case of a test with respect to a question with three or four possible answers, Cramer's V is used instead.[102] In the case of three possible answers, a value of 0.21 is considered a medium effect, and a value of 0.35 is considered a large effect (Zaiontz, n.d.). Regarding a test with respect to a question with four possible answers, a value of 0.17 is considered a medium effect, and a value of 0.29 is considered a large effect (Zaiontz, n.d.). Regarding the table below, please note that the expression "df" stands for "degrees of freedom". A question with two groups of interviewees and two possible answers has 1 df, a question with three possible answers has 2 df, and a question with three possible answers has 3 df. For a further discussion of this topic, see Field (2013).

df	small	medium	large
1	0.1	0.3	0.5
2	0.07	0.21	0.35
3	0.06	0.17	0.29

Table 1: Effect sizes for Cramer's V (Zaiontz, n.d.)

Finally, if the possible answers only include a "Yes" or a "No", the so-called odds ratio is also calculated and reported. The odds ratio indicates how

101 Instead of just "Chi-square", many computer programs, as for instance IBM SPSS, label that statistic "Pearson Chi-square" because it was Karl Pearson who introduced the Chi-square test.

102 For a further discussion of this subject see Field (2013).

much more likely a "Yes", or a "No" is, given that a participant belongs to the Nespresso, and not to the control group.[103]

6.2.2 An in-depth journey into the world of Nespresso enthusiasts: A hermeneutical analysis of the focus groups' contributions

As this study intends to analyse the contributions made by the three focus groups in the context they were made, the aim is to keep semantics and syntax integrated with one another, even in the process of the analysis. Thus, the data generated by the focus groups will be subjected to a hermeneutical analysis according to the tenets and categories of the theoretical framework synthesised in this study.

All the contributions made in the three focus groups were registered on audio-files and subsequently transcribed. Based thereon, the topics that were discussed are grouped and analysed according to the categories of analysis outlined above. In this process, the affirmations and statements made by the groups will be carved out. By the same token, commonalities and differences between the groups will be identified. For instance, the participants of both focus groups in Zurich felt, to some degree at least, manipulated by Nespresso's immaculate marketing campaign. What was noteworthy in that context is that the participants of the all-female group did not really worry about that, whereas the participants of the all-male group felt it was an issue. What both groups had in common, however, was their willingness to follow the ethos laid out by the marketing campaign. Yet, it needs to be stated that it is not the aim of this study, to either allege or show a gender-specific difference between the focus groups. The following references to gender simply serve the organisational purpose of clarifying, which one of the three focus groups is addressed.

All-male focus group, Zurich

In the all-male focus group that met in Zurich (Focus Group 1)[104], two out of three participants termed their coffee-drinking habits an addiction (FG 1, 04:00). Having said that, one of the two "addicts", participant A, immediately added that the addiction is rooted in the fact that "Nespresso, the

103 For a further discussion of the odds ratio, see Field (2013).

104 The references to the focus groups will henceforth be abbreviated to FG.

product, the coffee, really *is* very good"[105] (FG 1, 04:58). It is noteworthy that participant A said that Nespresso coffee *is* very good, he did not say that *he* thinks, or according to *his* view Nespresso coffee is very good. Participant A then stressed the constancy of Nespresso's high quality.

Having reached, right from the beginning, that "cruising-height", stressing Nespresso's seemingly ontological, innate qualities, participant B then added that for him, coffee-drinking is a ritual (FG 1, 06:15). Also, during the day, coffee-drinking is ritualised (FG 1, 06:39). What needs to be remembered is that all participants of the focus group are Nespresso drinkers. Therefore, for him, the ritual refers to the making of a Nespresso. When asked, whether he only drinks Nespresso, he denied it, and went on to say that drinking Nespresso, for him, is a question of convenience. However, that statement was immediately relativised and weakened when he conceded that he sticks to Nespresso and cannot explain to himself why he did not switch to other, less expensive capsule systems (FG 1, 07:53). He said that, rationally, he cannot explain his behaviour to himself, and that actually he is not the type of person that would behave in this way, but, in the case of Nespresso, he said that he would stick to it (FC 1, 09:26).

Following participant B's description of his behaviour, rationally inexplicable to him, participant C made a contribution, lifting the weight of the statements to a more intense level: He said that his behaviour, with respect to Nespresso, is of a compulsive nature: "In my case it is surely an addiction. In the morning at breakfast I try to do without coffee and then I am in a bad mood until I have the first cup of coffee (giggling)" (FG 1, 09:58). Interviewer: "Any type of coffee or ...?" Participant C: "No! any type of coffee?! If I have to get up early [...], I treat myself to a cup of coffee (participant C again begins to laugh and giggle) and then I look forward to (giggling again, the pitch of his voice is moving up), look forward to (he repeated the words, still joyfully giggling), to a Nespresso, and immediately, I am in a good mood (giggling). Here, I am subject to compulsion" (FG 1, 10:05).

When asked about Nespresso's aesthetics, participant C said: "Once, my partner came home with non-Nespresso capsules that also fit into the Nespresso machine (all three participants: laughter) [...]. I nearly threw a fit (participants A and B: laughter). I thought I wouldn't even try them, they look really daft. Then I noticed how I have really fallen for [Nespresso's]

105 The conversations in the two focus groups in Zurich were held in Swiss German, then transcribed to High German. Translation to English by the author, 2016.

entire aesthetics" (FG 1, 12:56). Participant A then added: "Me too, fully! That's just what I don't like, that I am obviously susceptible to such things. I think it's mad, the Nespresso shops in Berne, where everything is thought-through, everything fully styled, the design is top, from the capsule to the appearance of the shop assistant. It is truly mad and truly impressive and actually I'd rather elude this." Then, referring to the coffee-pads of rivalling brands he added: "However, I feel the same as you do, I don't need those gadgets wrapped in cotton wool in my house [...]" (FD 1, 13:16). To that, participant A added: "They look like sanitary products" (FD 1, 13:55). Everybody was now chuckling and giggling. Participant C then continued, implicitly alluding to being subject to Nespresso's model for the world, the ethos: "And this shows that you really do surrender to that stuff" (FG 1, 14:17).

Participant B then said, that Nespresso's aesthetic surface is not really important to him. He mentioned how impressed he is with Nespresso's recycling programme: "Just think how far they have come! A special collecting point for Nespresso capsules! *There I have satisfied my good conscience.*[106] [...] I didn't do any research; I feel I am in good hands, that's the point. I have the feeling that [with Nespresso] I get what I need. [...] I do not need anything else" (FG 1, 15:17). When asked by the interviewer whether he does not look around for rivalling products, he said: "No, because I am pleased [with the product]" (FG 1, 16:26). To that statement, the other participants both agreed (FG 1, 16:29).

The group then watched the latest Nespresso commercial How Far, featuring George Clooney and Jean Dujardin (How far, 2014). All the participants agreed that the commercial was well made. The interviewer then asked, whether there might be a positive side to being steered by advertising as obviously, Nespresso really manages to satisfy a consumer's distinct wants, and then added: "Would I go too far if I said that one could feel good about being steered by advertising in the sense 'Here I know I truly get what I would like to have'?" All participants immediately answered with a clear no: "No, no, absolutely not" (FG 1, 22:18). Obviously, the interviewer's suggestion did not, in the eyes of the participants, go too far. When the interviewer then asked, whether they consider testing alternatives, all of the participants unanimously said that they are not actually testing alternatives nor are they planning to do so in the future (FG 1, 37:22).

106 The conversation was held in Swiss German, however, the statement "There I have satisfied my good conscience" was pronounced in formal standard German.

The interviewer then asked them whether one can say that Nespresso succeeded in creating a model of the most optimal coffee consumption. All participants answered with a clear "Yes" (FG 1, 39:56).

With respect to moods, it is noteworthy that they were referred to, by the participants, throughout the entire duration of the conversation. Participant B, for example, referring to Nespresso's high quality and the comparatively high unit-price of a Nespresso capsule, said: "If one did not have the feeling of being in good hands, one would look around for alternatives. You pay more only if you feel good [with the brand]" (FG 1, 23:43). Later, when participant B told the story of how surprised he was to find a Nespresso machine in his hotel room in a remote place in Thailand, he said that he was "fascinated [...] [and] positively surprised," and went on to say: "I admire them for achieving such a feat" (FG 1, 30:46). Later, he added to that, that Nespresso did a good job in offering so many different flavours to choose from (FG 1, 38:50).

Later in the conversation, participant C, telling the story of how he bought a Nespresso machine, says, with joyful laughter, that he had "feelings of joy" in connection to the purchase (FG 1, 35:31). When asked by the interviewer whether those feelings of joy persisted, he replied: "Yes" (FG 1, 35:37). The interviewer then poses the question whether those feelings are constantly being renewed. Participant C replied: "Yes, when I order [the capsules] through the internet" (FG 1, 35:42). Later, in the context of having found "a home" with respect to coffee consumption, participant B said: "I am being confirmed again and again that all is well the way it is. What does it mean to have found "a home"? I simply have no reason to try anything else, because I am feeling good" (FG 1, 38:10). Toward the end of the conversation, participant B then told the story that, each time he is invited [for lunch or dinner] and offered a cup of coffee at a friend's place, if that friend still has one of those weird "I don't know what" [coffee machines], offering some 'broth', he would decline the offer, preferring to drink no coffee at all. He said: "Those moments remind me that at home I can have good coffee." Asked whether these thoughts come with a feeling of satisfaction or joy, he responds: "Yes, with joy, and then I think 'I'll stay with Nespresso.' Whenever I come across an alternative I am positively confirmed by Nespresso" (FG 1, 52:00).

Another issue discussed by the participants was Nespresso's comparatively high unit price. This issue was first addressed by participant C. Describing his reaction to an advertisement for organically grown coffee on Facebook, offering one kilogramme at a price of 20 Swiss francs, which, he said, made him think that that was too much, he expressed his unease with respect to feeling he has no means to withstand the effects of Nespresso's near-to-perfect marketing: "Just this week, there was an add on Facebook for organically grown coffee for 20 francs a kilo, well, everybody feels that this is too expensive, however, the [Nespresso] capsule would cost 80 francs a kilo. When I read that I thought 'Yes, you also belong to them for sure.'" (FG 1, 17:01).

Finally, regarding Nespresso's high unit price, participant B then said: "Yes, the price is undoubtedly very high. One also pays for the marketing. The beautiful sales assistants and the fact that everything is uniform and very soigné. That's what we finance with those capsules. However, if something is well done, why shouldn't I feel I am in good hands and think it is all right? I accept that." To which participant A then added: "It looks to me like it's handcrafted, something you also gladly pay for" (FG 1, 17:39). Clearly, all three participants consider the price of a Nespresso capsule to be very high, yet they are all willing to pay that high price.

All-female focus group, Zurich

In the all-female focus group, the discussion quickly zeroed in on one topic: "beauty". Responding to the question whether it is the taste of Nespresso that makes it so special, participant C said: "Yes, sure, the taste and the beautiful milk froth" (FG 2, 03:45). The interviewer then asked her, whether aesthetics also plays a role in choosing Nespresso: "[…] [Y]es that is true indeed, the capsules are something beautiful – choosing the capsule and putting it into the machine. I also think the machines are beautifully made. At home, I have a Nespresso machine and I think it is beautiful. I also now have the milk frother and that's in any event super and it is the most beautiful. It (beauty) does indeed matter, also the beautiful catalogues. I never have [i.e., drink] special editions, I just have my three to four coffee flavours I like […] – they are beautiful to look at, the Levanto is my favourite, the Arpeggio, hm, sometimes the Roma […] and the orange-one" (FG 2, 04:12). Participant A then said that for her, aesthetics is important, too, and that, if something is only of botched workmanship, she would not consider buying it. However, she would not drink the coffee, however beautifully presented, if its taste did not meet her standards (FG 2, 05:18). Also, participant B said that she chooses Nespresso first and foremost because of its taste. All participants considered Nespresso's taste superior to filter coffee as well as superior to the taste of all rivalling coffee brands. Only one exception was mentioned. Participant A said that in Italy, sometimes, coffee tastes better than Nespresso: "In Italy, they make coffee that tastes in earnest better than Nespresso. But only there, nowhere else" (FG 2, 05:46).

When asked how she got to know about Nespresso, participant B only gave a short response: "From people I know. Unfortunately, we do not [yet] have one, but the next one will be a Nespresso machine" (FG 2, 08:29). As it was obvious, from the context, that the "we" referred to her and her husband, the interviewer then asked whether she had decided about that together with her husband. She replied: "No, I made that decision." Everybody then giggled. Inquiring about her husband's reaction to her decision, or whether he even knew about it, she said: "No, he doesn't know it yet." Again, everybody giggled. "However, I know he likes it. It will be all right" (FG 2, 09:08).

Then, the interviewer played the Nespresso commercial How Far (2014) to the participants. They all liked that commercial. Participant A remarked: "That's a good one, very good", and then, to everyone's cheers and laughter, added: "Well, advertising can simply be marvellous!" (FG 2, 13:15). With a view to the commercials featuring George Clooney, the interviewer then asked whether the consumption of Nespresso is, to some degree at least, tantamount to participating in a beautiful, aesthetic world with charm and wit, (FG 2, 14:15). Participant C responded that she does not always think of the commercials when she drinks a Nespresso. "I also drink Nespresso just like that, I am truly fond of that coffee. However, I think, in the beginning, the thought that George Clooney also drinks a Nespresso when he is at home: that turns it into something special" (FG 2, 15:16).

Next, participant C testified that the commercial is like a confirmation, that the product [i.e., Nespresso] is a unique product. Then, she went on to say: "One can watch the commercial and still consider Nespresso a super product, or even more. It is linked to George Clooney. At home, my mother always says: 'Have a George!'" (FG 2, 18:32).

When confronted with the idea that Nespresso could go out of business, that there could be a time when there is no Nespresso, without any substitutes comparable to Nespresso available, all participants expressed their view that such a situation would be very bad. Participant B said: "Without Nespresso, something precious would be missing, there would be an empty void" (FG 2, 22:40). Here, participant B used an anaphora[107] to empha-

107 An anaphora is a rhetorical tool. It is used to add emphasis to the sentence's predicate. In an anaphora, some words (or synonyms) are deliberately repeated at the beginning of adjacent sentences.

sise the weight of her contribution. Participant C then added: “[…] It [the Nespresso experience] would be missing. […] Nespresso has a taste that you remember” (FG 2, 23:55). And participant A said: “I would no longer drink coffee, […] and I would pour out the bad coffee” (FG 2, 25:08).

When asked, whether Nespresso has introduced a coffee culture, participant A said that Nespresso has succeeded in the creation of a new need that previously had not existed, (FG 2, 26:00). To that, participant C added: “With my mother, a coffee culture was indeed awakened in her. After exercising together, my mother and her colleagues always go to her place to have a Nespresso with foamed milk. Me too, I hardly ever drink coffee at home; however, when brunching with a friend, we make a beautiful coffee and serve it in a glass. It is fun, also because you can choose your flavour. […] Something got started: the coffee klatch” (FG 2, 26:14). When asked, whether Nespresso enjoys a certain priority in the world of coffee, they all agreed that Nespresso has acquired such status. The interviewer then asked the participants whether they feel they are in good hands. To that, all the participants answered with a clear “Yes!” Participant A then added: “[…] [T]hey [Nespresso] have created a need, that previously had not existed at all. You cannot go back, of course not, now that it is here!” (FG 2, 30:20). Immediately, all the participants burst into spontaneous, happy laughter.

The interviewer then asked whether that situation could be likened to having a magnetic compass leading to such moments. Participant A responded: “Yes, it contains a certain ritual” (FG 2, 30:48). When asked whether they also try other coffee brands, one participant said: “⍰⍰⍰!”[108] All participants then, right away, burst into laughter (FG 2, 30:55).

Following that, the interviewer wanted to know whether such thoughts do not even arise in the first place. Participants A and C confirmed that, saying that they feel no need to switch to another brand, they are satisfied with Nespresso (FG 2, 31:15). Participant A then went on to say that Nespresso offers a wide variety of flavours, that her trying different brands has come to an end and, if she feels like a change, she now looks for a new flavour amongst the many different Nespresso capsules. Again, everyone burst in happy laughter (FG 2, 32:15).

When asked by the interviewer, whether they had a feeling of having arrived, all the participants answered with a clear “Yes!” (FG 2, 33:12). Participant C also added that she would not go back to another brand (FG 2,

108 This symbol, in the phonetic alphabet, describes a sound like the first “e” in the pronunciation of the word “better”, phonetic transcription “bɛtər”. In Swiss German, and English, “⍰⍰⍰” is a casual, sometimes funny way of saying “no”.

36:42). The interviewer then wanted to know whether they had ever considered taking the Nespresso machine with them when, if travelling by car, when they had to go on a trip away from home. Participant A responded: "Well, that's a good one! Considered? We did it!" (FG 2, 36:53). Everyone then burst into joyous laughter. What needs to be noted here is the use of a rhetorical question to add strength to the predicate of the subsequent sentence.

The discussion then moved on, addressing, from an ethical perspective, potentially challenging issues related to large corporations such a Nestlé; especially their power, their economic and financial clout, and their allegedly sole focus on profit were mentioned (FG 2, 40:18). However, none of the participants established a link between those downsides and Nespresso as a brand. Participant C then recounts to participant A the story portrayed in a Nespresso commercial. Participant A then said: "These commercials are ingenious, one just has to say that explicitly. I love this kind of humour" (FF 2 51:54).

Later in the discussion, participant C, also referring to the Nespresso commercials, said: "They [Nestlé] create a distinct world in its own right. Nestlé only marginally makes an appearance. Nespresso makes an appearance in its own right, together with George Clooney, and with him, everything is well" (FG 2, 1:02:39). To that, participant A added that it did not matter whether we live at the mercy of big government or of Nestlé (FG 2, 57:39), and anyhow: "People are being exploited all the time […] [W]e are surrounded by goods produced in sweatshops. Sadly, all the things we live with are possible only because we exploit other countries. That's global. Nestlé is not to be criticised more than others. They are just part of the system. I am making [a] compromise because their coffee [Nespresso] is simply the best. Basta![109] […] You cannot save the entire world by yourself, least of all if you do not drink Nespresso. […] The world will always revolve around money, and ours around coffee. […] If I can bring about a change, I do it, if I cannot, I have a Nespresso!" To that fervent apologia, almost a Marseillaise in favour of Nespresso, its worldview and ethos, participant C exclaimed: "What else?" On that note, on Nespresso's punch line, this focus group closed (FG 2, 1:04:52).

109 Italian for "That's it, enough!".

All-male focus group, Munich

Whilst the two Swiss focus groups mainly shed light on the models of and for the world and the accompanying moods and motivations as introduced by Geertz (1966), the German focus group, apart from providing insights into consumer identity and ethos, carved out two further aspects: that of the consumer's alienation through advertisement, as described by Williamson (2002), and Nespresso's club-good character as explained by Buchanan's economic theory of clubs (1965).

The three participants of the all-male focus group in Munich each had different approaches to coffee drinking. For participant A, coffee drinking is a ritual, a ritual he has become accustomed to (FG 3, 01:12), a ritual, furthermore, that appears to contribute to his personal well-being (FG 3, 01:17). For him, coffee is a luxury drink that enhances the status of everything connected to it. Participant B only drinks Nespresso at very special moments of inner focus, as he considers himself unable to access the pleasure offered by Nespresso in more profane moments. Finally, participant C differentiated between "coffee" and "good coffee" [*gescheiten*], meaning Nespresso, which he drinks at home: "In the afternoon, at work, I think, sometime soon you will go home, and then you can drink the good coffee again. At work, they have that weird, big coffee machine; that coffee is not so tingly. I then look forward to my Arpeggio, which I love, (FG 3, 07:22).

The interviewer asked what it is that makes Nespresso their first choice. Participant B responded that the reason lies in the convenience that comes with Nespresso's capsule system. For him, his choice is solely rooted in Nespresso's functionality (FG 3, 08:28). When the interviewer then questioned whether other brands did not also offer the same functionality, participant B was interrupted by participant A who said: "No, that is not so because, and that is why I believe the [Nespresso] capsule system is so successful, at a dinner party, you can offer each guest a choice of many different coffee flavours, beginning with decaffeinated coffee, Lungo, elegant and bitter all the way to sweet and creamy. With other espresso machines, with fully automatic coffee machines you don't have that option. There, you can only choose between two types of coffee beans, point one. Point two, if I brew a classic filter coffee, then I have eight cups in a pot, everyone has to drink the same coffee, in the same intensity, whether or not they want that. With the [Nespresso] capsule machine I can satisfy different tastes and needs. The functionality is perfect, it functions perfectly with all the original Nespresso capsules, furthermore, it is important that one does not get annoyed, the product has been brought to functional perfection, one can choose from different tasty flavours" (FG 3, 08:56). Regarding the price of a Nespresso capsule, participant A remarked that, even though a no-name coffee capsule sold at the discounter's only costs €0.20, he, as he can afford it, is willing to pay the €0.40 asked for one Nespresso capsule (FG 3, 37:38).

Participant A also testified that other capsule machines [offered by rivalling brands] are also perfect and come with appealing flavours. The interviewer then asked in which respect, according to him, they differ from Nespresso. He answered that "they round it up with a perfect design. They [Nespresso] offer different machines in combination with different flavours; and then there is the lifestyle, [...] one can bring faces like the one of George Clooney to your table" (FG 3, 10:26). That lifestyle, as participant A mentioned, includes the way he goes shopping for Nespresso: "One doesn't go shopping for coffee [Nespresso], one celebrates the buying of coffee. [...] One goes to a special shop. [...] One speaks of the individual flavours, referring to them by their names, Roma, Volluto, and so forth, or you only refer to their colours: 'Which capsule-colour do you desire?' Even if one celebrates this with the wink of an eye, this brings a lot of noblesse[110] to the table" (FG 3, 12:00). Participant C then said: "I must honestly say that some time ago we had that Nespresso shop at Karstadt's. [...] That was special, very special, very noble. I must say that one felt as if one were a member of the nobility [*man hat sich "von" gefühlt*] when you went shopping there. Now of course, me too, I only do my shopping at the [Nespresso] Flagship Store. That's different, one cannot see you from the outside. At the first shop, one could see you from the outside. So, if someone had passed by, someone who knew you, he would have thought, 'Oh! Look! *That one* goes to Nespresso!'[111] Man! That was awesome [*geil*]! That was so truly awesome [*so richtig geil*]! One felt so truly super!" (FG 3, 17:44). Here, participant C uses a rhetorical climax to convey the immensity of his good mood.

Regarding the Nespresso commercial How Far (2014), which they then all watched together, participant A remarked: "The scene with George Clooney was funny, you had to laugh, I found it witty, and it raised the appetite to try the coffee. I like the taste, it pleases me, I take it. If this is so, one can surrender oneself to the commercial [...], one becomes part of that world" (FG 3, 30:24). Later, referring to noblesse and George Clooney, participant A said: "For me, noblesse is the key to having fun, the key to try

110 "Noblesse" is the French word for "nobility".
111 This was said with great emphasis, in a voice full of admiration and respect.

the product. It is a witty story with George Clooney, it's fun to impersonate him in the kitchen. Mr. Volluto, signora Ristretto, that's witty, that was fun. However, I can re-enact the George Clooney gimmick also with a cup of Jacobs coffee[112] in my hand" (FG 3, 39:59). With respect to the Nespresso commercials, participant A furthermore remarked that "good commercials and [good] marketing, and that strategic wit with George Clooney [...]: these are stories that simply make one feel [like having a Nespresso] [da *hat man einfach Lust*]; and the commercials are so well made that – by serving Nespresso – one actually does not make a fool of oneself. That's the clue. One feels boundless desire to try it" (FG3 41:00).

Participant B then made the following contribution: For breakfast, he said, he does not drink Nespresso, because it is too early in the day and his taste buds are not yet fully awake and functioning. And so, it is irrelevant whether or not the coffee for breakfast, is a particularly good one (meaning Nespresso). To that, he added: "The exceptionally good (coffee) should remain as something exceptional" (FG 3, 1:04:40), meaning that Nespresso should be consumed only in exceptional moments. Later, with respect to those moments, he added: "[That moment has come] when all my tasks are completed, or nearly completed. I need to feel a certain inner calm and tranquillity. Now, I am done, I did a good job, and now I would like to have a cup of good coffee. One can consider that a reward" (FG 3, 1:09:50) Regarding those moments of inner calm and a possibly causal role of Nespresso, participant B then said: "At most, this is supported by Nespresso, [Nespresso] supports my relishing of those moments." When directly asked, whether Nespresso supports the process of reaching that inner focus, he immediately replied: "No, [in those moments of relishing] I am already there. *After* I have reached my inner focus, then Nespresso is something I relish. [However], if I am not there yet, then rather not. [...] When I am there, then yes. However, [it is] not [Nespresso], that takes me there. When I am there, then, Nespresso is adequate, because then, with respect to the pleasure, I am capable of feeling it, of experiencing it" (FG 3, 1:20:03). With that tautology, participant B completed that contribution.

When participant C was then asked by the interviewer, whether he would like to make a final contribution, he said: "Well, I have to say, for me, there is now no longer any other choice. I don't want to have any other coffee at all. [...] If Nespresso got more expensive, it would not matter to me. Back then, with the cigarettes, that was the same story, they continuously raised the price, one said to oneself, well, if they get so expensive, I'll

112 Jacobs coffee is a German coffee brand.

give up smoking, [...] however, one never did. A person would still buy it [i.e., Nespresso], perhaps a bit less, but they would still buy it. For me, it would be relatively awkward, if Nespresso no longer existed, one would just have to find another alternative (sic), however I believe, it would take me a long time to come to terms with that and find a replacement. I would be really very much upset, I'd be really upset. You get used to it, I like it very, very much, it just has my taste, I just really like it [...] (01:22:32). Later, participant C added: "I have to honestly say that for me, there is no other comparable coffee" (FG 3, 01:25:50), and continued: "With regards to the coming home, having a cup of coffee [i.e., Nespresso], unwinding and relaxing, [...] also having an inner focus: that's all one thing, that all belongs together, that saves the evening, whatever then might happen [next] (FG 3, 01:25:54). The interviewer then enquired whether Nespresso is part of that or not. Participant C responded: "Yes, on all counts; I have also come to depend a bit [on Nespresso] [*habe mich abhängig gemacht*], but I don't mind that at all" (FG 3, 01:26:12).

After some calculations regarding the comparatively low price of a Nespresso coffee machine and the high capsule price and how they strike a balance, participant A said: "In conclusion I would like to say that we are Nespresso clients, and as long as the quality remains high we are willing to buy the product, and also enjoy it. [...] Then, Nespresso has a place in our life, and we are willing to pay the price. Period. If the product got tarnished [...] due to a massive child labour or environmental scandal, then I would say I am longer at peace with myself with that product in the house; George Clooney could walk around butt-naked, I'd have an inner blockage to watching the advertisements. [...] I let myself be seduced to taste the product, if I like it, I will buy it again; if it is worth its price, I happily let myself be sedu..., hm used, hm entrapped. [...] If I like the product, and the price is all right for me, then I will buy [*benutze*] the product. [...] That's the issue" (FG 3, 01:29:39).

Regarding other Nespresso clients, participant A then remarked: "If you observe the people in the shop [i.e., the Nespresso boutique], who buy a piece of the quality of their lives from Nespresso and then boast, in front of other people, about the quality, then these are people who are, for brand experts, the best prey, that's clear. These are the people who only feel they are potent men if they drive a BMW, otherwise not. I, for myself, to some degree refuse to participate in that" (FG 3, 01:31:37). Participant C then said: "But actually, that was Porsche, wasn't it?" To which Participant B replied: "That doesn't matter at all!" Participant A then continued: "As a brand I just took BMW [for an example]. Well, today, for example, an Audi driver pushed us out of the way. They are assh... wonderful cars, only that, unfortunately, the wrong assholes always sit in them. [...] So! That's the issue (FG 3, 01:32:04). Referring to another brand, Coca Cola, he then continued: "If you have a sip of Coca Cola, holding the bottle, then of course you have, somehow, the advertisement in your head, don't you? [...] I am interested in advertising, I love those little films [i.e., commercials], hm, and of course, the advertisement also makes me laugh, I think it is funny. [...] Advertisements stay in your head, that is the way it is. I have the advertisement in my head" (FG 3, 01:32:58). And finally, he said: "If a client is willing to buy a branded product because he [or she] can afford it, it is important that the product is in the client's head. And Nespresso knows how to accomplish that. In the case of Nespresso, that works" (FG 3, 01:34:19).

6.3 *Findings of the socio-empirical analysis*

6.3.1 Quantitative survey

The statistical analysis was carried out with the help of IBM's SPSS 22. Based on the results of the Chi-square test, the results of the statistical analysis of the core questions are presented below.

All the eleven core questions presented in sub-chapter 6.1.1 show a marked difference in the response pattern between Nespresso clients and the control group. In all but one case, the difference is statistically significant at the 5% level[113], in three cases the difference is even highly significant at the 0.1 level of significance, with a reported p-value of ".000".[114] In two cases, a value of just marginally below 0.5 for Cramer's V shows a strong association between predictors and outcome. The pattern of the response, as is shown in this subchapter, does suggest that Nespresso clients relate to the brand of their choice in a way that is, in the statistical sense, distinctly different from the members of the control group.

The fact that an overall sample size of just below 200 yields such significant results indicates little variation *within* the two groups. This, in turn, indicates that Nespresso clients are indeed, in a fairly homogeneous sense, exhibiting a behavioural pattern and an attitude towards their chosen

113 Put in a very casual and informal way, this means that the risk of drawing the wrong conclusion is below 5%.

114 Again, put in a casual and informal way, the p-value is the risk of drawing the wrong conclusion.

brand that contrasts, in a statistically significant way, with the patterns characteristic for non-Nespresso drinkers.

Given the focus of this study, the questions aimed to capture, with respect to Nespresso clients, possibly, a present worldview with the corresponding ethos. Moreover, it was hoped that the patterns in the response would also allow for conclusions as to whether Nespresso clients regard their moods and motivations as "uniquely realistic". Finally, the questions also address the issue of whether or not the making of a Nespresso is a ritual.[115] The results of the statistical tests with respect to the eleven questions addressing these issues are presented below. For the reader's convenience, the objective of each question, outlined in subchapter 6.1.1, are briefly reiterated.

QUESTION 2

Question 2 aims to find out, whether the interviewees have a clear preference with respect to coffee brands, and whether there is a different pattern in the answers given between Nespresso clients and members of the control group. In this way, question 2 aims to address the issue whether Nespresso clients are, compared to members of the control group, more subjected to a certain model of the (coffee) world, resulting in a clear categorisation of coffee brands.

2. Which-one of the following statements do you most agree with? Please mark one (and only one) with a cross.

☐ I prefer my actual coffee brand to other brands. This is the brand of my choice, and I would not like to change brands. In a way, it has become a little bit part of my world.

☐ My current coffee brand tastes good, I like it. However, there certainly are other, good coffee brands. Why not try them sometime?

☐ My actual coffee brand is a random choice. I can't really say I prefer it to other coffee brands.

115 The question whether the drinking/tasting of a Nespresso is a ritual, too, was not addressed by the quantitative survey as Nespresso itself already *explicitly* makes that claim (Nestle-Nespresso n.d.b).

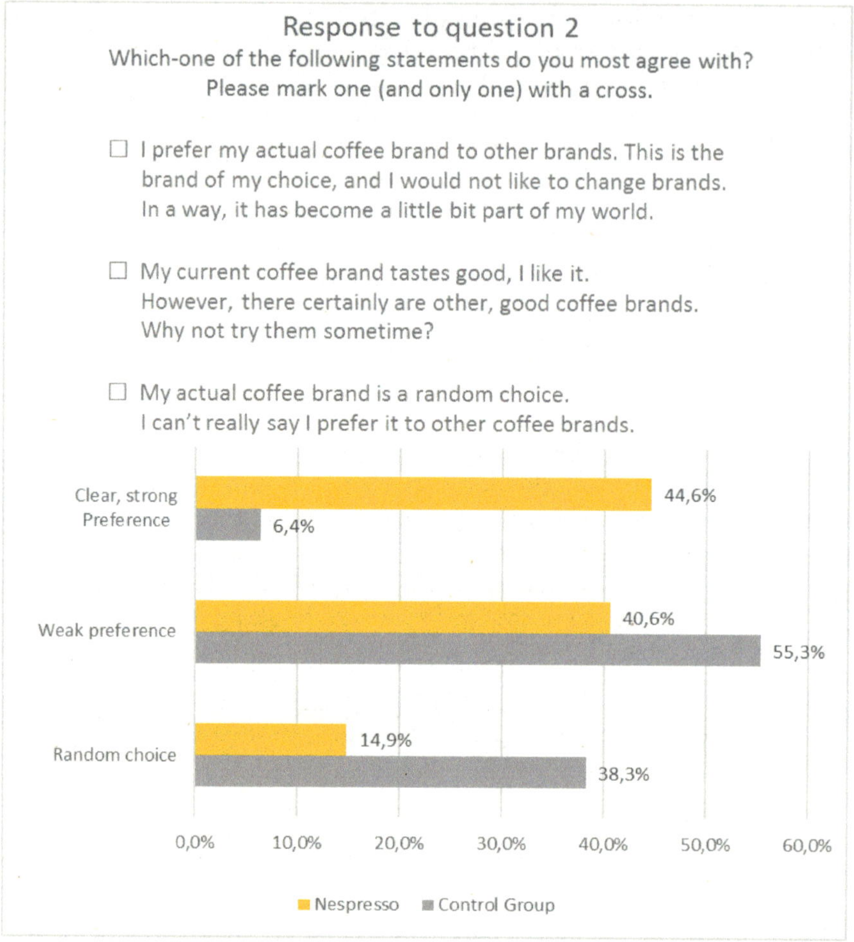

Chart 1: Output 6.1, response to question 2, generated with Excel from an SPSS output

Count

		Group		
		Control group	Nespresso	Total
Response	Random choice	36	15	51
	Weak preference	52	41	93
	Strong preference	6	45	51
Total		94	101	195

Table 2: Output 6.2, frequency count of responses to question 2, generated with SPSS

Chi-Square Tests

	Value	df	Asymp. Sig. (2-sided)
Pearson Chi-Square	39.571[a]	2	.000
Likelihood Ratio	43.718	2	.000
Linear-by-Linear Association	35.158	1	.000
N of Valid Cases	195		

a. 0 cells (0.0%) have expected count less than 5. The minimum expected count is 24.58.

Table 3: Output 6.3, results of Chi-square tests of responses to question 2, generated with SPSS

Symmetric Measures

		Value	Approx. Sig.
Nominal by Nominal	Phi	.450	.000
	Cramer's V	.450	.000
N of Valid Cases		195	

Table 4: Output 6.4, values of measures for the effect size, based on responses to question 2, generated with SPSS

The difference in the response between the two groups is highly significant. Whilst a clear preference represents the mode, that is, the most frequently occurring response, for Nespresso clients, a weak preference is the mode for the control group. With a p-value[116] of practically zero, the null hypothesis, stating that the response patterns are independent of the group association, that is, Nespresso or the control group, can safely be rejected. Therefore, the alternative hypothesis, stating that there is no independence, is validated. Moreover, a Cramer's V with a value of .45, which is furthermore statistically highly significant at the 0.1 percent level of significance, implies that there is indeed a very strong association between brand association and the strength of preference.[117]

QUESTION 3

Question 3 aims to find out, whether Nespresso clients give preference to their chosen brand or not. As they had already declared that they are Nespresso clients, the question wants to establish whether they consider their choice a preference. The interviewees who declared that they are not Nespresso consumers, were asked whether or not they have a preferred coffee brand. This allows us to fathom whether a difference exists between Nespresso clients and those who do not drink Nespresso regarding the existence of an established preference. A preference then not only implies a categorisation of the coffee world, it also implies an order, with the preference ranking first.

3. Is Nespresso your preferred coffee brand?

☐ yes ☐ no

This question, in the questionnaire for the control group, reads as follows:

3. Do you have a preferred coffee brand?

116 In the output tables, the p-value is labelled "Sig.".

117 Regarding the two tables "Chi-Square Tests" and "Symmetric Measures", the "Continuity Correction", the "Likelihood Ratio", the "Fisher's Exact Test", and the "Linear-by-Linear Association" all refer to statistical methods that are not used in this study.

Again, it is important to remember that the control group contains participants who also have a preferred brand, and those who do not. What they have in common is that they do not consider themselves Nespresso clients. It is not the aim of the socio-empirical survey to establish, whether a difference exists in the strength of brand affiliation between Nespresso clients and the sub-group of non-Nespresso drinkers who also have a clear brand affiliation. Instead, the aim is to establish, whether or not Nespresso drinkers, compared to non-Nespresso drinkers, are more or less likely to have a preference, that is, to respond in ways that can be explained by, and are in accordance with the Geertzian definition of religion.

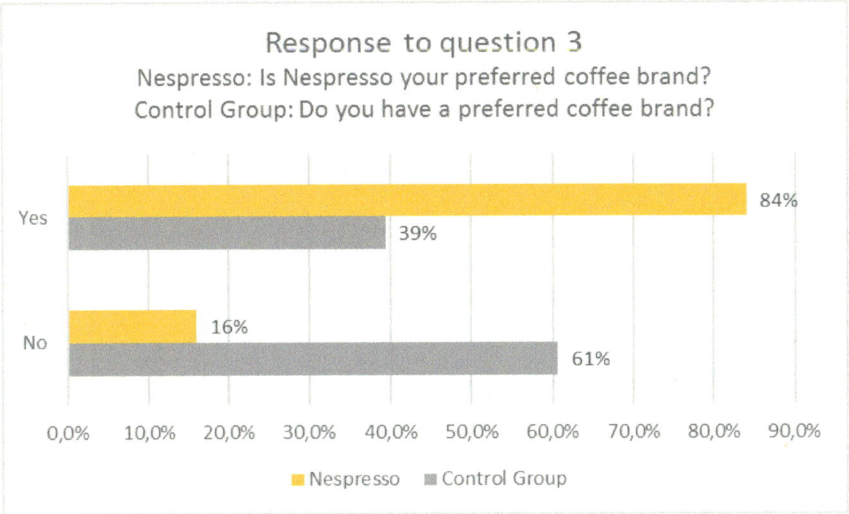

Chart 2: Output 6.5, response to question 3, generated with Excel from an SPSS output

Count

		Group		Total
		Control group	Nespresso	
Response	No	57	16	73
	Yes	37	84	121
Total		94	100	194

Table 5: Output 6.6, frequency count of responses to question 3, generated with SPSS

Chi-Square Tests

	Value	df	Asymp. Sig. (2-sided)	Exact Sig. (2-sided)	Exact Sig. (1-sided)
Pearson Chi-Square	41.137[a]	1	.000		
Continuity Correction[b]	39.257	1	.000		
Likelihood Ratio	42.983	1	.000		
Fisher's Exact Test				.000	.000
Linear-by-Linear Association	40.925	1	.000		
N of Valid Cases	194				

a. 0 cells (0.0%) have expected count less than 5. The minimum expected count is 35.37.

b. Computed only for a 2x2 table

Table 6: Output 6.7, results of Chi-square tests of responses to question 3, generated with SPSS

Symmetric Measures

		Value	Approx. Sig.
Nominal by Nominal	Phi	.460	.000
	Cramer's V	.460	.000
N of Valid Cases		194	

Table 7: Output 6.8, values of measures for the effect size, based on responses to question 3, generated with SPSS

Again, the difference in the response between the two groups is highly significant. With a p-value[118] of practically zero, the null hypothesis, stating that the response patterns are independent of interviewee's category, that is, Nespresso client or member of the control group, can safely be rejected. Therefore, the alternative hypothesis, stating that there is no independence, is validated. Moreover, the Phi coefficient with a value of .46, which is also statistically highly significant at the 0.1 percent level of significance, implies that there is indeed a fairly large effect size, that is, a rather strong association between the two categories of respondents (i.e., Nespresso clients and members of the control group) on one hand, and the answer given on the other.[119]

As can be seen in the above table, which is labelled "count", given a client is a Nespresso consumer, the odds of responding with "Yes" are 84 to 16, or 5.25. Instead, given a client belongs to the control group, the odds in favour of a "Yes" are only 37 to 57, or 0.649. If 5.25 is divided by 0.649, the result yields the so-called "odds-ratio". In this case, the odds ratio is 8.088, which means that the odds of a "Yes" are 8.1 times higher if the consumer is a Nespresso client.

QUESTION 10

Question 10 aims to find out, whether Nespresso clients consider, unlike members of the control group, their brand a part of a specific way of life. A way of life describes how people see "things", it gives indications with respect to specific value catalogues, it even indicates certain propensities to

118 Please see footnote 116 above.
119 Please see footnote 117 above.

act in a certain way. And it also differentiates between people, being a fertile ground for identity formation.

Question 10 then addresses such a potential cultural charge with respect to coffee brands:

10.	Do you believe, with the wink of an eye, that in a way, Nespresso is part of a way of life? ☐ yes ☐ no

This question, in the questionnaire for the control group, reads as follows:

10.	Do you believe, with the wink of an eye, that in a way, the coffee brand of your choice is part of a way of life?

Out of 101 Nespresso clients, 63, or 62 percent, said "Yes". Only 38 percent answered with a "No". Out of the 96 members of the control group, only 23, or 24 percent, said "Yes". 73, or 76 percent, answered with a "No" to that question. Naturally, the answer is given with a "wink of an eye". This wink of an eye, intending to add some humour to the question, making its cultural dimension appear less daunting.

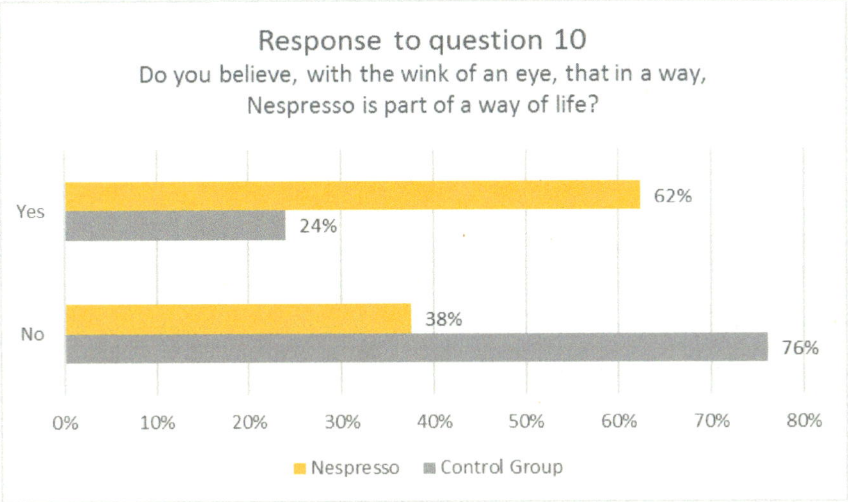

Chart 3: Output 6.9, response to question 10, generated with Excel from an SPSS output

Count

		Group		
		Control group	Nespresso	Total
Response	No	73	38	111
	Yes	23	63	86
Total		96	101	197

Table 8: Output 6.10, frequency count of responses to question 10, generated with SPSS

Chi-Square Tests

	Value	df	Asymp. Sig. (2-sided)	Exact Sig. (2-sided)	Exact Sig. (1-sided)
Pearson Chi-Square	29.533[a]	1	.000		
Continuity Correction[b]	27.992	1	.000		
Likelihood Ratio	30.441	1	.000		
Fisher's Exact Test				.000	.000
Linear-by-Linear Association	29.383	1	.000		
N of Valid Cases	197				

a. 0 cells (0.0%) have expected count less than 5. The minimum expected count is 41.91.

b. Computed only for a 2x2 table

Table 9: Output 6.11, results of Chi-square tests of responses to question 10, generated with SPSS

Symmetric Measures

		Value	Approx. Sig.
Nominal by Nominal	Phi	.387	.000
	Cramer's V	.387	.000
N of Valid Cases		197	

Table 10: Output 6.12, values of measures for the effect size, based on responses to question 10, generated with SPSS

The difference in the response between the two groups is highly significant. With a p-value of practically zero, the null hypothesis, stating that the response patterns are independent of an interviewee's category, that is, a Nespresso client or a member of the control group, can safely be rejected. Therefore, the alternative hypothesis, stating that there is no independence, is validated. Moreover, the Phi coefficient with a value of .387 is statistically highly significant, implying that there is indeed a fairly strong association.

Finally, for question 10, the odds ratio is 5.26, which means that the odds of a "Yes" are 5.26 times higher if the consumer is a Nespresso client.

QUESTION 15

Question 15 is preparing the interviewee for question 16, which addresses whether the making of a Nespresso is perceived as a ritual or not. Question 15 does not yet go so far as to refer to the making of a Nespresso as a special moment.

15. Imagine you are preparing, for yourself, the Nespresso of your choice. You have the peace of mind, and the time to deeply enjoy this moment.

Is this moment a little bit special, more than just the simple making of a coffee?

☐ yes, most definitely so	☐ not really
☐ yes, in a way	☐ no, definitely not

As in question 10, the equivalent question in the questionnaire for the control group is identical, only that instead of "Nespresso of your choice", meaning the chosen Nespresso flavour, it says "your coffee". As the subsequent questions that are asked in the control group questionnaire are all identical to the questions asked in the Nespresso questionnaire, they will no longer be separately listed.

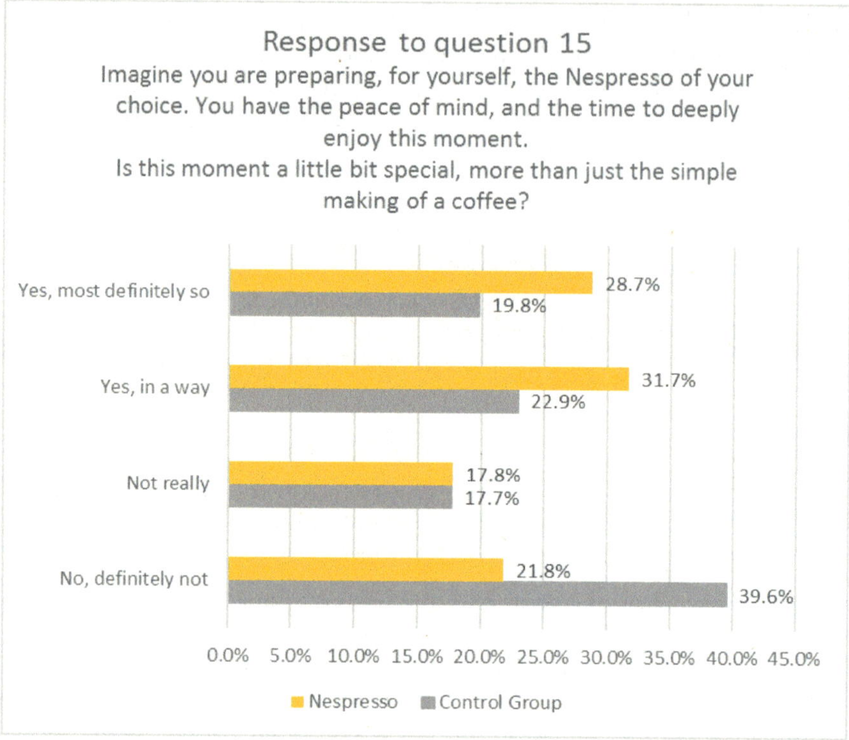

Chart 4: Output 6.13, response to question 15, generated with Excel from an SPSS output

Count

		Group		
		Control group	Nespresso	Total
Response	Definitely not	38	22	60
	Not really	17	18	35
	Yes, in a way	22	32	54
	Yes, most definitely so	19	29	48
Total		96	101	197

Table 11: Output 6.14, frequency count of responses to question 15, generated with SPSS

Chi-Square Tests

	Value	df	Asymp. Sig. (2-sided)
Pearson Chi-Square	8.109[a]	3	.044
Likelihood Ratio	8.182	3	.042
Linear-by-Linear Association	7.183	1	.007
N of Valid Cases	197		

a. 0 cells (0.0%) have expected count less than 5. The minimum expected count is 17.06.

Table 12: Output 6.15, results of Chi-square tests of responses to question 15, generated with SPSS

Symmetric Measures

		Value	Approx. Sig.
Nominal by Nominal	Phi	.203	.044
	Cramer's V	.203	.044
N of Valid Cases		197	

Table 13: Output 6.16, values of measures for the effect size, based on responses to question 15, generated with SPSS

The pattern of the responses to question 15 shows that there is a statistically significant (at the 5 percent level with a p-value of 4.4 percent) difference between Nespresso clients and the control group. The data in the count-table indicates that Nespresso clients are more likely than members of the control group to see the making of the coffee as a special moment with connotations that go beyond the simple making of a coffee. Only 21.8 percent of all Nespresso clients reject the idea that the making of a cup of coffee is a special moment, more than just the simple making of a coffee. Instead, in the case of the control group, 39.6 percent, almost twice as many, reject that idea. Finally, the value of Cramer's V (0.203) shows that the size of the above-described effect is a bit above medium.

QUESTION 16

Question 16 addresses the making of a coffee and whether it is seen as a ritual. The reader will recall that Nestle-Nespresso itself calls the tasting of a Nespresso a ritual (Nestle-Nespresso, n.d.b). A claim that is, by the way, confirmed by various participants of the focus groups. This question now aims to fathom whether or not the view that the making of a coffee is itself a ritual is spread evenly across the two groups (Nespresso clients and the control group).

16. Would you agree to the following statement?

"The making of my coffee is a pleasure in itself, I enjoy it almost as much as the coffee itself. In a special way, it has become a little ritual."

- ☐ yes, most definitely so
- ☐ yes, in a way
- ☐ not really
- ☐ no, definitely not

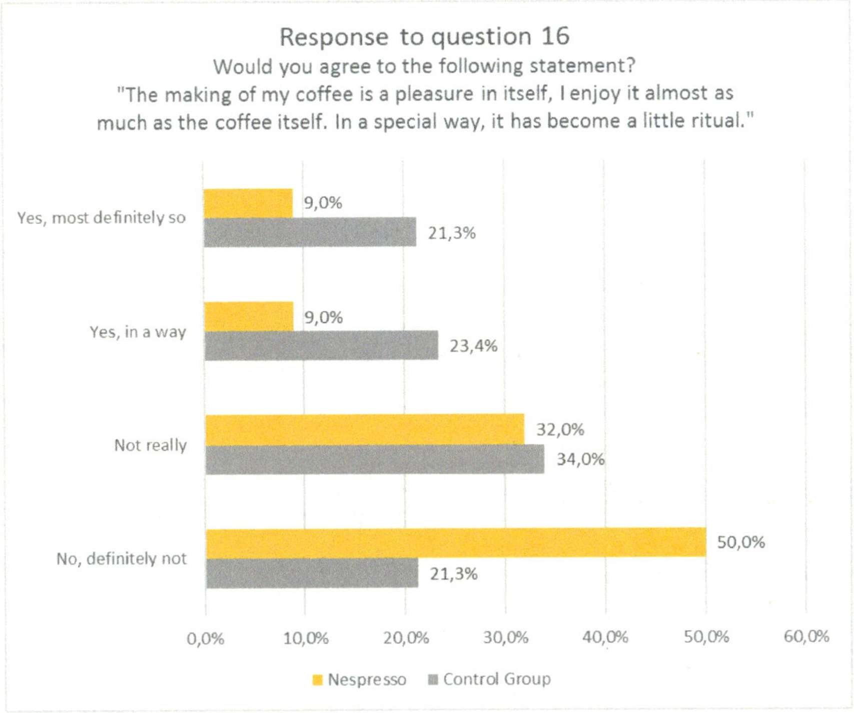

Chart 5: Output 6.17, response to question 16, generated with Excel from an SPSS output

Count

		Group		
		Control group	Nespresso	Total
Response	No	42	30	72
	Not really	16	22	38
	Yes, in a way	23	19	42
	Yes, most definitely so	15	30	45
Total		96	101	197

Table 14: Output 6.18, frequency count of responses to question 16, generated with SPSS

Chi-Square Tests

	Value	df	Asymp. Sig. (2-sided)
Pearson Chi-Square	8.207[a]	3	.042
Likelihood Ratio	8.312	3	.040
Linear-by-Linear Association	4.804	1	.028
N of Valid Cases	197		

a. 0 cells (0.0%) have expected count less than 5. The minimum expected count is 18.52.

Table 15 : Output 6.19, results of Chi-square tests of responses to question 16, generated with SPSS

Symmetric Measures

		Value	Approx. Sig.
Nominal by Nominal	Phi	.204	.042
	Cramer's V	.204	.042
N of Valid Cases		197	

Table 16: Output 6.20, values of measures for the effect size, based on responses to question 16, generated with SPSS

Compared to the control group, the percentage of group members that sees in the making of a coffee a ritual is nearly twice as high for the Nespresso group (29.7 percent for the Nespresso group and 15.6 percent for the control group). Moreover, the percentage of group members that clearly do not connote the making of a coffee with a ritual is considerably higher for the control group than for the Nespresso group (29.7 percent for the Nespresso group and 43.8 percent for the control group). Also noteworthy is the fact that the number of members of the control group that do not see a ritual in the making of a coffee is nearly three times higher than the number of members who see in it a ritual, 42 as compared to 15. Within the Nespresso group instead, an equal number of members, 30, see in the making of Nespresso a ritual as do not. Whilst the control group has a clear mode, rejecting the idea of a ritual, the Nespresso group is bimodal.

The results, that is, the chi-square statistic as well as Cramer's V are both statistically significant at the 5 percent level (with a p-value of 4.2 percent) and, with a Cramer's V of 0.204, show an effect size slightly above medium.

QUESTION 17

Question 17, addressing, head-on, the consumer's identity, establishes a link between the choice of brand and consumer identity. The pattern of the given answers is somewhat similar to question 16, but statistically weaker and, with a p-value of 5.9 percent, they are not significant at the 5 percent level of significance.

17. Do you believe, with the wink of an eye, that people who drink Nespresso are a little bit more special than other people?

☐ yes, most definitely so	☐ not really
☐ yes, in a way	☐ no, definitely not

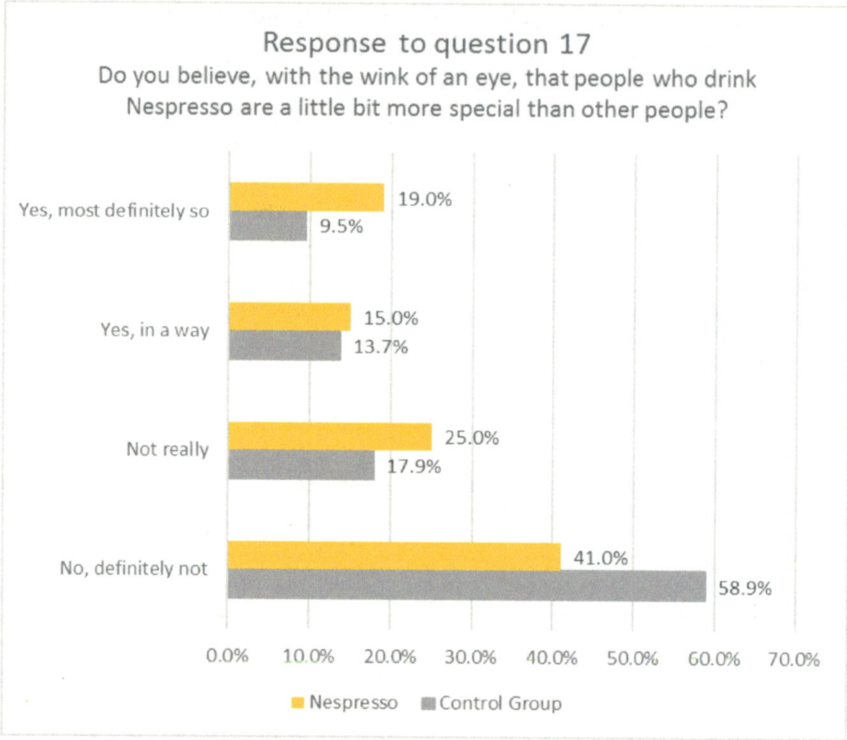

Chart 6: Output 6.21, response to question 17, generated with Excel from an SPSS output

Count

		Group		Total
		control group	Nespresso	
Response	No	56	41	97
	Not really	17	25	42
	Yes, in a way	13	15	28
	Yes most definitely so	9	19	28
Total		95	100	195

Table 17: Output 6.22, frequency count of responses to question 17, generated with SPSS

Chi-Square Tests

	Value	df	Asymp. Sig. (2-sided)
Pearson Chi-Square	7.434[a]	3	.059
Likelihood Ratio	7.528	3	.057
Linear-by-Linear Association	5.876	1	.015
N of Valid Cases	195		

a. 0 cells (0.0%) have expected count less than 5. The minimum expected count is 13.64.

Table 18: Output 6.23, results of Chi-square tests of responses to question 17, generated with SPSS

Symmetric Measures

		Value	Approx. Sig.
Nominal by Nominal	Phi	.195	.059
	Cramer's V	.195	.059
N of Valid Cases		195	

Table 19: Output 6.24, values of measures for the effect size, based on responses to question 17, generated with SPSS

The question might have seemed far-fetched to most interviewees: an absolute majority of the members of the control group, 58.9 percent and, in the case of the Nespresso group, a relative majority of 41 percent answered with a clear "No". Only 9.5 percent of the control group, the lowest frequency of all, answered with a clear "Yes". In the Nespresso group instead, 19 percent, twice as many, answered with a clear "Yes". Therefore, the data gives some indication that comparatively more Nespresso clients consider themselves "more special" than other people. Whether such feeling is rooted in the fact that they are Nespresso drinkers, or whether they are Nespresso drinkers because they consider themselves "more special", or whether there is no causal connection between the two characteristics at all, is left open.

With a p-value of 5.9 percent, the null hypothesis, stating that the affiliation of the interviewees (Nespresso drinker or member of the control group) and the patterns of the answers given are independent of one another, cannot be falsified at the 5 percent level of significance. Still, the results are an indication that members of the Nespresso group have a higher likelihood of answering with a "Yes".[120] The strength of that association with a Cramer's V of 0.195, though not statistically significant at the 5 percent level (p-value: 5.9 percent), is slightly above medium.

QUESTION 25

Question 25 addresses both, the model of the world as "right choice", and implies a contingent "wrong choice". This dichotomy provides a model of the coffee world, by providing a simple, but easy-to-grasp categorisation of the coffee world. Moreover, the question also addresses the model for the world as "choice" implies action and consumption. Finally, the question through the implied categorisation of the coffee world also alludes to the inside-outside dichotomy, which is mirrored in Nespresso's characteristic as a club-good.

25. Is Nespresso the "right choice"?

- ☐ yes, always the right choice
- ☐ yes, most of the time the right choice
- ☐ yes, sometimes the right choice
- ☐ no, it isn't

120 Sir Ronald Fisher stated that there is no reason why the 5 percent or the 1 percent level of significance should be the only meaningful levels of significance. For purely practical reasons, publishers began to only report the values of the z-, Chi-square, and t-statistic at the 5 percent and 1 percent levels. Therefore, it became customary to perform hypothesis tests at those levels of significance. However, with the help of the p-value, results that are, strictly speaking, not statistically significant at the 5 percent level of significance, are also included in the analyses.

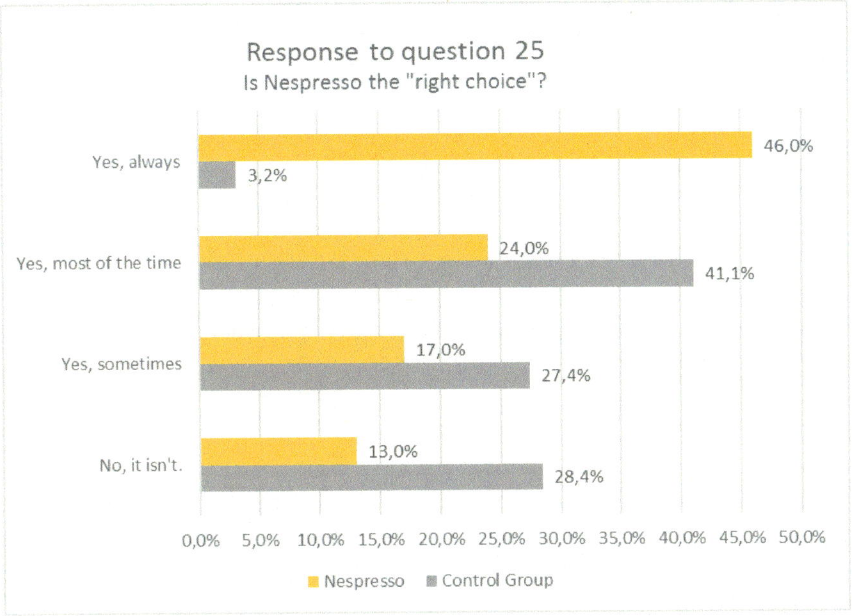

Chart 7: Output 6.25, response to question 25, generated with Excel from an SPSS output

Count

		Group		Total
		Control group	Nespresso	
Response	No, it isn't	27	13	40
	Yes, sometimes	26	17	43
	Yes, most of the time	39	24	63
	Yes, alway the right choice	3	46	49
Total		95	100	195

Table 20 : Output 6.26, frequency count of responses to question 25, generated with SPSS

Chi-Square Tests

	Value	df	Asymp. Sig. (2-sided)
Pearson Chi-Square	47.993[a]	3	.000
Likelihood Ratio	55.737	3	.000
Linear-by-Linear Association	29.820	1	.000
N of Valid Cases	195		

a. 0 cells (0.0%) have expected count less than 5. The minimum expected count is 19.49.

Table 21 : Output 6.27, results of Chi-square tests of responses to question 25, generated with SPSS

Symmetric Measures

		Value	Approx. Sig.
Nominal by Nominal	Phi	.496	.000
	Cramer's V	.496	.000
N of Valid Cases		195	

Table 22: Output 6.28, values of measures for the effect size, based on responses to question 25, generated with SPSS

Regarding question 25, the results of the Chi-square test are highly significant. The null hypothesis of no association between groups and types of answers can be rejected with a p-value of practically zero, that is, the remaining risk that the rejection of the null hypothesis is a mistake, is, for practical purposes, zero. For nearly half of the members of the Nespresso group, for 46 percent, Nespresso is always the "right choice". The corresponding figure for the control group is 3.2 percent. In the control group instead, 41.1 percent say that their brand is "most of the time" the right choice. Furthermore, 28.4 percent of the control group say that their brand is not always the "right choice", compared to 13 percent in the Nespresso group.

The results of the analysis show an exceptional strength of the association between groups and types of answers. According to statistical theory, a Cramer's V of 0.29 shows a very large effect size, implying a very strong association between group affiliation and the type of answers given. In the case of question 25, Cramer's V has a value of 0.496 and a corresponding p-value of practically zero.

QUESTION 26

Question 26 is a continuation and a deepening of the issues addressed in question 25. It aims to check whether consumers, at times, might wish to break through the ethos and the categories established by their brands.

> 26. Are there other coffee brands, which you prefer to Nespresso sometimes?
>
> ☐ yes ☐ no

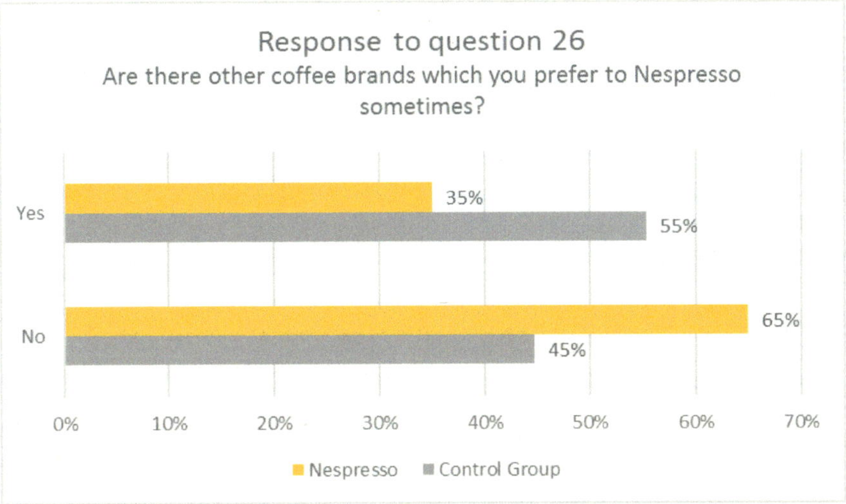

Chart 8: Output 6.29, response to question 26, generated with Excel from an SPSS output

Count

		Group		
		Control group	Nespresso	Total
Response	No	42	65	107
	Yes	52	35	87
Total		94	100	194

Table 23: Output 6.30, frequency count of responses to question 26, generated with SPSS

Chi-Square Tests

	Value	df	Asymp. Sig. (2-sided)	Exact Sig. (2-sided)	Exact Sig. (1-sided)
Pearson Chi-Square	8.088[a]	1	.004		
Continuity Correction[b]	7.287	1	.007		
Likelihood Ratio	8.140	1	.004		
Fisher's Exact Test				.006	.003
Linear-by-Linear Association	8.046	1	.005		
N of Valid Cases	194				

a. 0 cells (.0%) have expected count less than 5. The minimum expected count is 42.15.

b. Computed only for a 2x2 table

Table 24: Output 6.31, results of Chi-square tests of responses to question 26, generated with SPSS

Symmetric Measures

		Value	Approx. Sig.
Nominal by Nominal	Phi	-.204	.004
	Cramer's V	.204	.004
N of Valid Cases		194	

Table 25: Output 6.32, values of measures for the effect size, based on responses to question 26, generated with SPSS

The results are significant at the 1 percent level of significance with a p-value of 0.004 and show an effect size of a magnitude that lies between small and medium. The negative sign in front of the Phi coefficient mirrors the fact, that the respective structure of the answers given by the members of the two groups are opposite to one another: for the Nespresso group, the "No" is the answer that is given more often, whereas for the control group, it is the "Yes". Clearly, according to the data, if someone belongs to the Nespresso group, he or she is statistically more likely than a member of the control group to give "No" for an answer, testifying that he or she does not prefer, sometimes, other brands to Nespresso. The odds ratio is 2.299, indicating that a member of the Nespresso group is about 2.3 times more likely to answer question 26 with a "No".

QUESTION 27

The deepening of the issues connected to the model of and for the world is continued in question 27, testing whether the interviewee is tinkering with the idea of replacing Nespresso with another brand soon.

27. Are you presently presuming you could be replacing Nespresso with another coffee brand soon?

☐ yes, most definitely so ☐ not really

☐ yes, in a way ☐ no, definitely not

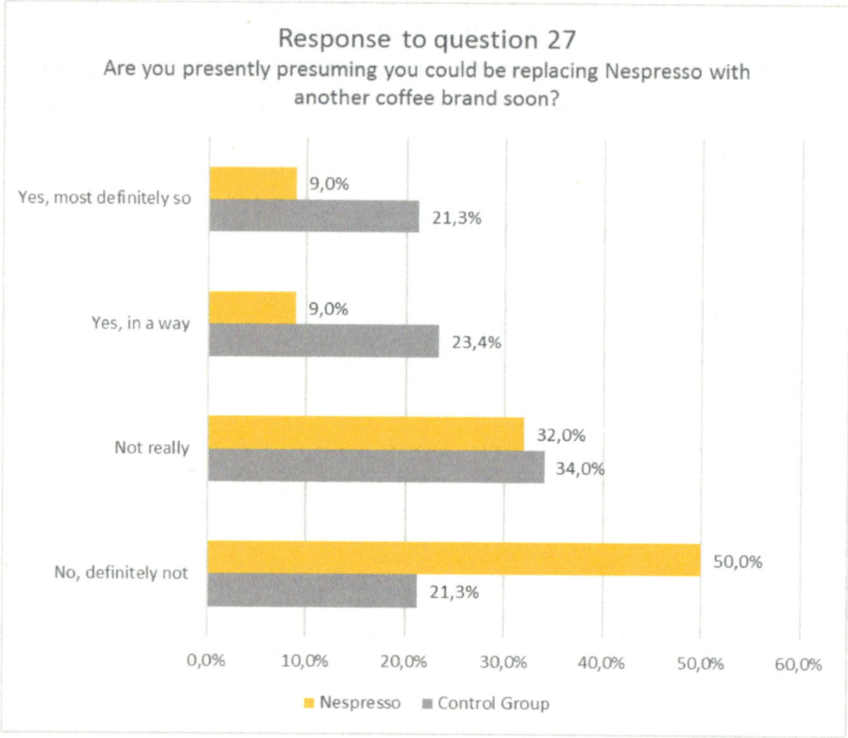

Chart 9: Output 6.33, response to question 27, generated with Excel from an SPSS output

Count

		Group		Total
		Control group	Nespresso	
Response	No, definitely not	20	50	70
	Not really	32	32	64
	Yes, in a way	22	9	31
	Yes, most definitely so	20	9	29
Total		94	100	194

Table 26: Output 6.34, frequency count of responses to question 27, generated with SPSS

Chi-Square Tests

	Value	df	Asymp. Sig. (2-sided)
Pearson Chi-Square	22.317[a]	3	.000
Likelihood Ratio	23.000	3	.000
Linear-by-Linear Association	19.911	1	.000
N of Valid Cases	194		

a. 0 cells (.0%) have expected count less than 5. The minimum expected count is 14.05.

Table 27 : Output 6.35, results of Chi-square tests of responses to question 27, generated with SPSS

Symmetric Measures

		Value	Approx. Sig.
Nominal by Nominal	Phi	.339	.000
	Cramer's V	.339	.000
N of Valid Cases		194	

Table 28: Output 6.36, values of measures for the effect size, based on responses to question 27, generated with SPSS

The results are highly significant with a p-value of practically zero. The value of Cramer's V, 0.339 shows a very large effect size indicating, that there is a very strong association between groups and types of answers.

In the case of the Nespresso group, 50 percent of the participants say that they are definitely not presuming, now, to replace Nespresso with another brand soon. That answer also is the mode, the most frequently given answer. For the control group, instead, the most frequently given answer is "not really". Only 21.3 percent of all members of the control group give "no, definitely not" as an answer. What is noteworthy in the pattern of the answers given is that, for the control group, frequencies are more or less evenly spread across all answers with the mode being moderately above the other possible answers, whereas for the Nespresso group, the mode really sticks out, it has by far the highest frequency, that is, clearly the largest number of participants who chose "no, definitely not" for an answer.

QUESTION 30

Question 30 aims to provide the categorisation of the coffee world, that is, the model of the world and the ethos, the model for the world, with a substantiation rooted in a personal experience of pleasure and gusto, thereby also providing a fundament supporting the perception of moods and motivations as uniquely realistic.

30. Could you imagine definitely replacing Nespresso with another coffee and to immerse yourself in the same experience of pleasure and gusto as before?

☐ yes ☐ no

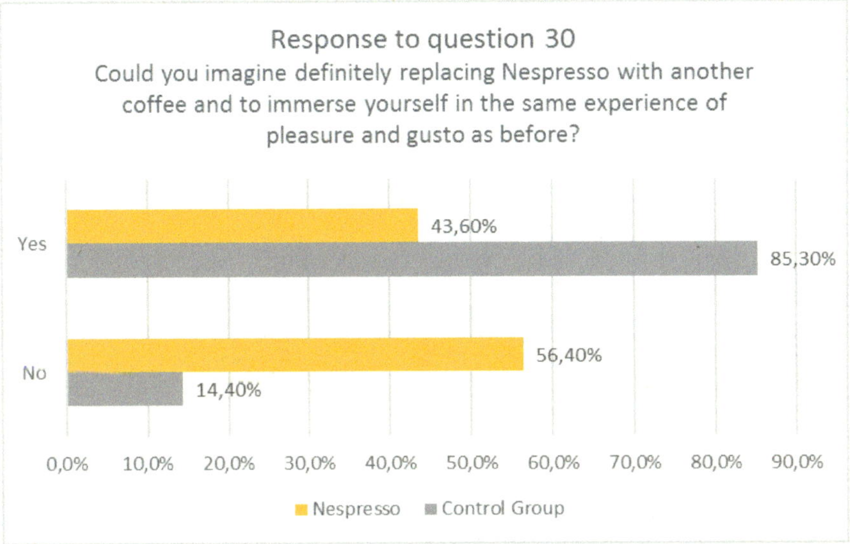

Chart 10: Output 6.37, response to question 30, generated with Excel from an SPSS output

Count

		Group		
		Control group	Nespresso	Total
Response	No	14	57	71
	Yes	81	44	125
Total		95	101	196

Table 29: Output 6.38, frequency count of responses to question 30, generated with SPSS

Chi-Square Tests

	Value	df	Asymp. Sig. (2-sided)	Exact Sig. (2-sided)	Exact Sig. (1-sided)
Pearson Chi-Square	36.845[a]	1	.000		
Continuity Correction[b]	35.062	1	.000		
Likelihood Ratio	38.862	1	.000		
Fisher's Exact Test				.000	.000
Linear-by-Linear Association	36.657	1	.000		
N of Valid Cases	196				

a. 0 cells (0.0%) have expected count less than 5. The minimum expected count is 34.41.

b. Computed only for a 2x2 table

Table 30: Output 6.39, results of Chi-square tests of responses to question 30, generated with SPSS

Symmetric Measures

		Value	Approx. Sig.
Nominal by Nominal	Phi	-.434	.000
	Cramer's V	.434	.000
N of Valid Cases		196	

Table 31: Output 6.40, values of measures for the effect size, based on responses to question 30, generated with SPSS

The results are, again, statistically highly significant, and indicate a fairly strong association between brand affiliation and the answers given. Both, the Chi-square statistic and Phi are significant at the 0.001 percent level, with a p-value of close to zero. Given that a Phi value of 0.5 indicates a large, and a value of 0.3 a medium effect size, the reported value of -0.434 can be read as a fairly large effect size. The negative sign is, for the purpose of the identification of the effect size's magnitude, ignored. The negative sign only indicates that, whilst most members of the Nespresso group answered with a "Yes", most members of the control group answered with a "No" instead. The odds ratio has a value of 7.495, a very high value. This indicates that the likelihood that a Nespresso client can imagine definitely replacing Nespresso with another coffee and to immerse themselves in the same experience of pleasure and gusto as before is about 7.5 times lower than for a member of the control group.

QUESTION 31

Question 31 addresses the models of and for the world as well as the accompanying moods. It aims to test whether the ethos has become firmly established in the Nespresso consumer's life.

31. Has Nespresso become a pleasant constant in your life?

☐ Yes, it has.	☐ well, not really
☐ well, in a way	☐ no, definitely not

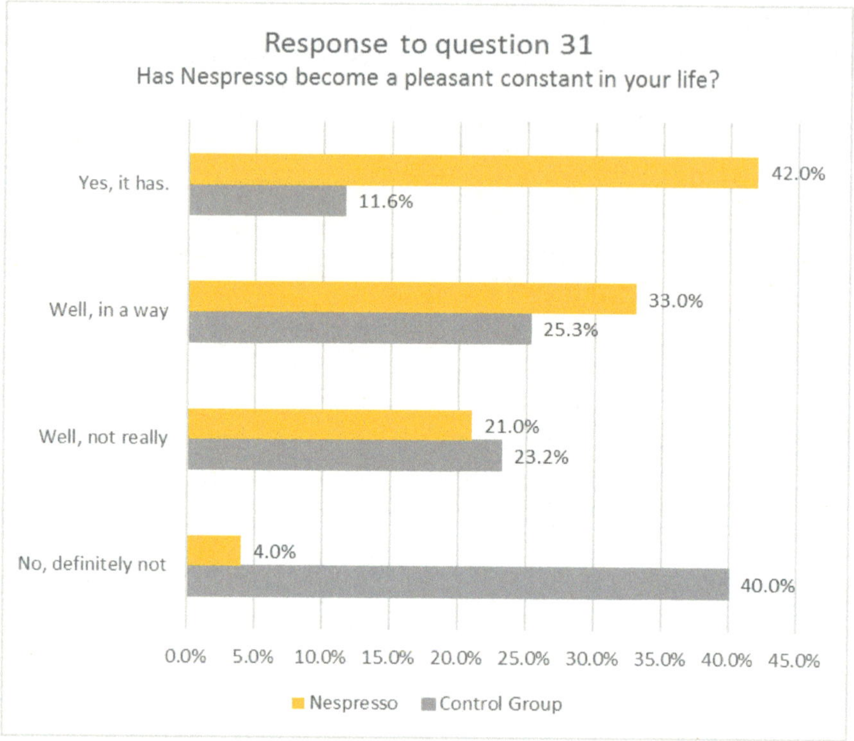

Chart 11: Output 6.41, response to question 31, generated with Excel from an SPSS output

Count

		Group		Total
		Controlgroup	Nespresso	
Response	No, definitely not	38	4	42
	Well, not really	22	21	43
	Well, in a way	24	33	57
	Yes, it has	11	42	53
Total		95	100	195

Table 32: Output 6.42, frequency count of responses to question 31, generated with SPSS

Chi-Square Tests

	Value	df	Asymp. Sig. (2-sided)
Pearson Chi-Square	47.003[a]	3	.000
Likelihood Ratio	52.470	3	.000
Linear-by-Linear Association	43.815	1	.000
N of Valid Cases	195		

a. 0 cells (0.0%) have expected count less than 5. The minimum expected count is 20.46.

Table 33: Output 6.43, results of Chi-square tests of responses to question 31, generated with SPSS

Symmetric Measures

		Value	Approx. Sig.
Nominal by Nominal	Phi	.491	.000
	Cramer's V	.491	.000
N of Valid Cases		195	

Table 34: Output 6.44, values of measures for the effect size, based on responses to question 31, generated with SPSS

The final question aiming to address whether or not the behaviour of Nespresso clients allows for inferences regarding a model of and for the world delivers statistically very significant results. Both, Pearson's Chi-square statistic as well as the Phi-coefficient are both statistically significant at the 0.1 percent level, with a p-value of close to zero. Moreover, the response patterns of both groups have a clear mode. A total of 42 percent of all members of the Nespresso group confirm that Nespresso has become a pleasant constant in their lives, and only 4 percent, the lowest frequency of all possible answers, testify that this is definitely not so. The pattern for the control group shows the exact opposite: 40 percent of the members of the control group definitely refuse the idea that their chosen brand has become a pleasant constant in their lives, and only 11 percent clearly agree to it. Clearly, as confirmed by a Cramer's V of 0.491, there is a strong association between groups on one hand, and the pattern of the given answers on the other. In other words, a member of the control group is almost as likely to reject the idea of the pleasant constant, as a member of the Nespresso group is likely to embrace it. For the members of the Nespresso group, a firm ethos is arrived at, for the members of the control group, however, this is not the case.

6.3.2 Qualitative survey

Regarding Nespresso's ranking against all other alternatives (other coffee brands), all nine participants of the three focus groups testified that Nespresso clearly, and without any doubt, comes first. One participant said the reason for that is due to Nespresso's convenience because of its system's clean easy handling and its superior taste. Four participants said the reason is Nespresso's superior taste only, three said it is because of Nespresso's immaculate technical functionality only, and finally, the participant who had said that for him Nespresso has become a compulsion, did not specify a reason.

Six out of the nine participants said, that Nespresso is always their first and only choice. The three exceptions were the following: One participant said that she does not yet have enough money to always drink Nespresso, yet, as soon as she does, she would only drink Nespresso, too. Another participant said that, besides not having enough money to always drink Nespresso[121], he only drinks Nespresso in special moments of inner focus, because he feels, he is only sufficiently centred, in those moments, so to be receptive to Nespresso's superior taste. The third participant who does not always exclusively drink Nespresso said it was for purely financial reasons only.[122]

Regarding the commercials, seven of the nine participants testified that their choice/the feeling they need a Nespresso, and/or their desire for Nespresso is connected to the commercials and/or Nespresso's entire marketing campaign. Seven of the nine participants also testified that Nespresso succeeded in the creation of a model, a (coffee) world of its own, where all is well. Moreover, eight of the nine the participants said that, with Nespresso, they felt they are in good hands, that they had, so to speak, found a home, or that Nespresso had obtained a place in their lives. Furthermore, for seven participants, an explicit connection exists between Nespresso and being in a good mood. Three participants testified that their good mood was connected to thc consumption of a Nespresso; three linked their good mood to the commercials, which they all liked, and the consumption of

121 He did not indicate that he expected his financial condition to improve.
122 He also did not indicate that he expected his financial condition to improve.

Nespresso; one participant testified, his good mood was connected to the commercials, which he considers very witty.
In one of the focus groups, the idea that Nespresso could go out of business was not addressed. In the two other groups, four out of six participants said that if Nespresso went out of business, it would leave a very big gap behind, one participant testified that she would even give up drinking coffee altogether. Across all three focus groups, for seven of the nine participants, Nespresso represents their model regarding coffee consumption. All of the nine participants testified that, in a general way, in their evaluation, and choice of coffee brands, Nespresso is given priority.

Eight of the nine participants made, in some way or another, a reference to Nespresso's comparatively high unit price. They all also said that Nespresso is worth the money. Five said that they enjoy that they can choose from various different flavours, one participant said that he was impressed with Nespresso's presence in other countries (i.e., Thailand).

Five participants made a clear reference to Nespresso's aesthetic surface, that is the conceived beauty regarding Nespresso and all the aspects/gadgets of the related marketing campaign. The cups were named, the interior of the Nespresso boutiques, even the apparent beauty of the shop assistants.

Regarding their future consumption, all participants said they would continue to drink Nespresso. More specifically, two participants made their pledge to consume Nespresso in the future dependent on the condition that Nespresso manages to keep up its quality. Two other participants testified that they had become dependent on Nespresso, another one said that now that there is Nespresso, there is no way of going back to another brand. Along the same lines, seven of the nine participants said that they never test alternatives. Only the two men who do not expect their income to increase testified that they were occasionally testing other brands, not to replace Nespresso, but to at least have acceptable coffee when they cannot, for financial reasons, allow themselves to have a Nespresso. One participant also said, that in her case an exception exists: When she is on holiday in Italy. On holidays to other countries she already has taken a Nespresso machine with her, but not to Italy: in Italy she drinks Italian coffee, not Nespresso, but only there, nowhere else.

In a concluding comment, one participant made a generalised statement regarding consumers of branded products saying that the self-image they have depends on the brands they consume, that is, they can only see themselves in a certain light if they buy a certain corresponding branded product. The choice of brand then, he said, depends on advertising: only if the advertisement has made it to the potential consumers' mind and stays there, in his, or her head, will a certain brand be chosen.

6.4 Discussion of the findings

Viewers, in their fabula construction, look for logical cues following the laws of cause and effect. The representation of the commercials' meaning by the syuzhet forces viewers to revise their prototype and default schemata in order to uphold the narrative's logic. Thereby, besides being informed of a specific behaviour, they create, with respect to the advertised commodity, a model of the world.

The commercials' syuzhet and style of representation, the commercials' narration, which put, alongside Nespresso, the exterior beauty of perfected form to the foreground, have strong implications regarding the truthfulness of the encoded message, once decoded by the viewer. As was shown by an exploratory study examining how Nespresso consumers form their judgement regarding the coffee's quality (Ulrich, 2017), a strong link exists between aesthetic beauty and truth. With respect to fabula construction, this has strong implications: The seeming truthfulness of the fabula possibly accrues from the syuzhet's aesthetic beauty. This style of representation encourages a fabula construction which makes the qualities attributed to Nespresso seem to be of an ontological nature. Furthermore, as will be discussed below, it makes the viewer's resulting moods and motivations seem "uniquely realistic", the seemingly only moods and motivations that make sense considering Nespresso's supremacy: Through the beauty of Nespresso's aesthetic representation, the seemingly ontological nature of the qualities attributed to Nespresso appears to be evident.

The ontological nature of Nespresso's qualities, as perceived by the interviewees, is also illustrated by another peculiar circumstance. Repeatedly, some members of the three focus groups, when they made a contribution that was connected to Nespresso's qualities, switched from the personal first-person singular "I" to the generic "one" in the third-person singular. For example, the participant who said that for breakfast, he does not drink Nespresso because it is too early in the day and his taste buds are not yet ready to be able to fully appreciate Nespresso's superior taste, and that he drinks Nespresso only after having finished his daily tasks: "Now, I am done, I did a good job, and now I would like to have a cup of good coffee. One can consider that a reward" (FG 3, 1:09:50). After attesting the attribute of "good coffee" to Nespresso, he switched to the third-person singular. It appears that the removal of the "I", the first-person singular, is an integral part in the establishment of seemingly ontological attributes pertaining to Nespresso. If the "I" were still used, it might dawn on the consumer that it is actually he himself, or she herself, who attributes the said qualities to Nespresso. The removal of the "I" after attribution has been made, however, makes the attributed qualities appear to innately belong to Nespresso. This ontologisation also has implications regarding the consumer's alienation as described by Williamson (2002). For instance, a participant of one of the three focus groups, describing a visit to a Nespresso boutique, testified: "I must say that one felt as if one were a member of the nobility [*man hat sich "von" gefühlt*] when you went shopping there" (FG 3, 17:44). He obviously did not say: "I felt like a member of the nobility." The withdrawal from the "I" to the "one", mirrors his alienation from himself. When attributing qualities to the product and to its purchase – qualities that he must at least have heard of, dreamt them up, or otherwise have come into contact with – he might not consider these qualities characteristic of his own identity. However, they are favourably connoted qualities he can relate to. By ascribing, as in this case, these qualities to the product's purchase, the viewer's *own* judgement is the origin of what might appear to him, or her to be ontologically related to that purchase. It is the viewer, induced by the commercials' narration, that is, their syuzhet and style, who attributes those characteristics to the product and its purchase. And, as Williamson (2002) has shown, through consumption of the commodity, the viewer, and consumer, manages to then consciously possess these qualities, and thereby enhance and complete his, or her identity.

This link between consumption and consumer identity is further illustrated by the contribution of another participant who said, regarding the Nespresso commercials and his connected motivation to drink Nespresso: "Good commercials and [good] marketing, and that strategic wit with George Clooney [...]: These are stories that simply make one want to try [the coffee], and the commercials are so well made that one does not make a fool of oneself if one serves Nespresso [to one's guests]. That's the clue. One feels boundless desire to try it" (FG3 41:00). If he had chosen Nespresso, as he had repeatedly claimed, for purely functional reasons rooted in Nespresso's superior quality and the easy-to-use capsule system, chances are he could serve Nespresso to his guests even if the commercials were judged to be embarrassing and silly. The product's superior quality would stand alone in its own right. However, this apparently is not so, illustrating that the consumption of the product is related to the consumer's identification with the world of Nespresso as portrayed in the commercials, and is thereby connected to the consumer's identity formation. He obviously does not want to be seen as a fool. Apparently, depending on the qualities attributed to the product, consumption potentially comes with the risk of forming an identity that invites ridicule and mockery. In the case of Nespresso, however, as participant stated, this is not so; by serving Nespresso, in his own words, "one does not make a fool of oneself" (FG 3, 40:19). Interestingly, that participant, using the "one" of the third-person singular, also withdrew from the realm of personally phrased statements. The distanced "one" gives that contribution the touch of a generally valid quality whose roots in the consumer's own fabula construction are not recognised. Instead, the statement seems to relate an apparently ontological truth.

This ontologisation was present throughout all focus groups. For instance, one participant testified that: "Nespresso, the product, the coffee, really *is* very good"[123] (FG 1, 04:58). These value judgements regarding Nespresso's qualities were not relativised. It remains undiscovered to the commercials' viewers and consumers, that it is actually they themselves who construct that meaning and attribute the corresponding qualities to the product. Instead, the product's attributes seem to just be there, justifying a categorisation and subsequent ordering of the world of coffee brands, giving rise to a model of the world, a worldview. For example, the participant testifying, regarding the special moments of inner focus, "When I am there, then, Nespresso is adequate, because then I am capable of feeling and experiencing the pleasure" (FG 3, 1:20:03), attributes to Nespresso the highest-ranking position in the world of coffee brands inasmuch as Nespresso's pleasure-inducing potential can only be accessed if the consumer himself has already reached that most special state of inner focus and tranquillity. For breakfast instead, a coffee other than Nespresso will be good enough. Herewith, that participant has created, regarding coffee brands, a model of the world.

Moreover, in that worldview, there is no room for possible ethical downsides connected to Nestlé SA, Nespresso's owner. Obviously, the representation of the commercials' coded message is such that, in their decoding, the viewers do not construct a fabula that connects Nespresso to Nestlé's, at times, challenged ethical reputation. The commercials are largely seen, as one participant testified, as brilliantly made, humorous entertainment: "These commercials are ingenious, one just has to explicitly say that. I love

123 The conversations in the two focus groups in Zurich were held in Swiss German, then transcribed to High German. Translation to English by the author, 2016.

this kind of humour" (FF 2 51:54). Another participant, also referring to the Nespresso commercials, testified: "They [Nestlé] create a distinct world in its own right. Nestlé only marginally makes an appearance. Nespresso makes an appearance in its own right, together with George Clooney, and with him, everything is well" (FG 2, 1:02:39). Here, that participant directly attributes the creation of a model of the world to the commercials; moreover, the metonymic power of George Clooney's presence, transferring "goodness" to everything that appears with him, is explicitly identified. The transfer of George Clooney's original signified to Nespresso, as encoded in the representation of all three commercials, is decoded in the corresponding manner by the viewers. As the commercials' syuzhet mirrors all the tenets of the economic theory of clubs, beginning with the insider-outsider dichotomy all the way to the display of all the different flavours offered by Nespresso (In the Name of Pleasure, shot 3, 00:04), the equilibrium, where consumer benefit is maximised, is implicitly present. Naturally, the implicit promise of maximised consumer benefit facilitates a fabula construction by the viewer that transfers George Clooney's signified to Nespresso. Again, it is not recognised, that it is the viewer who, through decoding, and guided by his, or her prototype and template schemata, constructs and produces the fabula and its meaning. In this sense, it goes unnoticed that advertising as a signifying practice, in order to achieve its effect, relies on the viewer to contribute his, or her meaning making powers to the process. That same participant also told the story that her mother, when suggesting that she, the daughter, should have a Nespresso, says: "Have a George!" (FG 2, 18:32). Prior to that contribution, that participant C had said that she presumed George Clooney also drinks Nespresso at home, as she does. She also testified that Nespresso is a "unique" product. Here, as illustrated by the analysis of the commercial What Else (2006), George Clooney's attributes are through metonymy, transferred to Nespresso, the signified is linked to a new signifier. This not only establishes a model of the world, but, as is apparent in her mother's suggestion "Have a George!", the model of the world flips over into a model for the world, an ethos.

There is only one singular exception to that worldview, and the corresponding ethos. One participant testified that in Italy, sometimes, coffee tastes better than Nespresso: "In Italy, they make coffee that tastes in earnest better than Nespresso. But only there, nowhere else" (FG 2, 05:46). So, with just one exception, all participants of the focus groups upheld that Nespresso tastes best. For all participants, their model of the coffee world centres around Nespresso, and only Nespresso. This view is also supported by the results of the quantitative survey. The responses to questions 25, 26, and 30 all indicate, that for Nespresso consumers, contrary to the members of the control group, their chosen brand is without alternatives. Actually, for one participant, that model of the world is so strong, that, should Nespresso go out of production, she would stop drinking coffee altogether: "I would no longer drink coffee, [...] and I would pour out the bad coffee" (FG 2, 25:08). Similarly, another participant testified that a world without Nespresso would be hard to cope with. He said that he would be very upset if Nespresso were no longer available, and that it would take him a long time to come to terms with that, implying the presence of a strong and effective model of the world, with Nespresso ranking first, and of the accompanying powerful and long-lasting moods. In his own words, he "honestly" admits that, as far as he is concerned, no other coffee brand exists for him, (FG 3, 01:22:32). For him, the good moments of coming home in the evening are tied to the consumption of a Nespresso, and so much so, that he speaks of being dependent on Nespresso, something he does not mind at all. With Nespresso, nothing can spoil the evening. Obviously, for him, the consumption of Nespresso had become a firm ethos supported by a powerful, good mood. For him, and for all other participants of the focus groups, as supported by the results of the quantitative survey, the value judgements regarding Nespresso, encoded in the commercials' audio-visual message reflecting a seemingly ontological hierarchy with respect to coffee brands, issue in both, a worldview and an ethos, in a model of, and for the world.

In the quantitative survey, questions 2 and 3 aim to address whether Nespresso clients, compared to the members of the control group, are more likely to express a clear preference regarding their chosen brand. As a preference implies a categorisation with a subsequent ordering, the statistically highly significant answers imply that yes, the Nespresso consumers are, compared to members of the control group, more likely to have both, a clearly established order regarding coffee brands and a tantamount preference regarding the coffee of their choice. This implies the presence of a model of and for the coffee world which has, as expressed by the clear preference, its reflection in an ethos, a blueprint for the "right" behaviour, that is, consuming Nespresso only.

Question 10 aims to find out whether Nespresso drinkers see their habit as part of a way of life. The result is staggering: A Nespresso drinker is 5.26 times more likely to see the choice of his, or her brand as part of way of life than a member of the control group. A way of life is not only about values, it is also about specific behavioural patterns. In the light of the answer given by nearly two thirds of the Nespresso clients, and only about a quarter of the participants of the control group, with a p-value close to zero, the result is intuitively comprehensible. Indeed, a statistically significant association exists between being a Nespresso client and seeing Nespresso, as a brand, as part of a way of life. That way of life, distinct from other ways of life devoid of Nespresso, not only reflects a specific ethos regarding consumption, it also, as will be discussed below, promotes a club-mentality, classifying human individuals into groups: those who consume Nespresso and those who do not. Moreover, seeing a difference between oneself and others is also conducive to identity formation. In this sense, Nespresso is also an identity donator. As the value of Phi is 0.387, indicating an association of notable strength, Nespresso's effect regarding determining a consumer's behavioural pattern and identity should not be underestimated.

One participant explicitly related Nespresso to a certain lifestyle: "[...] and then there is the lifestyle, [...] one can bring faces like the one of George Clooney to your table" (FG 3, 10:26). Here, the reference to *lifestyle*, addresses the ethos, as a lifestyle, any lifestyle, always implies a certain set of actions, of dos and don'ts. In the participant's own words: "One doesn't go shopping for coffee [Nespresso], one celebrates the buying of coffee. [...] One goes to a special shop. [...] One speaks of the individual flavours, referring to them by their names, Roma, Volluto, and so forth, or you only refer to their colours: 'Which capsule-colour do you desire?' Even if one celebrates this with the wink of an eye, this brings a lot of noblesse[124] to the table" (FG 3, 12:00).

As stated above, the participants do not establish a link between Nespresso and the ethical downsides related to a big corporation in a way that would compromise, or damage, their acquired model of and for the world. Moreover, as articulated by one participant, that untarnished worldview with Nespresso at its top, is also vehemently defended. That viewer, having that worldview with its corresponding ethos firmly in place, has no interest in having the construction of her fabula, which lies at the heart of worldview and ethos, questioned, lest the model of and for the world both get tarnished: "People are being exploited all the time [...] [W]e are sur-

124 "Noblesse" is the French word for "nobility". Assuming that today, most contemporaries might no longer be aware of the fact that prior to the French Revolution, the highest-ranking class was the clergy with the nobility only ranking second in the social pyramid, that participant, by invoking the notion of noblesse, alluded to a specific order, a model of the world, placing Nespresso at the top.

rounded by goods produced in sweat-shops. Sadly, all the things we live with are possible only because we exploit other countries. That's global. Nestlé is not to be criticised more than others. They are just part of the system. I am making [a] compromise because their coffee [Nespresso] is simply the best. Basta![125] [...] You cannot save the entire world by yourself, least of all if you do not drink Nespresso. [...] The world will always revolve around money, and ours around coffee. [...] If I can bring about a change, I do it, if I cannot, I have a Nespresso!" (FG 2, 1:04:52). It will be hard to top this apologia in favour of Nespresso. Not surprisingly, this firm ethos is seconded by a view, held by almost half of the interviewed Nespresso drinkers, that sees the making of a Nespresso as a ritual.

Enacted by George Clooney, in all of the three commercials, the representation of a model of and for the (coffee) world always includes the representation of all of the required steps involved in the making of a Nespresso. That repeatedly shown, identical behaviour not only facilitates learning, its ritualised character opens, as discussed in subchapter 4.1, the space where, according to Geertz (2010, p. 28) the two models, of and for the world, meet and meld. And of course, that ritual is an act that can easily be performed by the viewer. In this way, the commercials' syuzhet points towards a real-world locus where the decoding by the viewer, that is, the construction of meaning by the viewer can be reified. Thus, the meaning, constructed by the viewer, can easily be confirmed by him- or herself through consumption. And in and through such confirmation, the consumer obviously performs the ritual, consolidating, perhaps without consciously realising it, the model of and for the world. In this way, the consumer morphs into the referent of the commercials' symbolism – a role, self-enforcing and autopoietic that might be difficult to step out of.

Questions 15 and 16 of the questionnaire then address the issue of whether or not Nespresso consumers, contrary to members of the control group, consider the making of a cup of coffee, that is, Nespresso, a special moment or, even more than that, and a little ritual. The responses to both questions yield, at the 5 percent level of significance, statistically significant results. The likelihood that a Nespresso client who participated in the survey considers the making of a cup of Nespresso a special moment, more than just the simple making of a coffee, is considerably higher than the likelihood that a member of the control group sees in the making of a cup of coffee of his or her choice an equally special moment. Regarding the ritual, it can be said that the question of whether or not a coffee consumer

125 Italian for "That's it, enough!".

sees a ritual in the making of a coffee is not independent of the consumer's brand affiliation. The results, of course, do not allow for the conclusion that all members of the Nespresso group consider the making of a Nespresso a ritual. However, compared to non-Nespresso drinkers, the percentage of Nespresso drinkers that considers the making of a Nespresso a little ritual is almost twice as large as the corresponding figure in the control group. Also, compared to the control group, a considerably smaller number of Nespresso drinkers answered with an outright "No" (29.7 percent compared to 43.8 percent).

One of the focus groups' participants testified: "[...] [T]hey [Nespresso] have created a need, that previously had not existed at all. You cannot go back, of course not, now that it is here!" (FG 2, 30:20). To the interviewer's follow-up question, whether the participants feel they are guided by an internal compass towards those moments of consumption, that participant replied: "Yes, it contains a certain ritual" (FG 2, 30:48). This episode not only supports Bruner who said that "[a]bove the subsistence level, you do not need anything until you have it" (Bruner, 1979, pp. 145-146), shedding light on the successful mise en place of the model of and for the world, but also illustrates the participant's full awareness that she is performing a certain ritual. What is left open is, whether or not she is also aware of a ritual's implications regarding the strengthening of worldview and ethos. Yet, she is fully aware of the strength of the ethos, as it was she who said: "You cannot go back [...]!" (FG 2, 30:48).

The answers to question 17, whether Nespresso consumers are a little bit more special than other people, do not allow for the falsification of the null hypothesis at the 5 percent level of significance. Still, a p-value of 5.9 percent, just slightly above the critical 5 percent level, still provides some evidence that the members of the Nespresso group have a comparatively higher tendency to answer with "Yes". As meaning and identities are both constructed, this could be an indication that Nespresso drinkers are better "identity builders", that is, compared to members of the control group, Nespresso affiliates are more apt at both, the construction of identity and the construction of meaning regarding their chosen brand. The contributions of three participants of the focus groups at least point in that direction.

One participant testified that he caught himself thinking, 20 Swiss francs for a kilo of organically grown coffee was too much, whilst he is willing to pay the equivalent of 80 Swiss francs for a kilo of Nespresso. To that he added, that he has no means to withstand the power of Nespresso's marketing. Then he said: "Yes, you belong to them for sure" (FG 1, 17:01). That participant addresses the link between regulation and identity. The limitation of the number of club members through Nespresso's comparatively high unit price separates coffee drinkers into those who do belong to the Nespresso Club, and those who do not. Identity depends on exclusion and on difference. Two requirements fulfilled by Nespresso's high unit price, acting as a classificatory system. Regulation by the price creates insiders and outsiders, those who belong and those who do not. Belonging to a group then affects a person's cognition of his, or her identity. As this participant also testified that ordering Nespresso online always puts him in a good mood, it seems fair to conclude that as far as he is concerned, the identity in connection with Nespresso consumption is positively connoted.

Another participant said, describing his feelings in connection with visiting a Nespresso boutique: "I must honestly say that some time ago we had that Nespresso shop at Karstadt's. […] That was special, very special, very noble. I must say that you felt as if you were a member of the nobility [*man hat sich "von" gefühlt*] when you went shopping there. […] [O]ne could see you from the outside. So, if someone had passed by, someone who knew you, he would have thought, 'Oh! Look! *That one* goes to Nespresso!'[126] That was beautiful, that was awesome, that was really fully awesome! One felt great!" (FG 3, 17:44) Here, that participant directly addresses this issue of identity formation in conjunction with being a Nespresso client. As theoretically outlined above, identity depends on the exclusion of the other, in this case the non-Nespresso drinkers. Prices assume the function of a classificatory system, establishing the dividing line between those who can and those who cannot afford a certain product. In this sense, the practice of consuming Nespresso is conducive to identity formation by the consumer. Furthermore, that participant's testimony shows that he was in a very good mood when the buying took place. His good mood was linked to the idea that others, from outside the Nespresso boutique, might see him there inside the boutique, buying his coffee in that special place. In this scenario, that participant is not like all the others outside, he is inside, and they are excluded. Identity depends on exclusion. In this sense, that participant's imagined public perception of his consumption practice is a locus of identity formation. Moreover, the imagined public perception of his consumption practice, making him recognisable as a Nespresso client is a correlate of his good mood. His imagined ennoblement puts him in a very good mood. And, as was also theoretically outlined above, a good mood is also conducive to the motivation to act, to buy in this case. All of those theoretically established inter-relationships are

126 This was said with great emphasis, in a voice full of admiration and respect.

confirmed by that participant's contribution. In the Geertzian sense, participant C thereby has his ethos firmly established. Moreover, through the exclusion of the perceived other, the outsider, limiting the number of Nespresso clients to the level where consumer benefit is maximised, the model of the world, the order of things in the coffee world with Nespresso ranking first, is supported by the factuality of his imagined ennoblement making his intense moods[127] appear uniquely realistic.

Another participant also established a connection between the choice of brand and the consumer's identity. Relating his views regarding the identity of premium car drivers like Audi or BMW, he said: "They are assh... wonderful cars, only that, unfortunately, the wrong assholes always sit in them. [...] (FG 3, 01:32:04).

Questions 25, 26, 27, as well as 30, and 30 all address the model of the world and for the world. The results are all statistically highly significant showing that compared to members of the control group, Nespresso drinkers have created far stronger models of and for the world. Not only are their motivations to stick to their chosen brand, that is Nespresso, far stronger, as the results of the focus groups show, their worldview and ethos are also a source of joy and of a good mood. Their contributions, in accordance with the economic theory of clubs, testify that the benefits they obtain through their consumption of Nespresso are so large, that they not only justify Nespresso's comparatively high unit price, they also make their moods and motivations seem uniquely realistic.

The results of question 25, for example, indicate a very strong, and statistically highly significant association between choice of brand and a categorical labelling of that choice as the "right choice". Nespresso consumers, compared to members of the control group, are much more likely to always see their choice as the right choice. Members of the control group, instead, are less fixated on their chosen brands. This illustrates a stronger presence, regarding Nespresso consumers, of a brand-related worldview and the corresponding ethos. According to the results of question 26, members of the Nespresso group are, compared to members of the control group, 2.3 times less likely to prefer, at times, other brands. This is indicative of a comparatively strong brand affiliation, in the case of Nespresso consumers, mirroring both, worldview and ethos. This is further confirmed by the results of question 27 that show that also in the near future,

127 The intensity of his moods was underscored by his use of a rhetorical climax: "Man! That was awesome [*geil*]! That was so truly awesome [*so richtig geil*]! One felt so truly super!" (FG 3, 18:47).

for Nespresso consumers, their ethos is much less likely to change than for consumers of rivalling brands. Not surprisingly, members of the Nespresso group are about 7.5 times less likely, than members of the control group, to accept the idea, that they could immerse themselves in the same experience of pleasure and gusto even if they replaced their chosen brand, Nespresso, with another coffee.

As the results of question 30 indicate, for 85 percent of the Nespresso consumers who participated in the quantitative survey, Nespresso is simply without alternatives. Furthermore, as is illustrated by the results of question 31, for 75 percent of all members of the Nespresso group, their chosen brand has become in some way, a pleasant constant in their lives, whereas for 63.2 percent of all members of the control group, that has not happened. Not only is the model of and for the world much more firmly established for Nespresso clients, it also comes with the attribute "pleasant", indicative of a good mood being Nespresso's correlate. These interpretations of the quantitative survey's results are in the following, further substantiated by the contributions made by the participants of the focus groups.

As mentioned above, one participant testified that ordering Nespresso on the internet always puts him in a good mood. This connection between consumption and a good mood, naturally, issues in the continued motivation to consume Nespresso. As was theoretically outlined, moods are connected to emotions and, as Nussbaum points out, emotions are closely connected to actions (Nussbaum, 2001/2008, p. 135). In the case of one participant, those actions have, in his own words, actually resulted in compulsive, continued Nespresso consumption. Another participant said, that each time he is invited and offered a cup of coffee made with one of those "weird 'I don't know what' [coffee machines]", he would decline the offer. Then he made a comparison to Nespresso: "Those moments remind me that at home I have good coffee". To the interviewer's question, whether these thoughts come with a feeling of satisfaction or joy, he responded: "Yes, with joy, and then I think 'I'll stay with Nespresso'. Whenever I come across a counterexample I am positively confirmed by Nespresso" (FG 1, 52:00). Here, that participant almost reiterates all the important aspects of the Geertzian definition of religion. The categorisation and ordering of the models of and for the coffee world repeatedly, again and again, elicits a mood of joy in him, which, furthermore, appears to be totally justified by the characteristics attributed to Nespresso. Joy is a pervasive emotion, and in his case, a recurrent emotion; similar to the participant who is always put in a good mood when he orders Nespresso. Moreover, his joy is clearly rooted in Nespresso's perceived supremacy – a model of the world, which has become so firmly established for him, that his mood of joy seems to be uniquely realistic. The thought, however, that the model's perceived factuality could be a construction of his own, does not appear to cross his mind.

One participant then testified: "I have the feeling that [with Nespresso] I get what I need. [...] I do not need anything else" (FG 1, 15:17). To the interviewer's question whether or not he also looks around for rivalling products, he responded: "No, because I am pleased [with the product]" (FG 1, 16:26). To that statement, the other participants voiced their consent. Neither of them would ever consider switching to another brand. They all are intent on sticking to Nespresso (FG 1, 16:29). This episode shows that they are all motivated to stay with Nespresso. The ethos, the model for the world, is well established in their behavioural patterns. Moreover, it illustrates how the signifying practice of advertising, through encoding and subsequent decoding by the viewer, interprets the viewer and consumer's desire. Naturally then, the consumer has that desire met by consuming the advertised product. And consequently, the absence of the motivation to try out rivalling products seems to be uniquely realistic. When the interviewer then asked, whether it would go too far to suggest that one could feel good about being steered by advertising in the sense: "Here I know I truly get what I would like to have", all participants immediately responded with a clear no: "No, no, absolutely not" (FG 1, 22:18). Obviously, all participants testify that their desires, as perceived by them, are met. This leads to pervasively good moods, in relation to the product, and a continued motivation to consume it, solidifying the model for the world, and, by the same token, the model of the world. Not only does that world meet their coffee needs, it appears that it meets their perceived desires so well that, when asked by the interviewer, all of the participants unanimously say that they are neither testing alternatives nor planning to do so in the future (FG 1, 37:22).

Equally, when the interviewer asked the three participants of another focus group, whether they also try other coffee brands, one participant said: "⍰⍰⍰!"[128] All participants then, right away, burst into laughter (FG 2, 30:55). For those participants, the ethos, the model for the world has become most firmly established, to the point actually that a question aiming to challenge such ethos is a source of amusement and hilarity. Moreover, expressing the fact that such ethos is firmly established beyond questioning puts them in a very good mood. As this contribution shows, the com-

128 Please see footnote 108.

mercials' representation, the coding and commensurate decoding of its meaning, only has one vanishing point: continued consumption of Nespresso, and, connected thereto, sustained high operating profit margins. The three following contributions further highlight the connection between the firmly established models of and for the world on the one side, and powerful and pervasive moods and motivations on the other.

One participant who is married and does not yet have a Nespresso machine at home, told her fellow participants that the next coffee machine she will buy will definitely be a Nespresso one. When the other member of the focus group inquired as to whether or not her husband already knew about that, she replied: "No, he doesn't know it yet." Again, everybody giggled. "However, I know he likes it. It will just be all right" (FG 2, 09:08). Here, the model for the world is clearly visibly at work. Her ethos, her behaviour, and with it, apparently that of her husband's, have been determined. Moreover, the participants' talking about the ethos is supported by a good mood. Again, the link between mood and consumption is at work. After all, why shouldn't she be in a good mood? She will no longer be forced to step outside her home to have her desire for the best-tasting coffee fulfilled.

Later in the conversation, the interviewer then wanted to know whether the participants had ever considered taking the Nespresso machine with them on a trip away from home. One participant responded: "Well, that's a good-one! Considered? We did it!" (FG 2, 36:53). To that, everyone burst into happy laughter. Apparently, the firmly established ethos is a source of great joy, putting all participants in a good mood; and again, as described above, a good mood is related to emotions and thereby conducive to putting the ethos into action.

The participant of another focus group, with respect to the noblesse he sees connected with the consumption of Nespresso, said: "For me, noblesse is the key to having fun, the key to trying the product. It is a witty story with George Clooney, it's fun to impersonate him in the kitchen. Mr. Volluto, signora Ristretto, that's witty, that was fun. However, I can re-enact the George Clooney gimmick also with a cup of Jacobs coffee[129] in my hand." (FG 3, 39:59) Here, that participant addresses both: the good mood and the motivation to try the product. In this context, the motivation to try the product has far reaching implications. According to his statement, a re-enactment of George Clooney's portrayed actions seems to be something he could possibly want to do, implying that he has already learnt, or inter-

129 Jacobs coffee is a German coffee brand.

nalised, at least parts of George Clooney's behaviour shown in the commercials. His motivation to try the product is, through learning, translated into observable behaviour. Moreover, at the beginning of the focus group talk, he had said that coffee drinking is a ritual. This remark is insofar noteworthy as, according to Geertz, in the ritual, the model *of* the world merges with the model *for* the world, that is, in the ritual, the worldview and the ethos become one. Therefore, if the viewer is motivated to try the product, a seemingly harmless and inconsequential deed, then, through the power of the ritual, the model of the world is being constituted or solidified, respectively. To then subsequently solidify the ethos and to perpetuate the learnt behaviour, it is furthermore helpful if the viewer, at least to some degree, identifies with the commercials and the advertised product, something which is obviously the case here. Moreover, as was outlined in chapter 3.2.2, learning is facilitated if the commercials' viewer is put into a good mood (Liew & Tan, 2016, p. 113), a feat, with respect to this participant, the commercials apparently successfully accomplish. Considering all of these interrelations, a further contribution made by that participant with respect to the Nespresso commercial How Far (2014), is significant: "The scene with George Clooney was funny, you had to laugh, I found it witty, and it raised the appetite to try the coffee. I like the taste, it pleases me, I take it. If this is so, one can surrender oneself to the commercial [...], one becomes part of that world" (FG 3, 30:24). Here, he says that he is now able to see himself as a part of the world shown in the Nespresso commercials, a precondition for successful identification. Moreover, he makes a clear reference to his good mood and to being motivated to try the advertised product.

The connection between identification and motivation was also illustrated by the following contribution. One participant testified: "I also drink Nespresso just like that, I am truly fond of that coffee. However, I think, in the beginning, the thought that George Clooney also drinks a Nespresso when he is at home: that turns it into something special" (FG 2, 15:16). Here, the use of the conjunctive adverb "also" shows that that participant believes her habit is the same as George Clooney's. This facilitates identification, and, generally speaking, identification encourages learning. Moreover, the positive connotation of that overlap is likely to positively influence her mood, which has, in a multimedia learning system, as outlined in chapter 3.2.2, a positive influence on cognition as well as motivation. And it is motivation that translates learning into observable behaviour: the representation of a worldview, through decoding, thus establishes the viewer's ethos, resulting in his, or her habit. These examples mirror the successful completion of the mise en place of all the ingredients necessary for the models of and for the world to complete their task: a continued consumption of the advertised product.

Given Nespresso's commercial success, it can be said that, the clients' good moods in relation to Nespresso are conducive to a behaviour reflecting that mood, that is, to the consumption of Nespresso. Therefore, one of the aims, from the point of view of the firm, must be to put the commercials' viewers in a good mood. This is in parts achieved by the commercials' narration, which leads, according to all members of the focus groups, to the construction of a "witty" fabula. Furthermore, with a view to male viewers, it can be said that, inasmuch as they see George Clooney as an imagined adversary, or role model setting standards they cannot live up to, they can relax as all of those attributes that earned him his reputation obviously failed him. So, a man, even if he is not so handsome can relax as obviously, to tell by the commercials' fabula, handsomeness and sexiness obviously do not pay off. Moreover, as one male interviewee testified, the commercials are witty. And he therefore does not feel embarrassed to publicly admit that he likes them. And most likely, watching something you like is conducive to a good mood.

With respect to regular, female viewers, who might believe they would not have, given their looks, a chance of being approached by George Clooney, the commercials' message is equally assuasive: The women who obviously are approached by George Clooney do not care about him as something so much more desirable exists, something that is, and this is the good message, also within the reach of the ordinary female viewer, given her purchasing power is sufficient. So, male and female viewers alike, stand a good chance, viewing the commercials, of being put into a good mood. Thus, viewers have their good mood correlated to their fabula construction which, to say it again, includes the transfer of George Clooney's signified to Nespresso; as Geertz said, "[w]e interpret motives in terms of their consummations, but we interpret moods in terms of their sources" (Geertz, 1966/2010, p. 12).

Six of the nine focus groups participants explicitly remarked that they think the price of a Nespresso capsule is high. Yet, they all also testified, that they consider that high price to be justified. Obviously, Nespresso manages to create sufficient consumer benefit to make consumers pay the comparatively high asking price. The economic theory of clubs helps to explain how such a feat is accomplished. With a comparatively low price for a Nespresso coffee machine, the threshold to potentially be able to participate in the Nespresso Club is low. Once that threshold is overcome, however, the staying inside is connected to the continued purchase of the comparatively expensive Nespresso capsule. As the following contributions illustrate, Nespresso obviously manages to establish the equilibrium between regulation of the number of insiders, or Club members, through the high capsule price on the one hand, and the width of the offered product range and the degree of the diffusion of the product on the other – an equilibrium that issues in the maximisation of consumer benefit. As the contributions, illustrated in the following, will show, the line of argument, "consumers are willing to buy Nespresso capsules even though they are comparatively expensive" should possibly be replaced with "consumers are willing to buy Nespresso capsules *because* they are comparatively expensive, because only that high unit price successfully manages to regulate the number of Nespresso consumers to establish the equilibrium with the width of Nespresso's product range that maximises consumer benefit".

At one point, the interviewer mentioned to the participants of one focus group, who were discussing whether Nespresso's success is rooted in the capsule system's functionality, that other brands also offer systems with the same functionality, the participant, who had also remarked that Nespresso brings a lot of noblesse to the table (FG 3, 12:00), replied: "No, that is not so because, and that is why I believe the [Nespresso] capsule system is so successful, at a dinner party, you can offer each guest a choice of many different coffee flavours, beginning with decaffeinated coffee, Lungo, elegant and bitter all the way to sweet and creamy. With other espresso machines, with fully automatic coffee machines you don't have that option. There, you can only choose between two types of coffee beans, point one. Point two, if I brew a classic filter coffee, then I have eight cups in a pot, everyone has to drink the same coffee, in the same intensity, whether or not they want that. With the [Nespresso] capsule machine I can satisfy different tastes and needs. The functionality is perfect, it functions perfectly with all the original Nespresso capsules, furthermore, it is important that one does not get annoyed, the product has been brought to functional perfection, one can choose from different tasty flavours" (FG 3, 08:56). Here, that participant gives testimony of some of the main tenets of Buchanan's economic theory of clubs. As mentioned, and outlined in chapter 4.2, that theory states that, for a given number of club members, the individual club member's utility is maximised if he or she, by virtue of being a club member, or a Nespresso client for that matter, can choose from a product range which is neither too small nor too large. If the product range is too small, the benefits of being a club member are below their point of maximum, which is reached if the product range is increased. In the case of filter coffee, or the choice between two types of coffee beans only, the product range is so limited that the consumer's benefit is, compared to Nespresso, simply too small.

If, on other hand, the product range is too large, each individual option, or flavour, appears to be only of little value because the large number of choices is tantamount to the removal of scarcity. As value comes with scarcity, less scarcity means that less value is attached to each individual flavour. The aim always is to strike an equilibrium between the number of flavours from which to choose and the number of club members, or Nespresso clients in this case. That equilibrium maximises, in the client's view, his or her utility, which then, as will be seen, translates into the client's willingness to pay a very high unit price for a Nespresso capsule. The presence of noblesse, obviously, is worth its price. Clearly, for that participant, an equilibrium, as described by the economic theory of clubs is established. This is further substantiated by his subsequent remark that, even though a no-name coffee capsule sold at the discounter's only costs €0.20, he, as he can afford it, is willing to pay the €0.40 asked for one Nespresso capsule (FG 3, 37:38). This statement implies that there are people who do not have the sufficient purchasing power to spend €0.40 on a single coffee capsule. This regulation by the market price makes that participant, contrary to the many with insufficient purchasing power, a club insider. And obviously, the benefit derived therefrom is sufficiently large to make that consumer pay twice the unit price of a capsule sold at the discounter's.

Finally, another participant, referring to Nespresso's wide variety of flavours, testified that she no longer tries different brands; if she feels like a change, she now looks for a new flavour amongst the many different Nespresso capsules. A contribution that was, by the way, met by the other participants with happy laughter (FG 2, 32:15). This statement exemplifies the contributions made by Buchanan's economic theory of clubs, whereby club members maximise their utility by staying inside the club if the number of club members and the width of the offered product range strike a happy balance, which obviously seems to be the case here. Naturally, maximisation of consumer benefit is also conducive to the establishment of a firm ethos. Another participant then added that, when she had her first Nespresso, she had thought: "Ah, super!" and that after a few more cups [of Nespresso], that flavour had already anchored itself inside of her (FG 2, 33:15).

The discussion of this study's findings has shown, that with the synthesised theoretical framework, the results of the audio-visual as well as the socio-empirical analyses can be explained and accounted for. The mechanisms at work, leading to Nespresso's high operating profit margins, are, in a comprehensible and traceable manner, laid open. As will be shown in the following final chapter 7, what perhaps appears to be, at first sight, a lucky strike of a big multinational corporation owed to chance, is in fact the result of a marketing campaign based on a system of symbols with, in the Geertzian sense, strong structural and functional analogies to religion.

6.5 Summary

The socio-empirical survey created a sufficiently broad database to check, on all counts, whether or not the predictions that can be made according to theory can be confirmed. The analysis of that data permits a detailed look at the evidence, piece by piece, to see, whether the tenets of the theoretical frame of this study can be upheld, or whether they fail in the explanation of the scrutinised phenomenon.

The chosen approach for the quantitative analysis, the Chi-square test for independence, presupposes a set of categorical data. To facilitate categorisation, the possible answers that the interviewees could give were mostly limited and pre-formulated. That, it can be argued, constitutes a bias in the data, and that, had the questions allowed for more open answers, a different picture might have emerged. That is why the quantitative survey was followed by a qualitative survey with focus groups where the participants had the possibility to frame their answers as they saw fit. As the subsequently presented findings of the analysis will confirm, the participants of all focus groups remained, of their own accord, within the categories that were already present in the quantitative survey. Again, it could be argued that the participants had been conditioned by the preceding quantitative interview. However, there were several months between the quantitative and the qualitative survey, that is, between the interview and the focus groups, and, in the focus groups, the interviewer mostly took a back seat and let the talk evolve according to the participants' contributions. In their own words then, the participants drew up a map that is dominated by the key concepts of the theoretical frame, such as the model of and a model for the world, a map that illustrates a consumer's alienation, a map that highlights the benefits of a club-good. In this sense, the findings of the socio-empirical survey, presented in this chapter, confirm the adequacy of the theoretical framework.

7 Conclusion

Nespresso, one of Nestlé's coffee brands, has earned its owner exceptionally high operating profit margins, a multiple of the industry average. That outstanding commercial success has, so far, gone largely unexplained. This study then addressed the question of whether or not the Nespresso marketing campaign possesses a dimension that has, so far, gone unnoticed – a dimension inviting consumers into a world of branded coffee consumption, which, once inside, does not seem to provide for a way out again. The question was raised whether or not Nespresso's commercial success is possibly rooted in the campaign's effective creation of a model of coffee consumption, as well as a model for coffee consumption – worldview and ethos – and the role the consumer plays therein. This study aimed to find out, whether the secret of Nespresso's marketing campaign could be revealed, if, based on Geertz's definition of religion, the campaign is approached with a theoretical framework pertaining to the study of religion.

In this final chapter, this study's principal question, asking whether or not Nespresso's exceptional commercial success could be explained, on the theoretical level, by a structural, and functional analogy between Nespresso's marketing campaign, on the one hand, and religion, on the other, will be addressed. First, the results are presented below. They show that the question is answered in the affirmative. The chapter then proceeds with a critical reflection on the theoretical framework, followed by methodological reflections on this study's interdisciplinary approach, addressing the question of the choice of adequate methods. The chapter closes with an outlook addressing potential topics of future research.

7.1 The results of the audio-visual and the socio-empirical analysis

This study is based on a corpus of two different kinds of data, audio-visual data and primary consumer data collected by me with the help of four assistants. The audio-visual data consists of three Nespresso commercials, What Else (Michel Gondry, 2006), Like a Star (Grant Heslov, 2012), and In the Name of Pleasure (Grant Heslov, 2013), all featuring George Clooney. Those commercials were chosen for two reasons: First, unlike other Nespresso commercials, they do not contain explicitly religious symbolism. Instead, they all, as their strong semiotic overlap illustrates, work with codes whose rearrangement, provoked by their narratives, issues in structural and functional analogies to religion. Second, if they are analysed in the chronological order of their release, a telling, syntagmatic semiotic progression can be identified.

In the audio-visual analysis, each of the three commercials was approached with the question regarding their meaning making power with respect to worldview and ethos. Additionally, as worldview and ethos, in the Geertzian sense, presuppose the presence of a system of symbols, that question also includes the dichotomic aspect of inside-outside, as any system implies a demarcation.

Against the background of that question, the three commercials were analysed focussing on three different aspects: their aesthetic surface, the codes present in their narratives, and the cues that induce the viewer (receiver), given he or she has the required previous knowledge regarding George Clooney's star-persona, to create new codes by transferring a sign's signified to a new signifier. In the following, these three aspects will be addressed in the sequential order of their occurrence in the commercials' narrative. First, however, the overlap of the three commercials' narrative and its semiotic implications are addressed. Subsequently then, the results of each of the commercials' analysis are presented individually, revealing the syntagmatic progression across the three commercials and its semiotic meaning. Furthermore, to make the presented results retraceable, the commercials' narratives will be briefly recapitulated.

The aesthetic surface of the commercials is, without exception, immaculate and fashionable. In addition thereto, they all begin by showing George Clooney entering, from the outside world, a Nespresso boutique. This creates an inside-outside dichotomy, setting the world of Nespresso consumers apart. Nespresso consumers are presented as insiders. As mentioned above, this is a precondition regarding the formation of a system of symbols.

In all three commercials then, George Clooney shows how he makes a cup of Nespresso for himself, with the Nespresso capsule clearly visible. This making of a Nespresso is shown in detail, and when the final drop falls into the cup, it rebounds, adding to the beauty of the aesthetic surface. In this sense, the cup with Nespresso emerges as a second protagonist. The third protagonist, or protagonists, in all three commercials are female. They are all totally indifferent to George Clooney's charms, who, in the commercials, plays himself, or rather his star-persona, that is, the person a viewer with the required previous knowledge, is likely to believe him to be.

What Else (Michel Gondry, 2006) features two young women, already present in the boutique when George Clooney enters, having a conversation and drinking Nespresso. They mention qualities like "dark, very intense, unique, an intense body, delicate and smooth, a strong character, rich, very rich", and finally, "Latin American temperament" – qualities, a viewer is likely to attribute to George Clooney. The narrative then shows George Clooney as he overhears to two women's conversation and, with a cup of Nespresso in his hand, walks over to them, enquiring as to what they are talking about. Bewildered and bemused, the two women, not showing the slightest interest in George Clooney, make him understand that they are talking about Nespresso. In this way, the commercial's narrative only makes sense to the viewer, if the signified, originally attached to George Clooney as the signifier, is transferred to a new signifier, Nespresso. In this way, the viewer is cued to rearrange preestablished codes, thereby creating an order, a worldview with respect to coffee brands. The two young women prefer their conversation about, and the uninterrupted consumption of Nespresso, to making the acquaintance of George Clooney. Obviously, Nespresso trumps George Clooney. As mentioned, this transfer of meaning by the viewer then presupposes the he, or she has the required previous knowledge regarding George Clooney and his star-persona. Furthermore, as discussed in chapter 1.3, the transfer is made possible, in the first place, by the annulment of the separation of thing and concept, a typical characteristic of a postmodern consumerist society. As will be shown below, this also has strong implications with respect to consumer's identity formation.

In Like a Star (Grant Heslov, 2012), George Clooney, on a very rainy, dark evening, is let into the Nespresso boutique after closing hours, "But only because it is you, Mr. Clooney", the shop assistant says. The viewer is led to believe that George Clooney's celebrity status affords him that preferential treatment. Then, as he is shown making a cup of Nespresso for himself, another late-coming Nespresso consumer is let in, and the shop assistant says, "But only because it is you, Mrs. Martin". This is followed by a tinkling sound, underscoring the creation of a new code: The viewer is cued to rearrange the narrative's code to make sense of the story. It might have appeared obvious to the viewer that the shop assistant knows George Clooney's name, but the fact that also Mrs. Martin, who is clearly not a celebrity, is addressed by her name indicates that she must be a regular client. Obviously, preferential treatment is not owed to celebrity status, but to being a regular Nespresso client. This new code is confirmed by Mrs. Martin, who says to George Clooney that whenever she visits a Nespresso boutique, she feels like a star. In this commercial then, the signified, originally taken from George Clooney, is passed on to yet another signifier, the consumer him- or herself with the corresponding ramifications to consumer identity. As discussed in chapter 2.1.2, this study presupposes a postmodern consumer, able to live different selves alongside one another, being playful with his, or her identity. It is this playfulness that allows for the above-described transfer of the signified from Nespresso to the consumer. The signified is now shared between the consumer and Nespresso. And as that sharing is linked to consumption, this provokes the emergence of an ethos, a specific consumer behaviour, that is, the continued consumption of Nespresso.

In IN THE NAME OF PLEASURE (Grant Heslov, 2013), George Clooney is shown as he leaves a lift that leads directly into a Nespresso boutique on the top floor of a high-rise building in a developed urban area. The boutique opens to a roof garden where the clients consume their Nespresso, sitting on beautifully designed chairs and settees. Again, the inside-outside dichotomy is clearly established right at the start of the commercial. Again, as in the other two commercials, George Clooney is shown as he makes his cup of Nespresso, showing, in a close-up, how the cup is slowly being filled with Nespresso, the final rebounding drop then is underscored by a tinkling sound, introducing Nespresso as a second protagonist. With his Nespresso, George Clooney walks out to the terrace and asks a beautiful young and unaccompanied woman, whether he may join her. As she has just finished her cup of Nespresso, he offers to fetch her another one. The viewer is cued to believe that this could be the beginning of a club acquaintance, a romance even. However, as he walks away, heading towards the entrance to the coffee serving area inside the building, she jumps up and shouts, pointing to the entrance: "George Clooney is inside!" All the female customers then, with screaming voices, run to the entrance, blocking the way so George Clooney cannot return to the terrace. The female protagonist then sits back in her armchair, takes George Clooney's cup and, undisturbed by him, revels in the consumption of another Nespresso. The female protagonist's desire is for Nespresso. Now, a viewer's decoding of the narrative, in a manner that makes sense of the female protagonist's portrayed behaviour, implies a rearrangement of the codes, that is, the signified "desirable" is transferred from George Clooney to Nespresso. With a view to the syntagmatic semiotic progression present in the chronological order of the two previously analysed commercials, the female protagonist's choice makes sense. As Nespresso's signified, appropriated from George Clooney, is also transferred, through consumption, to the consumer, her choice is between being with a star, or taking George Clooney's Nespresso and feeling like a star herself. Obviously, she went for the latter. And, if "being famous", or perhaps in its milder version of "being someone that matters" is part of a viewer's fantasy, then, through identification, the viewer has his, or her desire interpreted for him, or for her. The viewer's desire then is for Nespresso, which is tantamount to the establishment of a firm ethos.

The socio-empirical analysis then is based on two types of data: quantitative data collected through convenience sampling and qualitative data collected in three small focus groups of three Nespresso consumers in each group, providing the framework to gain access to those Nespresso consumers' emic view. The quantitative data was generated by questionnaires and the participants were divided into two groups: Nespresso clients and members of the control group, that is consumers of other coffee brands or non-branded coffee. That database allowed for statistical tests to find out whether or not there are, in the statistical sense, significant differences between the Nespresso consumers that participated in the survey and members of the control group. The questions aimed to find out whether 1) the coffee drinkers' choice mirrors a strong preference or whether it is a random choice, 2) they see in their choice a part of a way of life, 3) they see in the making of a cup of coffee a little ritual 4) their choice means they, as consumers, are "more special" than people who prefer other brands, 5) they see their choice, in a categorical way, as the "right choice", 6) they sometimes prefer other brands, 7) they are considering replacing their brand by another brand soon, 8) they could imagine to switch to another brand and still have the same experience of pleasure, and finally, 9) whether their choice has become a pleasant constant in their lives. The questions addressed to the participants of the focus groups were more open, the aim was to let them share their experience with Nespresso with the other members of the group. Those questions were grouped into three categories: 1) Nespresso's position at the top of available coffee brands, 2) moods associated with Nespresso, and 3) the motivation to continue being a Nespresso client. In the following, first the results of the statistical analysis based on the questionnaires are presented, followed by the results of the analysis of the focus groups.

The results are presented following the order of the questions listed in the above paragraph. The percentage figure in brackets indicates the likelihood, that the statement made here are not correct. In the statistical sense, any value below 5 percent is acceptable and indicates a statistically valid statement. If the statement cannot be considered statistically valid and has to be rejected, that will be indicated by an asterisk*. Compared to members of the control group, the Nespresso drinkers who participated in the survey 1) express a much stronger preference for their brand (0 percent), 2) are much more likely to see in their choice of brand a part of a way of life (0 percent), 3) are more likely to see in the making of a cup of coffee, that is Nespresso, a little ritual (4.2 percent), 4) are more likely to consider themselves to be "more special" than consumers of other brands* (5.9 percent), 5) are much more likely to see in their choice a categorically "right choice" (0 percent), 6) are much less likely to prefer, at times, other brands (0.4 percent), 7) are much less likely to consider replacing their brand by another brand soon (0 percent), 8) are much less likely to be able to imagine to switch to another brand and still have the same experience of pleasure (0 percent), and 9) are much more likely to see in their choice of brand a pleasant constant in their lives (0 percent).

In the following, the results of the focus groups are given. They are ordered in the same way as the questions presented above. 1) For all Nespresso consumers who participated in the focus group, Nespresso occupies an unrivalled first position in the myriad of available coffee brands. Only those with a limited purchasing power testified, that they do not always drink Nespresso, for financial reasons. 2) For all but one of the participants, the consumption of Nespresso is related to a pervasively good mood, which issues, for all those participants, 3) in a powerful, pervasive, and a long-lasting motivation, to continue with their consumption of Nespresso. This establishes a firm ethos. The participant who does not connect Nespresso with a good mood, finds his motivation to consume Nespresso in his endeavour, to crown the special moments in his life.

The question then arises regarding this study's external validity, or, in other words, whether or not the above conclusions can be generalised. Generalisation is warranted as the data, collected between 2013 and 2015 across a time span of 21 consecutive months, shows very little variation and has consistent patterns, that is, most Nespresso consumers that participated in the survey gave identical or similar answers. This applies also to the members of the control group. Therefore, statistical reliability, a precondition for validity, is achieved. It is argued that if due consideration to the conditions stated below is given, this study's conclusions can be generalised. The conditions are that the marketing campaign must succeed in involving would-be consumers in the creation of a system with the advertised commodity at its centre, clearly setting it apart from rivalling products and brands. The failure to create a system of its own is tantamount to failing in the creation of worldview and ethos. Moreover, if a system of symbols is to cause a substantial rise in the commodity's exchange-value, the advertised commodity's placement in the existing cultural map must be such, that the transfer of a signified, from a previous signifier to the commodity, is not a priori highly unlikely. Moreover, the code of the original signifier, in Nespresso's case George Clooney, must be understood in the same way, irrespective of individual backgrounds and biographies, by a considerable number of the targeted consumers, facilitating identification and the merging of the advertising's and the viewer's fantasies by large numbers of viewers. Finally, the commodity's representation, as is the case with Nespresso's representation as a club good, must be such that the viewer's decoding invariably attaches a high exchange value to the commodity.

Regarding the limitations of the above generalisation, it must be remembered that meaning is always created within a context. This study's context, a largely secularised, consumer-oriented postmodern society, limits the degree to which the study's results and conclusions can be generalised. The use of the term postmodern itself, introduced and discussed in subchapter 1.3, comes with limitations. Whilst the delineation and categorical demarcation of the notions modern and postmodern in their socio-cultural meaning and implications is in itself the issue of a debate, a generalisation of this study's conclusions, including also would-be consumers living in societies whose socio-cultural history and development cannot possibly be described as postmodern, must be avoided.

Regarding the benefits of the results of the audio-visual and the socio-empirical analysis presented above, it can be said that they allow the shedding of light, from different angles, on Nespresso's outstanding success. These different angles then permit a wider and more in-depth understanding of that commercial phenomenon which has, so far, remained largely unexplained. As humans are not born with an intrinsic sense of what can be called "culturally right behaviour", they are open to models of and for the world. This openness constitutes the inroad for the Nespresso's marketing campaign to the heart and mind of consumers. The results of the audio-visual analysis allow for the interpretation that the viewer's decoding of the commercials, steered by his, or her intent to uphold a narrative logic, issues in the categorisation (inside-outside) and subsequent ordering (attributing ranks) of the world of coffee brands. As evidenced by the results of the socio-empirical analysis, the decoding of the commercials' narrative is a meaning-producing process so powerful that it leaves the consumer no option other than to create a worldview that issues in an ethos of continued Nespresso consumption. The results of both, the audio-visual and the socio-empirical analyses, allow, from different angles, for the interpretation that, through the language of advertising – a signifying practice – Nespresso's marketing campaign was successful in ultimately locking consumers into a worldview and an ethos, that is, a model of and for the world with strong accompanying moods and motivations that also seem, given their perception of Nespresso, to be perceived as uniquely realistic. In other words, the study's results, discussed in chapters 5 and 6, support the view that the marketing campaign has indeed resulted in the transformation of the use-value of a coffee capsule into a super-elevated exchange value, successfully placing Nespresso at the top of a myriad of available coffee brands. Furthermore, as discussed in chapter 6, the results of the socio-empirical survey favour the interpretation that, once inside, as the two models mutually reinforce one another, the consumer will find it difficult to escape the models' stranglehold. As several participants of the Nespresso focus groups testified, they, even if they have some understanding of the mechanics at work, either see themselves unable to break out, demonstrate no intent to do so, or they are only willing to opt out if Nespresso should suffer a major reputation, and/or quality crisis – put succinctly: once a Nespresso consumer, always a Nespresso consumer: Nespresso becomes firmly established in the consumers' lives. Obviously, the signifying practice of the language of advertising, co-involving the consumer in the production of meaning, guarantees the continued consumption at high unit prices, issuing in Nespresso's sustained and high profit margins.

7.2 A retrospective look at the study's theoretical framework

In the above chapter, the results of the two analyses were presented. The question now arises, how these results were possible in the first place. This question is answered in the following by a meta-theoretical reflection regarding the use of a theory pertaining to the study of religion in a study addressing a commercial, business-related phenomenon.

Explaining the commercial success of a marketing campaign with a theoretical body rooted in the study of religion might at first appear to be counterintuitive. This impression reflects a conditioned way of reasoning that tacitly refuses to consider whether a theory from another academic discipline, opening the field for new perspectives, might be better suited to explain a specific phenomenon than the theories readily available within the discipline. A case in point is the immensely strong preference of Nespresso consumers for their brand, which remains ultimately unaccounted for by the theoretical body prevalent within the field of marketing. Yet, if (1) advertising is understood as a cultural language, and (2) if that language is analysed according to Geertz's semiotic approach, the power, effect, and impact of Nespresso's marketing campaign, that is, the successful transfer of meaning, the signified, from George Clooney to a new signifier, Nespresso, and ultimately – owed to the aforementioned annulment of thing and concept – to the consumer, are laid open and become accessible

In order to better understand why the Geertzian approach indeed provides the pivotal point of this study's theoretical framework, it needs to be understood that, as will be discussed below in chapter 7.3, the Geertzian approach to religion is best accessed if Geertz is read as a practice theorist[130], wherein practice, and the ritual assume a pivotal role in the production of meaning. As evidenced by the results of the analyses, in the practice of consumption, the production of the Nespresso campaign's meaning is completed and continually reproduced. They suggest that, at a high level of abstraction that allows for the application of the Geertzian "general order of existence", or worldview, to a commercial remit, Geertz's definition of religion not only helps to explain practices and belief systems that are generally referred to as religious, but also makes it possible to understand and explain, on the theoretical level, a commercial phenomenon that would remain unexplained, if approached with a theoretical body pertaining to the field of marketing.

In the sense that the new codes suggested by the commercials' narratives constitute a system of symbols, formulating a specific order, or worldview regarding Nespresso consumption, the analogy between the marketing campaign and religion is of a structural nature. Of course, the concept of a worldview, in the context of a coffee brand, does not include eschatological dimensions; it describes a specific classification, and ordering of the many coffee brands that are available to consumers. By the same token, the analogy is functional in the sense of the commercials' narratives effective power to co-involve consumers in the production of new codes, and thereby, of an ethos, a specific behaviour, rooted in powerful, pervasive and long-lasting moods and motivations.

The results support the view that the high performativity of symbolism, extensively practised in religion, has been appropriated by an important member of the business community. It can be maintained that, if Geertz is read as a practice theorist, his work contributes to an in-depth understand-

130 For further reading on this topic, please see Springs (2008).

ing of a phenomenon that, at first sight, neither falls within the remit of anthropology nor of the study of religion. This study's theoretical approach then sheds light on the largely overlooked potential of the study of religion regarding the procurement of satisfactory and paradigmatic theoretical frameworks that help to explain commercial and economic phenomena. The theoretical identification of structural and functional analogies between religion and the Nespresso marketing campaign shows the relevance of the economic dimension within the study of religion. If they care to look, scholars might indeed find, in the field of the study of religion, a theoretical bonanza explaining commercial and economic phenomena that have remained, so far, largely unaccounted for.

7.3 Methodological reflections on this study's interdisciplinary approach

This study, approaching a commercial phenomenon with a theoretical body pertaining to the field of the study of religion, aimed to shed light, from different angles, on a so-far largely unexplained commercial phenomenon. The high level of abstraction and the contextual qualities of the Geertzian definition of religion made this approach possible in the first place. Regarding the commercial phenomenon itself, it must be remembered that it includes two principal counterparts: Nespresso and its marketing campaign, on the one hand, and the consumer, or receiver of the meaning coded in the campaign, on the other. The scrutiny of those two counterparts and their different aspects required a choice of adequate methods. This is the reason why this study includes approaches and methods from different research paradigms: hermeneutics and empiricism. For the same reason, within the socio-empirical survey, a mixed-method approach was chosen, combining qualitative and quantitative methods. These various methods represent a continuum, ranging from hermeneutical methods to a mixed-method research, including convenience sampling, and focus groups, allowing an in-depth scrutiny of the different aspects of the Nespresso's commercial success. This approach obviously precludes the establishment of seemingly objective results, results that could be replicated under what might be compared to laboratory conditions. Yet, this has never been the aim of this study. The aim was to shed light, from different angles, on a multi-layered, largely unexplained commercial phenomenon.

Finally, a reflection on the researcher's hermeneutical perspective is needed. The researcher's own cultural map, the questions that he posed to the audio-visual corpus, and to the participants of the socio-empirical survey, and the many questions that could have been asked but were omitted, clearly reflect a hermeneutical perspective. As my alma mater is the London School of Economics and Political Science, steeped in microeconomic theory that aims to explain, amongst other things, the behaviour of firms, I am acutely aware that firms are under constant and relentless market pressure to generate high cash flows, or, in other words, high profits. In his postgraduate studies, the I turned to the study of religion and cultural studies, where he acquired, amongst other insights, an understanding of the constitutive power of symbol systems. Following a path of paradigm pluralism, the integration of microeconomic reasoning with theories and concepts pertaining to the study of religion was made possible. This also describes my hermeneutical position that enabled me to scrutinise Nespresso's commercial success by doing this interdisciplinary study. In conclusion, it should perhaps be added that I am aware that my perspective and way of reasoning, culturally bounded as it is for everyone, did not allow me to look for answers beyond the possibilities of my cultural language. Other researchers then, who approach the same phenomenon, might indeed come to different answers.

7.4 Outlook and future research

In his concluding comments, one of the focus groups' participants described how consumers re-appropriate, through consumption, the characteristics, which they themselves attributed to the product. In his remarks, he did not differentiate between different brands or different types of consumer goods. His statement was of a most generic nature, making a broad generalisation. In his view, Nespresso clients buy, through the purchase of Nespresso, a piece of the quality of their lives. It was clear to him that they are the best prey for brand experts. He then described the type of a brand-oriented consumer in more detail as, for example, men who only feel potent if they drive a BMW, or a Porsche, or an Audi. The choice of brand is irrelevant. What matters is that the advertising stays in the consumer's head, as it does, according to him, with the Coca Cola consumer who, holding a Coca Cola bottle in his, or her hands, takes a sip. According to that participant, a consumer considering the purchase of a branded product must have that product imprinted in his, in her head. Then, advertising and marketing have completed their task.

This study's evidence suggests that that participant is correct in saying that a branded product must make it to the consumer's head. What he does not address, however, is how exactly the product gets anchored there. An approach based on neuromarketing is likely to produce new insights regarding that question, as could an approach based on cognitive psychology. Advertising does not function like a remote control that steers the consumer's actions. It is the consumer him-, or herself that, triggered by the commercials' codes, that completes the construction of a product's superelevation, attributing a set of values and characteristics to the product. Those values must be, prior to the event of seeing the advertisement, part of his or her cultural map, otherwise the consumer would not even recognise a code as a code, it would simply go unnoticed. The consumer then, if he or she wishes to possess or enjoy those qualities and attributes, needs to acquire and appropriate them through the purchase of the branded product. However, why a consumer cannot feel he or she possesses those qualities without having to acquire them through consumption, or, going back to that participant's example with male drivers of premium cars, why some drivers cannot feel potent behind the steering wheel of another car, is an issue that is not addressed by this study. Yet, that is possibly a field that merits further and closer attention.

Could it be that consumers are subject to a lack of self-worth, disallowing them to see the characteristics and qualities attributed to the branded product as part of their innate identity? Possibly, with a view to this study's postmodern, largely secularised backdrop, religious traditions, their hidden implications and shadowy socio-cultural maps are still very much present in today's society and in the personal lives of many of its members – albeit not in their know manifestation and outer appearance of religiously motivated self-humiliation and self-depreciation, but in the less easily recognisable forms of conspicuous consumption and brand-based identity formation. The human need for upliftment might have remained unaltered, only, it is no longer connected to explicitly religious symbols. Furthermore, given a consumer's required previous knowledge, upliftment then is attained through consumption, irrespective of the individual consumer's cultural identity. Future research, looking carefully into the causes that possibly prevent humans from directly owning the qualities attributed, by themselves, to branded products, might shed light on these issues.

Finally, future research might simply also follow the same approach as this study, however, collect the data for the socio-empirical survey in a different manner. Perhaps, even an approach under laboratory conditions is chosen, or an approach, wherein coffee consumers are digitally accompanied wherever they order, make, or consume their coffee and are asked to immediately report their personal experience related thereto. Or embedded field research is undertaken wherein the researcher chooses to share a brand adherent's life, aiming to fathom the consumer's worldview and ethos, moods and motivations.

8 Reference List

Aaker, D. A., Stayman, D. M., & Vezina, R. (1988). Identifying Feelings Elicited by Advertising. *Psychology and Marketing, 5*(Spring), 1-16.

ABC news. (n.d.). *People Magazine's sexiest man alive through the years.*

Retrieved from http://abcnews.go.com/Entertainment/photos/people-magazines-sexiest-man-alive-years-12024905/image-12024923

AMA online dictionary. (n.d. a). Retrieved from https://www.ama.org/resources/Pages/Dictionary.aspx?dLetter=M

AMA online dictionary. (n.d. b). Retrieved from https://www.ama.org/resources/Pages/Dictionary.aspx?dLetter=A

Amesbury, R. (2002). The Truth of Religion and Religious Truths. In *International Journal for Philosophy of Religion, 51*(3), 159-173.

Amici (n.d.). Retrieved from https://www.amici.ch/de/blog/die-familie-amici-n61

Atkin, D. (2004). *The Culting of Brands: Turn Your Customers Into True Believers*. London, UK: Penguin Books Ltd.

Assies, W. (2003). David versus Goliath in Cochabamba: Water Rights, Neoliberalism, and the Revival of Social Protest in Bolivia. *Latin American Perspectives, 30*(3), 14-36. Retrieved from http://www.iheal.univ-paris3.fr/sites/www.iheal.univ-paris3.fr/files/%21%20cochabamba%20De%20assies.pdf

Barthes, R. (1964/1967). *Elements of Semiology*. New York NY: Hill and Wang.

Barzelay, M. (1993). The Single Case Study as Intellectually Ambitious Inquiry. In *Journal of Public Administration Research and Theory: J-PART, 3*(3), 305-318.

Belk, R. W., Wallendorf, M., & Sherry, Jr., J. F. (1989). The Sacred and the Profane in Consumer Behavior: Theodicy on the Odyssey. *Journal of Consumer Research, 16*(1), 1-38.

Belk, R. W., & Tumbat, G. (2006). The Cult of Macintosh. *Consumption, Markets and Culture, 8*(3), 205-217. (Original work published in 2005)

Benjamin, W. (1991a). Aufzeichnungen und Materialien. In R. Tiedemann (Ed.), *Walter Benjamin: Das Passagen-Werk – Gesammelte Schriften Bd. V•1*. Frankfurt a.M.: suhrkamp taschenbuch wissenschaft.

Benjamin, W. (1991b). Aufzeichnungen und Materialien. In R. Tiedemann (Ed.), *Walter Benjamin: Das Passagen-Werk – Gesammelte Schriften Bd. V•2*. Frankfurt a.M.: suhrkamp taschenbuch wissenschaft.

Beverfood. (n.d.) Retrieved from http://www.beverfood.com/boom-vendite-capsule-caffe-mokarabia-grazie-ai-accordi-distributivi-pubblicita/

Beverland, M. B., & Lindgreen, A. (2010). What makes a good case study? A positivist review of qualitative case research published in Industrial Marketing Management, 1971–2006. *Industrial Marketing Management, 39*(1), 56-63.

Binswanger, H. C. (2011). *Die Glaubensgemeinschaft der Ökonomen – Essays zur Kultur der Wirtschaft*. Hamburg: Murmann Verlag.

Bolz, N. (2002). *Das konsumistische Manifest*. München: Wilhelm Fink Verlag.

Bordwell, D. (1997). *Narration in the Fiction Film*. London UK: Routledge. (Original work published in 1985)

Brown, S. (1993). Postmodern Marketing? *European Journal of Marketing, 27*(4), 19-34.

Bruce, S. (1999). *Choice and Religion: A critique of Rational Choice Theory*. Oxford UK: Oxford University Press.

Bruce, S. (2014). Authority and Freedom: Economics and Secularization. In J. Stolz, & J.-C. Usunier (Eds.), *Religions as Brands: New Perspectives on the Marketization of Religion and Spirituality* (pp. 191-204). Farnham UK: Ashgate Publishing Ltd.

Bruck, M. & Ceci, S. J. (1999). The Suggestibility of Children's Memory. *Annual Review of Psychology*, *50*, 419-439.

Bruner, J. S. (1979). *On Knowing: Essays for the Left Hand*. Cambridge, MA: Belknap Press of Harvard University Press.

Buchanan, J. M. (1965). An Economic Theory of Clubs. *Economics, New Series*, *32*(125), 1-14.

Burawoy, M. (1991). The Extended Case Method. In M. Burawoy, A. Burton, A. A. Fergusson, K. J. Fox, J. Gamson, N. Gartrell, et al. (Eds.), *Ethnography Unbound: Power and Resistance in the Modern Metropolis* (pp. 271-290). Berkley, CA: University of California Press.

Casanova, J. (1994). Public Religions in the Modern World. Chicago, IL: The University of Chicago Press.

Cassone, A., & Marchese, C. (1999). The Economics of Religious Indulgences. *Journal if Institutional and Theoretical Economics (JITE)/Zeitschrift für die gesamte Staatswissenschaft*, *155*(3), 429-442.

Cornes, R., & Sandler, T. (1986). *The Theory of Externalities, Public Goods, and Club Goods*. Cambridge, UK: Cambridge University Press.

Cova, B. (1996). The Postmodern Explained to Managers: Implications for Marketing. *Business Horizon*, *19*(6), 15-23.

Cowie, E. (1990). Fantasia. In P. Adams & E. Cowie (Eds.), *The Woman in Question: m/f* (pp. 149-196). Cambridge, MA: The MIT Press.

CSI Market. (2014). Retrieved from https://csimarket.com/Industry/industry_Profitability_Ratios.php?ind=505&hist=12

Czycholl, H. (2013, July 21). Die ganze Wahrheit über Kaffee – und seinen Preis. *Welt*. Retrieved from http://www.welt.de/finanzen/verbraucher/article118234110/Die-ganze-Wahrheit-ueber-Kaffee-und-seinen-Preis.html

Daily Mail Reporter. (2010, November 30). The saga continues: George Clooney and John Malkovich star in a second Nespresso coffee ad. *Mail online*. Retrieved from http://www.dailymail.co.uk/tvshowbiz/article-1334469/George-Clooney-John-Malkovich-star-second-Nespresso-coffee-ad.html

Davis, W. (2011). *A General Theory of Visual Culture*. Princeton, NJ: Princeton University Press.

Dawson, A. (2011). Consuming the Self: New Spirituality as ‚Mystified Consumption'. *Social Compass*, *58*(3), 309-15.

Denzin, N. K. (2012). Triangulation 2.0. *Journal of Mixed Methods Research*, *6*(2), 80-88. Retrieved from

file:///C:/Users/Ulrich/Downloads/Denzin_2012_80-88%20(1).pdf

DerGloeckel. (2008, April 26). *Red Bull-Werbung: Geschmacklosigkeit oder Rechteverstoss?* Retrieved from https://www.youtube.com/watch?v=nEJ_WPguDxw

Derrida, J. (1996). *Randgänge der Philosophie*. Wien: Passagen Verlag.

Doherty, D. (2013, February 13). Bloomberg. Retrieved from

http://www.bloomberg.com/news/2013-02-12/nestle-2-a-shot-nespresso-propels-premium-brand-profit.html

du Gay, P., Hall, S., Janes, L., Mackay, H., & Negus, K. (1997). Introduction. In *Doing Cultural Studies: The Story of the Sony Walkman (Culture, Media and Identities series)*. London: SAGE Publications.

Eco, Umberto. (1986). *Travels in Hyperreality*. Open Library: Gruppo editoriale Fabbri-Bompiani, Sonzogno, ETAS.

Einstein, M. (2008). *Brands of faith*. Abingdon, UK: Routledge.

Ellingson, L. L. (2009). *Engaging crystallization in qualitative research*. Thousand Oaks, CA: SAGE.

Ellingson, L. L. (2011). Analysis and representation across the continuum. In N. K. Denzin & Y. S. Lincoln (Eds.), *Handbook of qualitative research* (4th ed., pp. 595-610). Thousand Oaks, CA: SAGE.

Ellrich, L. (1999). *Verschriebene Fremdheit: Die Ethnographie kultureller Brüche bei Clifford Geertz und Stephen Greenblatt*. Frankfurt a. M.: Campus Verlag.

Elveren, E. (2013, April 26). Apple Market Share is Growing. iPhonePedia. Retrieved from http://www.iphonepedia.com/apple-market-share-is-growing/

Eurostat. (2017). Retrieved from http://ec.europa.eu/eurostat/statistics-explained/index.php/File:Gross_operating_rate_within_the_non-financial_business_economy,_EU-28,_2014_(%25)_YB17.png

Explorable. (n.d.). Convenience Sampling. Retrieved from https://explorable.com/convenience-sampling

Femalefirst. (n.d.). Retrieved form http://www.femalefirst.co.uk/celebrity/George+Clooney-2021.html#ixzz4CcJWkb4v

Field, A. (2013). *Discovering Statistics Using IBM SPSS Statistics*. London: SAGE Publications Ltd.

Firat, A. F. (1991). The Consumer in Postmodernity. *Advances in Consumer Research*, *18*(1), 70-76. Retrieved from http://www.acrwebsite.org/volumes/7141/volumes/v 18/NA-18

Firat, A. F., & Venkatesh, A. (1993). Postmodernity: The Age of Marketing. *International Journal of Research in Marketing*, *10*(3), 227-249.

Firat, A. F., Dholakia, N., & Venkatesh, A. (1995). Marketing in a Post Modern World. *European Journal of Marketing, 29*(1), 40-56.

Firat, A. F., & Shultz, C. J. II. (1997). From Segmentation to Fragmentation: Markets and Marketing Strategy in the Postmodern Era. *European Journal of Marketing, 31*(3/4), 183-207.

Firat, A. F., & Shultz, C. J. II. (2001). Preliminary Metric Investigations into the Nature of the „Postmodern Consumer. *Marketing Letters, 12*(2), 189-203.

Flick, U. (2007). *Designing qualitative research*. London, England: SAGE. (Original work published in 2002)

Forbes. (2014). Retrieved from https://www.forbes.com/powerful-brands/list/

Gauthier, F., Martikainen, T., & Woodhead, L. (2013). Introduction. In Gauthier, F. & Martikainen, T. (Eds.), *Religion in Consumer Society: Brands, Consumers, and Markets*. Farnham UK: Ashgate Publishing Ltd.

Geertz, C. (1962). The Growth of Culture and the Evolution of Mind. In J. Scher (Ed.), *Theories of the Mind* (pp. 713-740). New York, NY: The Free Press.

Geertz, C. (1964). Ideology as a Cultural System. In D. Apter (Ed.), *Ideology of Discontent* (pp. 47-76). Glencoe, IL: The Free Press of Glencoe.

Geertz, C. (1973). *The Interpretation of Cultures*. New York, NY: Basic Books.

Geertz, C. (2010). Religion as a Cultural System. In M. Banton (Ed.) *Anthropological Approaches to the Study of Religion* (pp. 1–46). Abingdon, England: Routledge. (Original work published in 1966)

Gergen, K. J. (1991). *The Saturated Self*. New York, NY: Basic Books.

Gilroy, P. (2012). Diaspora and the Detours of Identity. In K. Woodward (Ed.), *Identity and Difference* (pp. 299-341). London: SAGE Publications Ltd. (Original work published 1997)

Hall, S. (1993). Encoding, Decoding. In S. During (Ed.), *The Cultural Studies Reader* (pp. 477-487). Abingdon, UK: Routledge.

Hall, S. (2003a). Introduction. In S. Hall (Ed.), *Representation: Cultural Representations and Signifying Practices* (pp. 1-11). London, UK: SAGE Publications Ltd. (Original work published 1997)

Hall, S. (2003b). The Work of Representation. In S. Hall (Ed.), *Representation: Cultural Representations and Signifying Practices* (pp. 13-64). London, UK: SAGE Publications Ltd. (Original work published 1997)

Hall, S. (2003c). The Spectacle of the 'Other.' In S. Hall (Ed.), *Representation: Cultural Representations and Signifying Practices* (pp. 223-279). London, UK: SAGE Publications Ltd. (Original work published 1997)

Hall, S. (1997). The Centrality of Culture: Notes on the Cultural Revolutions of our Time. In K. Thompson (Ed.), *Media and Cultural Regulation* (pp. 207-238). London, UK: SAGE Publications Ltd.

Hamouda, M., & Gharbi A. (2013). The Postmodern Consumer: An Identity Constructor? *International Journal of Marketing Studies, 5*(2), 41-49.

Hastie, R. (1981). Schematic Principles in Human Memory. In E. T. Higgins, C. P. Herman & M. P. Zanna (Eds.), *Social Cognition: The Ontario Symposia on Personality and Social Psychology* (Vol. 1, pp. 39-88). Hillsdale, NJ: Erlbaum.

Hirschman, A. O. (2013). *The Passions and the Interests: Political Arguments for Capitalism before its Triumph*. Princeton, NJ: Princeton University Press. (Original work published 1977)

Holt, D. B. (2002). Why do Brands Cause Trouble? A Dialectical Theory of Consumer Culture and Branding. *The Journal of Consumer Research, 29*(1), 70-90.

Höpflinger, A.-K. (2014). "Tomorrow, Christ on the Cross Will beSelling Socks". References to Christianity in Contemporary Advertising Campaigns". In J. Schlehe, & E. Sandkühler (Eds.), *Religion, Tradition and the Popular: Transcultural Views from Asia and Europe* (pp. 225-242). Bielefeld: Transcript Verlag.

Hörisch, J. (2011). *Tauschen, sprechen, begehren – Eine Kritik der unreinen Vernunft*. München: Carl Hanser Verlag GmbH & Co. KG

Horizont. (2009, November 6). Ein himmlisches Duo für Nespresso: George Clooney und John Malkovic. Retrieved from http://www.horizont.net/marketing/nachrichten/-Ein-himmlisches-Duo-fuer-Nespresso-George-Clooney-und-John-Malkovic-88327

Houston, J. P., Bee, H., & Rimm, D. C. (1985). *Essentials of Psychology*. Orlando, FL: Academic Press Inc.

Iannaccone, L. R. (1992). Sacrifice and Stigma: Reducing Free-riding in Cults, Communes, and Other Collectives. *Journal of Political Economy, 100*(2), 271-291.

Iannaccone, L. R. (1998). Introduction to the Economics of Religion. *Journal of Economic Literature, 36*(3), 1465-1495.

Illycupscollection. (n.d.). Retrieved form http://illycupscollection.com/index.php/design-and-features/menu-styles

Investopedia. (2015). Retrieved from http://www.investopedia.com/ask/answers/071015/what-profit-margin-usual-company-food-and-beverage-sector.asp

Jameson, F. (1991). *Postmodernism, or, The Cultural Logic of Late Capitalism*. Durham, NC: Duke University Press.

Kirchenbund. (2013). *Diaconia*. Retrieved from http://www.kirchenbund.ch/en/tags/diaconia

Ko, E., & Megehee, C. M. (2012). Fashion marketing of luxury brands: Recent issues and contributions. *Journal of Business Research, 65*, 1395-1398.

Kolig, E. (1988). Australian Aboriginal Totemic Systems: Structures of Power. *Oceania, 58*(3), 212-230.

Königkrämer, V. (2011, November 16). Benetton-Werbung empört den Vatikan. *Stern*. Retrieved from http://www.stern.de/panorama/papst-kuesst-imam-benetton-werbung-empoert-den-vatikan-3441534.html

Lades, L. K. (2015). Impulsive Behavior. In M. Altman (Ed.), *Real-World Decision Making: An Encyclopedia of Behavioral Economics* (pp. 215-217). Santa Barbara, CA: Greenwood.

Landeskriche. (n.d.). *Diakonie*. Retrieved from http://gr-ref.ch/Diakonie

Langer, S. K. (1960). *Philosophy in a New Key. A Study in the Symbolism of Reason, Rite, and Art* (4th edition). Cambridge MA: Harvard University Press.

Lavazza. (1995a). *Benvenuti in Paradiso*. Retrieved form

http://www.lavazza.it/it/mondo_lavazza/comunicazione/tv/

Lavazza. (1995b). *Benvenuti in Paradiso*. Retrieved form

https://www.youtube.com/watch?v=6EJvhPQm1ic

Lavazza. (1995c). *Leonardo*. Retrieved form http://www.lavazza.it/it/mondo_lavazza/comunicazione/tv/

Lavazza. (1995d). *Leonardo*. Retrieved form https://www.youtube.com/watch?v=urK-Ly1jUwDo

Lavazza. (2012a). *Giardini dell'Eden 40"*. Retrieved from https://www.youtube.com/embed/9ggpwrgiY-8?rel=0

Lavazza. (2012b). *Giardini dell'Eden 40"*. Retrieved from

https://www.youtube.com/watch?time_continue=14&v=9ggpwrgiY-8

Le Goff, J. (1985). *L'imaginaire médiéval: Essais*. Paris: Éditions Gallimard.

Lehmann, J. (1986). *Buddha – Leben, Lehre, Wirkung: Der östliche Weg zur Selbsterlösung*. Frankfurt a. M.: Fischer Verlag GmbH.

Lévi-Strauss, C. (1971). *Totemism*. Boston, MA: Beacon Press.

Lewis, J. (2008). *Cultural Studies*. London, UK: SAGE Publications Ltd.

Liew, T. W., & Tan, S.-M. (2016). The Effects of Positive and Negative Mood on Cognition and Motivation in Multimedia Learning Environment. *Journal of Educational Technology & Society, 19*(2), 104-115.

Luidens, D. A., & Nemeth, R. J. (1994). Social Sources of Family Contributions: Giving Patterns in the Reformed Church in America. *Review of Religious Research, 36*(2), Special Issue: Patterns of Financial Contributions to Churches), 207-217.

Lyden, J. C. (2003). *Film as Religion: Myths, Morals, and Rituals*. New York, NY: NYU Press.

Lyon, D. (2000). *Jesus in Disneyland: Religion in Postmodern Times*. Cambridege, UK: Polity Press.

Mäder, M.-T. (2012). *Die Reise als Suche nach Orientierung: Eine Annäherung an das Verhältnis zwischen Film und Religion*. Marburg: Schüren Verlag GmbH.

Madsen, K. B. (1974). *Modern theories of motivation: A comparative meta-scientific study*. New York, NY: John Wiley & Sons.

MailOnline. (2011, November 17). Benetton withdraws ad campaign image of Pope kissing Egyptian imam after Vatican complains it is disrespectful. Retrieved from http://www.dailymail.co.uk/news/article-2062423/Benetton-Unhate-advert-Pope-kissing-imam-withdrawn-Vatican-calls-disrespectful.html

Makowski, M. (2009, April 1). Religion, Clubs, and Emergent Social Divides. *Munich Personal RePEc Archive MPRA* (MPRA Paper No. 14359). Retrieved from http://mpra.ub.uni-muenchen.de/14359/

Manstetten, R. (2004). *Das Menschenbild der Ökonomie: Der homo oeconomicus und die Anthropologie von Adam Smith*. Freiburg i. B.: Karl Alber Verlag. (Original work published 2000)

Markides, C. C. (1999). A Dynamic View of Strategy. *Sloane Management Review, 40*(3), 55-63.

Marx, K. (2009). *Das Kapital* (Reprint of the 2nd ed., 1872). Köln: Anaconda Verlag GmbH. (Original work published 1867)

Marx, K. (2002). *Das Kapital: Volume I* (Translation of the 4th edition (1890) by Hans G. Ehrbar. Original work published 1867). Retrieved from http://content.csbs.utah.edu/~ehrbar/cap1.pdf

Maslow, A. H. (2013). *A Theory of Human Motivation* [Kindle ebook]. Retrieved from Amazon.com (Original work published 1943)

Matzler, K., Bailom, F., von den Eichen S. F., & Kohler, T. (2013). Business model innovation: coffee triumphs for Nespresso. *Journal of Business Strategy, 34*(2), 30-37.

McCracken, G. (1986). Culture and Consumption: A Theoretical Account of the Structure and Movement of the Cultural Meaning of Consumer Goods. *Journal of Consumer Research, 13*, 71-84.

Megehee, C. M., & Woodside, A.G. (2010). Creating Visual Narrative Art for Decoding Stories That Consumers and Brands Tell. *Psychology and Marketing, 27*(6), 603-622.

Micheelsen, A. (2002). I don't do systems: An interview with Clifford Geertz. *Method and Theory in the Study of Religion, 14*(1), 2-20.

Mick, D. G. (1998). Semiotics in Marketing and Consumer Research: Balderdash, Verity, Pleas. In S. Brown & D. Turley (Eds.), *Consumer Research: Postcards from the Edge* (pp. 249-262). Milton Park, UK: Taylor & Francis

Mick, D. G., Boroughs, J. E., Hetzel, P., & Brannen, M. Y. (2004). Pursuing the meaning of meaning in the commercial world: An international review of marketing and consumer research founded on semiotics. *Semiotica, 152*(1/4), 1-74.

Mick, D. G., & Oswald, L. R. (2006). The Semiotic Paradigm on Meaning in the Marketplace. In Belk, R. W. (Ed.), *Handbook of Qualitative Research Methods in Marketing*. Cheltenham, UK: Edward Elgar Publishing Ltd.

Miles, M. R. (1996). *Seeing and Believing*. Boston, MA: Beacon Press.

Miller, T. (2006). What it is and what it isn't: Introducing ... Cultural Studies. In T. Miller (Ed.), *A Companion to Cultural Studies* (pp. 1-20). Malden, MA: Blackwell Publishers Inc.

Mokarabia. (2013, November 26). *Mokarabia, l'arte italiana del buongusto.* Retrieved from https://www.youtube.com/watch?v=wDhLPWeEjyQ&list=PLqCvj5w7_KdJDtGWt5uZQsVzmRFQ8of4E

Morgan, D. (2005). *The Sacred Gaze: Religious Visual Culture in Theory and Practice.* Berkley, CA: University of California Press.

Morris, W. N. (1989). *Mood: The Frame of Mind.* New York NY: Springer-Verlag New York Inc.

Mukhopadhyay, A., & Johar, G. V. (2007). Tempted or Not? The Effect of Recent Purchase History on responses to Affective Advertising. *Journal of Consumer Research, 33*, 445 – 453.

Muniz, A. M. Jr., & O'Guinn, T. C. (2001). Brand Community." *TheJournal of Consumer Research*, *27*(4), 412-432.

Muniz, A. M. Jr., & Schau, H. J. (2005). Religiosity in the Abandoned Apple Newton Brand Community. *The Journal of Consumer Research*, *31*(4), 737-747.

Murdock, G. (1995). Across the Great Divide: Cultural Analysis and the Condition of Democracy. *Critical Studies in Mass Communication*, *12*(1), 89-95.

Nardella, C. (2015). *La migrazione dei simboli: Pubblicità e religione*. Milano: Edizione Angelo Guerini e Associati SpA.

Nehring, A. (2008). Religion und Kultur: Zur Beschreibung einer Differenz. In A. Nehring & J. Valentin (Eds.), *Religious Turns – Turning Religions. Veränderte kulturelle Diskurse – neue religiöse Wissensformen* (pp. 11-31). Stuttgart: Kohlhammer.

Nespresso Accessories Ritual Collection. (2015, March 4). Retrieved from https://www.youtube.com/watch?v=DjSDNdde3SA

Nestlé FAQs. (2014). Retrieved from http://www.nestle-nespresso.com/about-us/faqs/brandrelated

Nestlé Media Press Releases. (2013, February 14). Good performance across the board, Nestlé model delivered again. *Nestlé*. Retrieved from http://www.nestle.com/media/pressreleases/allpressreleases/full-year-results-2012

Nestlé-Nespresso. (2009, November 7). [Eric Garnier]. *It's Heaven.* Retrieved from https://www.youtube.com/watch?v=23j1B4-lroM

http://www.werbeblogger.de/2009/11/10/george-clooney-john-malkovich-robert-rodriguez-was-sonst/ (Third video: Nespresso, Sofa)

Nestlé-Nespresso. (2016a). Unique Business Model and Route to the Market. Retrieved from https://www.nestle-nespresso.com/asset-library/Documents/Nespresso%20-%20Business%20Model%20Factsheet.pdf

Nestlé-Nespresso. (2016b). Global Brand Community. Retrieved from

https://www.nestle-nespresso.com/asset-library/documents/nespresso%20-%20global%20brand%20community%20factsheet.pdf

Nestlé-Nespresso. (n.d.a). *Facts and Figures*. Retrieved from https://www.nestle-nespresso.com/about-us/facts-and-figures

Nestlé-Nespresso. (n.d.b). Nespresso Les Collections *by world-class designers enhance the coffee tasting ritual.* Retrieved from http://www.nestle-nespresso.com/newsandfeatures/nespresso-les-collections-by-world-class-designers-enhance-the-coffee-tasting-ritual

Nestlé-Nespresso. (n.d.c). *Global Presence*. Retrieved from https://www.nestle-nespresso.com/about-us/global-presence?char=All

Neumeyer, M. (2005). *The Brand Gap: How to Bridge the Distance Between Business Strategy and Design*. (n.p.): New Riders.

Neumeyer, M. (2015). *The Brand Flip: Why customers now run companies and how to profit from it*. (n.p.): New Riders.

Norris, P., & Inglehart, R. (2004). *Sacred and Secular: Religion and Politics Worldwide*. Cambridge, UK: Cambridge University Press.

Nussbaum, M. (2008). *Upheavals of Thought*. Cambridge, UK: Cambridge University Press. (Original work published 2001)

Nussbaum, M. (2009). *Therapy of Desire*. Princeton, NJ: Princeton University Press. (Original work published 1994)

Oliver, R. L. (1992). An Investigation of the Attribute Basis of Emotion and Related Affects in Consumption: Suggestions for a Stage-Specific Satisfaction Framework. In J. F. Sherry, Jr. & B. Sternthal, *Advances in Consumer Research*, *19*, 237-244. Provo, UT: Association for Consumer Research.

Ortner, S. B. (1984). Theory in Anthropology since the Sixties. *Comparative Studies in Society and History*, *26*(1), 126-166.

Ortner, S. B. (2006). *Anthropology and Social Theory: Culture, Power, and the Acting Subject*. Durham, NC: Duke University Press.

Panofsky, E. (1982). *Meaning in the Visual Arts*. Chicago, IL: University of Chicago Press. (Original work published 1955)

Peirce, C. S. (1974). *Elements of Logic*. Cambridge, MA: The Belknap Press of Harvard University Press. (Original work published 1931)

Pezzoli-Olgiati, D. (2008). Film und Religion: Blick auf Kommunikationssysteme und ihre vielfältigen Wechselwirkungen. In A. Nehring & J. Valentin (Eds.), *Religious Turns – Turning Religions. Veränderte kulturelle Diskurse – neue religiöse Wissensformen* (pp. 45-66). Stuttgart: Kohlhammer.

Pezzoli-Olgiati, D. (2011). Images in Images. In D. Pezzoli-Olgiati & Ch. Rowland (Eds.), *Approaches to the Visual in Religion* (pp. 21-38). Göttingen: Vandenhoek &Ruprecht GmbH & Co. KG.

Pezzoli-Olgiati, D., & Rowland, C. (2011). Preface. In D. Pezzoli-Olgiati & Ch. Rowland (Eds.), *Approaches to the Visual in Religion* (pp. 9-13). Göttingen: Vandenhoek &Ruprecht GmbH & Co. KG.

Pezzoli-Olgiati, D. (2012). Religion und Visualität. In M. Stausberg (Ed.), *Religionswissenschaft* (pp. 343-364). Berlin: Walter de Gruyter GmbH & Co. KG.

Pezzoli-Olgiati, D. (2015). Religion in Cultural Imaginary: Setting the Scene. In D. Pezzoli-Olgiati (Ed.),*Religion in Cultural Imaginary: Explorations in Visual and Material Practices* (Vol. 13, pp. 9-38). Zürich: TVZ Theologischer Verlag Zürich AG.

Pimentel, R. W., & Reynolds, K. E. (2004). A Model for Consumer Devotion: Affective Commitment with Proactive Sustaining Behaviors. *Academy of Marketing Science Review*, *8*(7), 1-45.

Plate, B. S. (2008). *Religion and Film: Cinema and the Re-Creation of the World*. London, UK: Wallflower Press.

Pollack, D. (2011). Still alive – das Säkularisierungsparadigma. In A. Liedhegener, A. Tunger-Zanetti, & S. Wirz (Eds.), *Religion – Wirtschaft – Politik: Forschungszugänge zu einem aktuellen transdisziplinären Feld* (pp. 41-60). Zürich: Pano Verlag.

Prigg, M., Parsons, C., & Margolis, J. (2012, November 2). I've got one! Jubilant Apple fans around the world finally get their hands on the iPhone 5 - so what IS all the fuss about? *Mail Online*. Retrieved from http://www.dailymail.co.uk/sciencetech/article-2206143/iPhone-5-release-day-2012-Apple-fans-Sydney-New-York-finally-hands-latest-iPhone.html

Ragas, M. W., & Bueno, R.J. (2002). *The Power of Cult Branding: How 9 Magnetic Brands Turned Customers into Loyal Followers (and Yours Can, Too!)*. New York, NY: Crown Business.

Research Methodology. (n.d.). Convenience Sampling. Retrieved from https://research-methodology.net/sampling-in-primary-data-collection/convenience-sampling/

Revill, J. (2012, November 21). Nespresso Reshuffles as Rivals Wade. In. *The Wall Street Journal*. Retrieved from https://www.wsj.com/articles/SB10001424127887324352004578132943986605034

Richins, M. L. (1997). Measuring Emotions in the Consumption Experience. Journal of Consumer Research, 24(2), 127-146.

Roederer, C. (2012). Stratégies expérientielles et dimensions de l'expérience: La quête de l'avantage concurrentiel commercial. *Décisions Marketing*, *67*, 63-74.

Rose, G. (2012). *Visual Methodologies*. London: SAGE Publications Ltd.

RP Online (2017). Retrieved from

http://www.rp-online.de/panorama/leute/sexiest-man-alive-liste-der-heissesten-maenner-bid-1.1966380

Ryle, G. (2009a). *The Concept of Mind: 60th Anniversary Edition*. Abingdon, UK: Routledge. (Original work published 1949)

Ryle, G. (2009b). *Collected Essays 1929 – 1968: Collected Papers Volume 2*. Abingdon, UK: Routledge. (Original work published 1971)

Sandler, T. (2013). Buchanan Clubs. *Constitutional Political Economy*. Vol. *24*(4), pp. 265-284. Retrieved from: http://link.springer.com/article/10.1007%2Fs10602-013-9148-5#page-1

Saussure, F. (1986). *General Course in Linguistics*. Chicago: Open Court Publishing Company. (Original work published 1972)

Schiffman, L. G., Lazar Kanuk, L., & Wisenblit, J. (2010). *Consumer Behavior* (10th ed.). Upper Saddle River, NJ: Prentice Hall.

Schilbrack. K. (2005). Religion, Models of, and Reality: Are we through with Geertz? *Journal of the American Academy of Religion*, *73*(2), 429-452.

Schouten, J. W., McAlexander, J. H., & Koenig, H. F. (2007). Transcendent customer experience and brand community. *Journal of the Academy of Marketing Science*, *35*(3), 357-368.

Seel, M. (2015). Beauty: A Brief Conceptual Journey. *Aesthetic Investigation*, *1*(1), 165-173.

Seele, P. (2008). *Philosophie der Epochenschwelle: Augustin zwischen Antike und Mittelalter (Quellen und Studien zur Philosophie, Band 80)*. Berlin: Walter de Gruyter GmbH & Co. KG.

Selwyn-Holmes, A. (2009, June 5). Kissing nun. *Iconic Photos*. Retrieved from https://iconicphotos.wordpress.com/2009/06/05/kissing-nun/

Sherry, J. F. (1998). The Soul of the Company Store: Nike Town Chicago and the Emplaced Brandscape. In J. F. Sherry (Ed.), *Service Scapes: The Concept of Place in Contemporary Markets* (pp. 109-146). Chicago, IL: American Marketing Association.

Solomon, M. R. (2013). *Consumer Behavior.* Harlow, UK: Pearson Education Ltd.

Springs, J. A. (2008). What Cultural Theorists of Religion Have to Learn from Wittgenstein; Or, How to Read Geertz as a Practice Theorist. *Journal of the American Academy of Religion, 76*(4), 934-969.

Spitzenpfeil, R. (2010, November 11). George Clooney und das Huhn. *Neue Zürcher Zeitung.* Retrieved from http://www.nzz.ch/autxnespresso-werbung-1.8337630

Sternborg, A. (2015, May 13). Kritik zu Victoria. *film*. Retrieved from http://www.epd-film.de/filmkritiken/victoria

Stock Analysis on Net. (2014). Retrieved from http://www.stock-analysis-on.net/NASDAQ/Company/Apple-Inc/Ratios/Profitability

Stolz, J. (2010). A Silent Battle: Theorizing the Effects of Competition Between Churches and Secular Institutions. *Review of Religious Research, 51*(3), 253-276.

Stolz, J. (2013). Entwurf einer Theorie religiös-säkularer Konkurrenz. *Kölner Zeitschrift für Soziologie und Sozialpsychologie*. Wiesbaden: Springer VS.

Stolz, J., & Usunier, J.-C. (2014). Religions as Brands: New Perspectives on the Marketization of Religion and Spirituality. In J. Stolz, & J.-C. Usunier (Eds.), *Religions as Brands: New Perspectives on the Marketization of Religion and Spirituality* (pp. 3-25). Farnham, UK: Ashgate Publishing Ltd.

Stonewallgazette. (2010). Benetton's most controversial ad campaigns. Retrieved from http://www.stonewallgazette.com/2010/08/benettons-most-controversial.html

Tiedemann, R. (1991). Einleitung des Herausgebers. In R. Tiedemann (Ed.), *Walter Benjamin: Das Passagen-Werk – Gesammelte Schriften Bd. V•1* (pp. 9-41). Frankfurt a.M.: Suhrkamp Taschenbuch Wissenschaft.

Trowitzsch, M. (2012). *Karl Barth heute* (2nd ed.). Göttingen: Vandenhoeck & Ruprecht.

Ulrich, M. (2017). An Unexpected Overlap between Civil Religion and Consumption: The Unseen Role of Conscious Commodity Design. *Journal of Religion in Europe, 10*(1-2), 218-239.

Venkatesh, A., Sherry, J. F. Jr., & Firat, F. A. (1993). Postmodernism and the Marketing Imaginary. *International Journal of Research in Marketing, 10*(3), 215-223.

Walmart. (2019). Retrieved from https://www.walmart.com/ip/Aluminum-Yellow-Diamond-Caution-Slippery-When-Wet-Car-Road-Sign-Commercial-Metal-Square-Sign-12x12/175919140

Williamson, J. (2002). *Decoding Advertisements*. London: Marion Boyars. (Original work published 1978)

Woodhead, L. (2011). Five Concepts of Religion. *International Review of Sociology*, 21(1), 121-143.

Woodruff, R. B. (1997). Customer Value: The Next Source for Competitive Advantage. *Journal of the Academy of Marketing Science, 25*(2), 139-153.

Woodward, K. (2012). Concepts of Identity and Difference. In K. Woodward (Ed.), *Identity and Difference* (pp. 7-61). London, UK: SAGE Publications Ltd. (Original work published 1997)

Yarow, J. (2014, February 13). Apple Collects 87% Of All The Profits In The

Smartphone Handset Industry. *Business Insider*. Retrieved from http://www.businessinsider.com/apple-smartphone-profit-share-2014-2

Yin, R. K. (2014). *Case Study Research: Design and Methods*. London, UK: SAGE Publications Ltd.

Zaiontz, Ch. (n.d.). Real Statistics Using Excel. Retrieved from http://www.real-statistics.com/chi-square-and-f-distributions/effect-size-chi-square/

9 Audio-visual Sources

- Victoria, Sebastian Schipper, DE 2015
- What Else, Michel Gondry, 2006
  Retrieved from https://www.youtube.com/watch?v=DfyeXrdZZ1o
- Like a Star, Grant Heslov, 2012
  Full length version, retrieved from
  https://www.youtube.com/watch?v=tPsm2r7uCi4
  Shortened version, retrieved from https://www.youtube.com/watch?v=LiyM5fGow9U
- In the Name of Pleasure, Grant Heslov, 2013
  Retrieved from https://www.youtube.com/watch?v=VQA3DyKJ1yw
- How Far, Grant Heslov, 2014
  Retrieved from https://www.youtube.com/watch?v=jaLw8bklpgc&t=45s